PN
2277
.N5
A85

Atkinson, Justin
Brooks, 1894-

The lively years,
1920-1973

DATE		

○ ○

THE LIVELY YEARS

○ ○

OTHER BOOKS BY BROOKS ATKINSON

Broadway
Once Around the Sun
Broadway Scrapbook

OTHER BOOKS BY ALBERT HIRSCHFELD

The World of Hirschfeld
The American Theatre As Seen by Hirschfeld
Show Business Is No Business

The Lively

BROOKS ATKINSON and
ALBERT HIRSCHFELD

ASSOCIATION PRESS • NEW YORK

"Wintergreen for President" by George and Ira Gershwin copyright © 1932 New World Music Corporation. Copyright renewed. All rights reserved. Used by permission of Warner Bros. Music.

"Soliloquy" is from *Carousel.* Music by Richard Rodgers, words by Oscar Hammerstein II. Copyright © by Williamson Music, Inc. U.S. copyright renewed 1973. Used by permission.

"A Cock-eyed Optimist" is from *South Pacific.* Words by Oscar Hammerstein II, music by Richard Rodgers. Copyright © 1949 by Richard Rodgers and Oscar Hammerstein II. Williamson Music Inc., New York, N.Y. publisher and owner of publication and allied rights for all countries of Western Hemisphere. All rights reserved. Used by permission.

The song from *Lost in the Stars* by Maxwell Anderson and Kurt Weill is copyright © 1946 by Chappell & Co., Inc. Used by permission of Chappell & Co., Inc.

Lyrics from "Fugue for Tinhorns" by Frank Loesser copyright © 1950 by Frank Music Corp. Used by permission.

"Tonight" from *West Side Story* copyright 1957, 1959 by Leonard Bernstein and Stephen Sondheim. Reprinted by permission of G. Schirmer, Inc.

Quotations from *J.B.* by Archibald MacLeish. Copyright © 1956, 1957, 1958 by Archibald MacLeish. Reprinted by permission of Houghton Mifflin Company.

Quotations from *A. Raisin in the Sun* by Lorraine Hansberry. Copyright © 1958, 1959 by Robert Nemeroff as executor of the estate of Lorraine Hansberry. Used by permission of Random House, Inc.

Quotation from "Dream Deferred," a poem by Langston Hughes, is from *The Panther and the Lash.* Copyright 1951 by Langston Hughes. Reprinted by permission of Alfred A. Knopf, Inc.

Library of Congress Cataloging in Publication Data

Atkinson, Justin Brooks, 1894–
    The lively years, 1920–1973.

    1. Theater—New York (City)—History. 2. Drama—
20th century—History and criticism.   I. Hirschfeld,
Albert, joint author.   II. Title.
PN2277.N5A85   792'.09747'1   73-14659
ISBN 0-8096-1856-7

Printed in the United States of America
Designed by The Etheredges

o o o o o o o o o o o o o o o o o o o o o o o o o o o o o o o o o o o o o o o o o o o o o

CONTENTS

o o o o o o o o o o o o o o o o o o o o o o o o o o o o o o o o o o o o o o o o o o o o o

V

CONTENTS · VII

1960 – 1973

o o o o o o o o o o o o o o o o o o o o o o o o o o o o o o o o o o o o o o o o o

THE LIVELY YEARS

o o o o o o o o o o o o o o o o o o o o o o o o o o o o o o o o o o o o o o o o

In the American theatre—or, specifically, on Broadway—the lively years began at the end of World War I. Several enterprising playwrights, of whom Eugene O'Neill was the foremost, began to write thoughtful plays about human beings instead of stereotypes; and several producers, of whom the directors of the Theatre Guild were the most notable, began to put them on the stage.

The plays about people did not constitute a revolution. But they did widen the scope of the theatre and give the art of the theatre new values that have never depreciated. The change is illustrated by the experience of the Pulitzer Prize committee, which gave the first prize in 1918 to Jesse Lynch Williams for *Why Marry?*—a routine comedy in the familiar vein of bright mediocrity. "That was surely a creditable performance in its day," William Lyons Phelps wrote seventeen years later, "but during the last ten years it would not even have been considered."

The committee could not find a play worthy of an award in 1919. But in 1920 it gave the prize to Eugene O'Neill for *Beyond the Horizon*. Two years later he received the prize for *Anna Christie*. Not all the prize-winning plays since then have been of conspicuous merit.

1

But routine entertainment in a box-office style has never again been regarded as prize material.

During the two decades preceding World War I there had not been an American play that would be taken seriously today. The theatre was formula entertainment—generally in a melodramatic form with a happy ending. With one or two exceptions, the producers had elementary taste; they were hucksters. William Vaughn Moody's *The Great Divide,* in 1906, is often cited as a play with a real theme and a pioneer in serious theatre. It contrasted the manners of a female Eastern schoolteacher with those of a rough Western man. But in reality *The Great Divide* is an example of the intelligent play that was finally destroyed by adherence to the formula. Although it did define the differences between Eastern and Western manners, it concluded with the standard sentimentality that makes most plays of that period intolerable today.

During this period of America's adolescence many plays from abroad offered the public provocative ideas about human beings and their problems. The foreign theatre was more sophisticated than ours. Plays by Ibsen, Strindberg, Shaw and Galsworthy seasoned the bland theatre diet of American audiences. When John Galsworthy's *Justice* was produced in 1916 with John Barrymore starring, Channing Pollock, a critic and playwright, made a particularly discerning comment: "Overnight the theatre has ceased to be a toy, a plaything—and it has become a vital part of every day."

Justice was not a mechanical trick; it was an imitation of humanity. To people accustomed to the child's garden of sweet banalities, a play that faced up to reality was startling. Charles Klein, one of the most successful playwrights of the early 1900's, said that when he was getting ready to write a play the characters were only "mental abstractions." Mechanics of playmaking came first. "The characters are mere puppets, bobbing about at the will of the monarch Mechanics," he said. He was not much interested in people.

The innocent values of playwriting in the early years are illustrated by Elmer Rice's experience with his first play, *On Trial,* in 1914. It was the dramatization of a murder trial and it exploited an idea Mr. Rice had read in an article by Clayton Hamilton. Mr. Rice interrupted the narrative sequence by introducing a scene from the past out of context—"flashback," it is called today. Arthur Hopkins, an imaginative producer, bought the play. He liked the startling crafts- manship but not the setting or the characters. Mr. Rice accordingly gave the play a new setting and new characters. Although characters are the essential elements in all forms of art, they were only the pup- pets of craftsmanship and mechanics in the theatre of that day.

Why did the change come so decisively after World War I? Did the national experience create a new point of view? Nothing so basic as that can be proved. But it is a matter of record that thousands of young Americans went abroad for the first time and were drawn into the mass savagery of war. It shook the traditional provinciality of the nation. The experience was bitter on a colossal scale and just about everyone was convinced that it "must not happen again." Since the young men were in the trenches during an Administration that had campaigned on "keeping us out of war," many of these civilian sol- diers lost respect for the integrity and authority of their Govern- ment. The braggart war song, *Over There*, which came out of the Broadway theatre district, was the best we could do for the war when America joined the Allies. After the war was over, the theatre took an adversary role: *R.U.R.*, *What Price Glory?*, *Bury the Dead*, *Idiot's Delight*, *Tiger at the Gates*, *Mister Roberts*, *Sticks and Bones* put an end to martial bombast. Human beings had taken the theatre away from the mechanics.

The plays discussed in this book are not "the best" of the 1920 to 1973 period—not necessarily "the best," that is. But some of them are definitely among the best, such as *The Adding Machine*, *Our Town* and *The Visit*. These say something original and important about people, and in a forthright style. Many memorable plays that are entitled to be called "the best" are not discussed because they do not come within the particular province of this book. This book is con- cerned with plays that criticize life, that wrestle with the dilemmas of civilized life.

Once in a Lifetime, by Moss Hart and George S. Kaufman, does not appear here although it is an expert and hilarious farce. But its *dramatis personae,* to use the old term, consists of caricatures—humorous distortions of people. The comedy that had the longest run, *Life With Father* by Russel Crouse and Howard Lindsay, is not here because it has no significance outside the domestic circle of a self-contained family. Even Eugene O'Neill's *Long Day's Journey Into Night* is missing because it is confined to the ingrown life of one particular neurotic family.

If the theatre were limited to plays of social significance, it could not fulfill its traditional function of drawing people out of themselves and into an imagined world in which wit, humor, romance, excitement and audacity are as valid as reality. *Reunion in Vienna* is a better play than *They Shall Not Die*—better organized, better written. But this book is committed to comments on, and drawings of, plays that mirror important issues of their times.

I have recently reread all the plays listed in the table of contents, and the comments I make about them in this book are new. Some of my opinions differ sharply from the opinions I had of these plays originally. Mr. Hirschfeld has drawn the actors in the process of giving performances. He has caught the vitality of the plays on the stage, which is the fundamental art of the theatre. Although I have tried to write the new comments in terms of the texts, my impressions are still conditioned by the original performances, because a text is only the dry bones of a play. In my opinion *There Shall Be No Night* has lost the harrowing pertinence it had in 1940 when World War II was darkening our skies, but my memory of the play is still colored by the exalted performances of Lynn Fontanne and Alfred Lunt. *Strange Interlude* now seems like a sophomoric melodrama, but my memories of Miss Fontanne's cool, detached, menacing *femme fatale* (the American flower of evil) are still vivid. *Lost in the Stars* now seems like hackwork, but I can still hear Kurt Weill's rushing music. Once a play has been seen it cannot be isolated from the performance; that is why revivals seldom seem as iridescent as the originals.

Here and there in this book I have referred to the actors who originally brought the play alive. But this is not a book of memories.

Rather it is an outline of the plays that have given the modern theatre a new dimension and which have made it an integral part of our cultural life since World War I. Although the theatre has lost size and scope in the last quarter of a century, it still criticizes life as angrily or contemptuously as it did in 1920. John Howard Lawson, who wrote *Processional,* and Clifford Odets, who wrote *Awake and Sing,* were no more passionately critical than are David Rabe, who wrote *Sticks and Bones,* and Jason Miller, who wrote *That Championship Season.*

To renew acquaintance with these plays is a pleasant excursion. It is like a stroll through the history of the last half century—some of it barbaric, some of it tender, some of it amusing, but all of it sociable. The plays are part of the world chronicle. Most of them are not timeless plays. But all of them are—or were—timely. In the Twenties, when disillusion about the war was torturing the spirit of the men who had been through it, the theatre was in the forefront of public opinion. The Capeks' *R.U.R.* and *The World We Live In* held up to ridicule the accepted standards and myths about war and society. Conspiring with Laurence Stallings and Maxwell Anderson, the theatre laughed the glories of war out of *What Price Glory?*

The theatre not only reflected but also created public opinion. The causes, the political issues, the human predicaments of the successive years are still vivid in these plays by writers who were part of their time. The dehumanization of industry, the segregation of Negro citizens, political corruption, political revolution, psychiatric probes into personalities, the Great Depression and our methods of dealing with it, Sacco and Vanzetti, fascism, freedom of speech, character assassination, organized crime, the emptiness of a business career—all are bared here in the work of contemporaries who were articulate and who stated their ideas dramatically.

In the Twenties and Thirties and part of the Forties the American theatre was aggressive, intelligent and dynamic, and it pioneered in many forms. The leadership is less visible today. After World War II European and British writers struck out in a style that has always eluded Americans—the negative point of view about the whole structure of civilization, universal doom, madness, hopelessness. *No Exit,*

Waiting for Godot, Rhinoceros, The Homecoming, all are devastating attacks upon normal values. They cut everything that is rational out from under us. Indeed, there are very few optimistic plays among those discussed in this book—*Our Town* and *The Skin of Our Teeth* by Thornton Wilder, *The Time of Your Life* by William Saroyan, and possibly Archibald MacLeish's *J.B.* which ends on a rising note after a series of catastrophes. Optimism is in short supply in the theatre, as in life. The overwhelming majority of these plays are critical and the most recent are the most critical. In the Twenties dramatists attacked their subjects as if the inequities could be resolved. Some of the traditional optimism of America lurked behind most of the early plays. But not now. There is no conviction now that problems will be solved and that happy days are just over the horizon.

If all this sounds depressing, I must add that the plays in this book are stimulating to read and think about today. They express the minds of some very interesting people—in some cases wrongheaded perhaps, but never boring. Whatever their points of view may be, the plays retain the passion, wit, independence, conviction and fervor of writers with minds and personalities. Even in the cases where, in my opinion, the scripts have lost the distinction they seemed to have originally, they still awaken enchanting memories of days of doubt, hope and inquiry. They are a part of the human experience.

Robert Sherwood, for example, began as a playboy of the western world in ruminative comedies like *The Road to Rome* and *The Queen's Husband.* But who shall say that his mind and convictions were less interesting when he became a propagandist of contemporary ideas in *Idiot's Delight* and *There Shall Be No Night*? He grew in moral stature as he declined in sophistication and exuberance. He did not have to give his life for his country, as many of his contemporaries did. But he did give his career for his country; although I find *There Shall Be No Night* prosaic, diffuse and ingenuous today, I still feel enriched by Robert Sherwood's high-mindedness.

None of the writers of the plays discussed in this book failed in his mission in life. All of them said what was on their minds at specific moments. All their plays are pertinent to the human tradition; and the actors, directors, designers, company managers and house **man-agers**—and audiences—did the best they could by them at the time. The record is both bright and honorable.

This is the second occasion on which Al Hirschfeld and I have collaborated on a book. The first was *Broadway Scrapbook* in 1947. The illustrations for that book consisted of reproductions of theatre drawings he had made for the Sunday drama pages of *The New York Times,* and the text consisted of seventy of my Sunday articles. Neither one of us had to do much new work. But for *The Lively Years* Mr. Hirschfeld has had to make new drawings for almost all the plays discussed. For these he had to consult the files at the Library of the Performing Arts (one of the most civilized places in New York) for material on which to base his drawings.

No problem. Mr. Hirschfeld likes to draw, likes to go to the theatre, and likes just about everything—friends, arguments, art exhibitions, dinner parties around his monumental dining table, and books, magazines, and newspapers. I have just looked up a sketch about him that I wrote in the Introduction to *Broadway Scrapbook.* All of it is still as valid now as it was then. Let me quote one section: "Friends of Chekhov used to say they never knew when he did his writing since he always seemed to have so much time for sociability. That's one of the mysteries of Hirschfeld. I know he does a prodigious amount of work, but he never gives the impression of working. He is never too busy to go to the theatre, on short notice, too, nor too busy to plunge wholeheartedly into the muddled affairs of his friends, for he has a versatile healing hand for all kinds of people, and he is never too busy to drop everything and plunge into an argument."

In the quarter of a century since those comments were made, nothing about Al has changed except that his smashing black beard has become white and venerable. The sparkling eyes still betray the impudence that bubbles behind them. And his drawings: In comparison with the lively sketches he was making twenty-five or thirty years ago the drawings have become more spontaneous; they are more like improvisations in design, with the lines nimbler and more mischievous. If they were not so entertaining, people would realize that they rank with Forain, Toulouse-Lautrec, Cruikshank, Rowlandson, and the friskier aspects of Hogarth.

I have been a friend of Al's ever since we met on the Soviet steamer *Sibier* in 1936 on the way from London to Leningrad and then on to a theatre festival in Moscow. Since it is a matter of honor for the Soviet administration to promote its worst art as its best, the theatre festival was a ludicrous disaster. But Al and I had a very good time, and have had very good times ever since. I am glad to be in the same book with him again.

BROOKS ATKINSON

o o o o o o o o o o o o o o o o o o o o o o o o o o o o o o o o o o o o o o o o o

Dedicated with Thanks to
the Lincoln Center Library
of the Performing Arts
and the Walter Hampden Memorial Library at
The Players.

Pauline Lord in ANNA CHRISTIE

Eugene O'Neill

ANNA CHRISTIE

Since Eugene O'Neill was the first American dramatist to write about human beings, as distinguished from fictional stereotypes, this book inevitably begins with one of his plays. *Anna Christie* was produced on November 2, 1921, at the Vanderbilt Theatre in New York. Although it came early in O'Neill's career, which had another thirty-two years to run, he was already a turbulent force in the theatre. His lonely sea plays, now collected under the generic title of *S.S. Glencairn*, and also *The Emperor Jones* had been produced in the Provincetown Playhouse in Greenwich Village, named for the Cape Cod community where O'Neill's plays were first produced. *Beyond the Horizon* was produced in 1920 at the Morosco Theatre in the Broadway district where it was an immediate success. Alexander Woollcott, critic for *The New York Times*, said it had "greatness in it." O'Neill did not have to wait for public recognition.

We have chosen *Anna Christie* instead of *Beyond the Horizon* to introduce this book because it is a pithier play. It dramatizes the private agonies of three inarticulate people trapped in the sprawling snare of life—Chris, an ineffectual, superstitious captain of a sea-going barge, Anna, his rootless daughter recently discharged from a tuberculosis hospital, and Burke, a stoker in a steamship. In the course of the drama Anna confesses to Burke, who wants to marry her, and to her father, who wants her to remain with him, that she has been a prostitute. Her news is devastating; both Burke and her father instinctively try to rid themselves of her. In the last act there is a desperate reconciliation of all three—one problem solved, but others looming on the future. In the last speech Chris faces the future apprehensively: "Fog, fog, fog, all bloody time," he mutters. "You can't see where you vas going, no. Only dat ole davil, sea—she knows!"

The production of *Anna Christie* represented the most perceptive talent in the New York theatre. Arthur Hopkins, a producer of taste and insight, directed the performance. Robert Edmond Jones, the pioneer in dramatic design, provided the battered, moody settings. Pauline Lord, a luminous actress with a reticent style of speaking, played Anna with an introverted pride that gave the play immediacy and power.

Just about everyone happily surrendered to *Anna Christie* as soon as it opened. It was obvious that something fresh and challenging had come into the theatre. But since O'Neill was already known as a tragic writer who despised the conventional theatre, some theatregoers took exception to what they described as the "happy ending." They regarded it as a surrender to the commercial theatre. A controversy broke out in the newspapers. O'Neill, a young man quick to take offense from any Establishment point of view, retorted that the last act was anything but a happy ending—that it indicated nothing happier than the continuance of the hopeless lives of three blundering people.

O'Neill had not skimped on the quality of his dramatic writing. *Anna Christie* is a masterpiece of characterization. Although all the characters are drenched in the gloominess of O'Neill's point of view, they are all vigorously individualistic. They are separate but equal and invariably consistent. Products of a purposeless environment, they all live without purpose or direction—hardly more than tokens of life floating on some dark current rolling on to oblivion. For all their worldliness, they have a kind of innocence about life.

O'Neill knew them and their environment. The first act is set in

"Johnny-the-Priest's" saloon (actually "Jimmy-the-Priest's" saloon) near the waterfront on Fulton Street in New York where O'Neill had lodged and often drunk himself into a stupor with other derelicts in the days before his first marriage.

O'Neill was a romantic rebel. He liked to shock the public with the bitterness of his assaults on American optimism. Since he was Strindbergian but not an intellectual like Arthur Miller, for example, or T. S. Eliot, or Jean-Paul Sartre, he could never define his philosophy lucidly. But one speech he gave to Anna comes close to his general attitude toward life: "We're all poor nuts and things happen, and we just got mixed in wrong, that's all." Not very profound. But from a drifter like Anna it recognizes, on the one hand, the helplessness of her life and, on the other, the need for compassion in all human relations.

In 1921 *Anna Christie* was a vivid fragment of reality. It won the Pulitzer Prize in 1922, two years after O'Neill had won his first with *Beyond the Horizon*.

o o o o o o o o o o o o o o o o o o o o o o o o o o o o o o o o o o o o o o

Eugene O'Neill

THE HAIRY APE

o o o o o o o o o o o o o o o o o o o o o o o o o o o o o o o o o o o o o o

If proof were needed that O'Neill was a dramatist, and not merely a playwright, *The Hairy Ape* would be the most effective evidence. It takes leave of the familiar world of physical reality, where the commercial theatre had been amiably at home for several decades, and goes off into the stratosphere of fantasy. It explores not so much the life as the soul of a primitive man. The hairy ape is Yank, a powerful, ignorant, braggart stoker in the engine room of a transatlantic liner. A wealthy girl who is making a patronizing tour of the engine-room is horrified by Yank's brutish appearance, talk and behavior. "Take me away," she screams. "Oh, the filthy beast!" and she faints. Through the rest of the play Yank tries to find her and get revenge for the insult. He never finds her. In the last scene he is destroyed by the system of which she is an important part.

In other hands, *The Hairy Ape* might have been an agitprop play with a political message, for it is alive with political implications. But O'Neill is not a propagandist. He translates the message into a roaring exercise in dramatic improvisation. He calls it "a comedy of ancient and modern life," an ironic phrase since Yank dies in the last scene. Any comedy it contains is black and malicious.

There is an element of autobiography in *The Hairy Ape*. O'Neill was indulging in the youthful pleasure of feeling sorry for himself in a world dominated by conventional people. But the genius of the play is its brawling expression of the personalities of seamen and water-front characters whom O'Neill knew more intimately than any other writer did.

There are at least two remarkable qualities in the writing of *The Hairy Ape*. In the first place, it is basically an expressionistic play. Despite a few scenes of direct writing, like the lyrical description of sailing ships, the below-deck scenes are for the most part expressed in group dialogue, like chants from an ominous underworld. In some of the group scenes the characters wear identical masks and thus represent a featureless class alienated from the rest of the world. Although Strindberg, who was O'Neill's chief mentor, had written expressionistic plays, the style was new to the American theatre. Ernst Toller's *From Morn to Midnight*—pure expressionism—was produced by the Theatre Guild on May 21, 1922. But *The Hairy Ape* had been produced two months earlier at the Provincetown Playhouse. O'Neill was not influenced by the Toller play.

In the second place, *The Hairy Ape* is pure existentialism in the vein of Jean-Paul Sartre's *No Exit*, which was produced in 1946. Yank

Louis Wolheim in THE HAIRY APE

is an existential character who owes nothing to anyone and gives nothing to anyone and lives alone in a totally indifferent world. When a suspicious policeman asks him what he has been up to, Yank answers: "I was born, see? Sure, that's the charge. Write it on de blotter. I was born, get me!" Being born was his only crime.

Nothing could be bleaker than the philosophy of *The Hairy Ape*. In May the chief magistrate of New York City, William MacAdoo, considered prosecuting the producers of *The Hairy Ape* for obscenity, indecency and impurity. He dropped the charges; he might have done better to prosecute *The Hairy Ape* for disturbing the peace.

The great strength of the original production was the animalistic acting of Louis Wolheim as Yank. While playing football in college years previously Wolheim had broken his nose; throughout the rest of his life it remained flat against his face and gave him a barbaric appearance. An excellent actor, he turned *The Hairy Ape* into a savage hubbub with devastating philosophical and political overtones. Arthur Hopkins, who had produced *Anna Christie,* and Robert Edmond Jones, who had designed it, were both involved as friends in the original production. After it had had a modest run in Macdougal Street, Hopkins brought it uptown to the Plymouth Theatre. He replaced the Oriental actress in the part of the society girl with Carlotta Monterey, a spectacular beauty and mediocre actress who was much admired on Broadway. When she took the part O'Neill did not pay much attention to her and she resented what she regarded as his rudeness. Seven years later—in 1929—she became his third wife, and had a fundamental and constructive influence on the rest of his career. In 1922 O'Neill resented the topside people as snobs and oppressors. In 1929 he was no longer in the fo'c's'le. He was a first-class passenger himself, and reveled in it.

○ ○

Karel and Josef Čapek

R.U.R. and
THE WORLD WE LIVE IN

ʊ ʊ

When *R.U.R.* and *The World We Live In* were produced—both in the month of October 1922—Czechoslovakia was only three years old. It had been created by the Versailles Treaty of 1919. Americans did not expect to be taking instruction from a nation as young as that. But the brothers Čapek—Karel and Josef, friends of the illustrious President Tomáš Masaryk—made a shattering impression on Broadway that year in two satiric plays about the ignorance and perfidy of the human race. Having been brought up to regard the theatre as a magic box that bore no relation to life, American playgoers were jolted out of their complacence. They had won World War I, or so they assumed, and they saw no reason to be pessimistic about their present or future.

Karel Čapek was the sole author of *R.U.R.*—the initials stand for "Rossum's Universal Robots." It is a brilliant satiric melodrama on the mechanization of life. Rossum and his son have discovered how to manufacture the near equivalent of human beings—everything essential being present except the soul. The "robots" do the physical work and much of the bureaucratic work in an industrial society. They are more efficient—two and one-half times more efficient—than people. They do not waste time on painting, weaving, playing the piano, or

A Robot in R.U.R.

going to church. Rossum believes that he has made God unnecessary. His industrial heirs now manufacture robots in some unidentified country and sell them in lots of five thousand or fifteen thousand to enterprising nations that want to cut the cost of manufacturing sensationally.

Eventually an engineer with a conscience begins to introduce some humanity into the manufacture of robots. Instead of "universal" robots he starts making "national" robots. That is the undoing of the system. When they are endowed with human attributes the robots start hating one another, and especially human beings. They revolt. "Slaughter and domination are necessary if you would be human beings. Read history," the last human being tells the victorious robots.

Some people were shocked by the audacity of Čapek's satire. Since it turned up in New York only five years after the Communist revolution, it was suspected of being Communist propaganda. One writer in the *Philadelphia Public Ledger* suggested the spectacular career of Gerard Swope, president of General Electric Company, as an antidote: "In the American-plan career of Mr. Swope is offered the best answer to the purveyors of such ideas as have their expression in such plays as *R.U.R.*," he declared sanctimoniously.

R.U.R. was written with great wit by a virtuoso playwright who could catch all the ideas he frivolously tossed into the air; and the flawless Theatre Guild production, with Basil Sydney, Dudley Digges, Helen Westley and Louis Calvert in the cast, had a run of 184 performances. *R.U.R.* provided a philosophical scandal that most people relished. Now we know that they were enjoying a prophetic play. For our system is today dehumanized by the computer. Like Rossum's Universal Robots, the computer is mechanically proficient and has extraordinary intelligence. It can absorb and systematize information more rapidly than human beings can. But it has also contrived an autonomous civilization separated from human civilization. It is a law unto itself; it has no moral or ethical standards. It perpetuates errors. It mechanically blocks communication with individual people who may be victims of computer errors. Since it is tireless and assumes omniscience it can become more formidable than the human beings who have conceived it. It can produce a monstrous, separate future in which human truth is overwhelmed. Karel Čapek was creating a philosophical joke in 1922. But the philosophical conclusion of the robots in his play: that man is "an outlaw in the universe," does not seem to be so fantastic now. The nerve that Karel Čapek struck in 1922 is still a live nerve today. He was dreaming of the plausible.

THE WORLD WE LIVE IN

In the same month in which the Theatre Guild produced *R.U.R.*, William Brady, a commercial producer, put on a more comprehensive satire by Karel and Josef Čapek—*The World We Live In*. It opened at the Al Jolson Theatre on October 31, 1922. In the original text the play was called *The Insect Comedy* because it represented the mass behavior of civilized human beings as being identical with the mass behavior of moths, crickets, beetles, ants—mindless, merciless, instinctive, voracious, cruel—quite the opposite of the ethical concept the human race has of itself. Incidentally, it was a matter of ironic amusement on Broadway that this terrible indictment of the social system was produced by a commercial manager and adapted for the American stage by Owen Davis, a commercial dramatist known at that moment as the author of hundreds of hack plays.

There are none of the familiar social amenities in *The World We Live In*. Among the insects love and courtship is full of malice and deception, and no one gets what he wants. Every insect is greedy. If a beetle accumulates a fortune he is immediately obssessed with the necessity of making another fortune. "Everyone who has made one pile has to try to make another," one beetle says to another. "Oh, what a treasure . . . what a precious little fortune," says a female beetle to her male. "It is our only joy. To think how we've saved and scraped, toiled and moiled, denied ourselves," says the male, although it turns out, as the authors say, that it is harder to keep a fortune than to make it.

In the midst of all this carnage and ferocity, a human being, called the Vagrant in the program, tries to convince himself that human beings are a cut or two above the insects because they work for others —"the price we owe for life, not to ourselves, to others." But the Čapek play will have none of that. It sweeps on into the pious barbarisms of war—a subject that the Čapek brothers knew more intimately than most Americans. Their dialogue is full of sanctimoniousness and double-think: "We are waging the battle of peace by waging war." "We are a nation of peace. Peace means work. And work strength. And strength war." The side that is losing the war convinces itself that it is winning. When the news comes back that his troops are losing, the Dictator says it is "according to plan," and the Quartermaster tells the public: "Our heroic men are fighting in magnificent spirits." Light at the end of the tunnel, no doubt.

But the Čapeks' ultimate assault on the hypocrisy of war is the humbug of the Dictator's prayer to God: "Great God, thou hast granted victory unto Justice. I appoint Thee, Colonel! Third Division, forward against the enemy! Spare nobody! No prisoners! Forward! Righteous God of strength, Thou knowest that our holy cause is Thine! Thou knowest that in our victory lieth the victory of right and justice over base and evil enemies, and in Thy divine will I bow my heart in humbleness! After them! Hunt them down! Kill! Kill! Slaughter all!" The leader of the opposing army addresses God in the same unctuous style.

Since *The World We Live In* is written in the expressionistic style many theatregoers—accustomed to the Belasco type of realism— left the theatre disgruntled and certain that they had been swindled. But the critics took the play very seriously. They urged their readers to see it. And it is interesting a half century later to note that several actors who had small parts in the play later became leaders in the theatre: Kenneth MacKenna, who was to accomplish many things in Hollywood, played a beginner's part in the Čapek play. Mary Blair, one of the pioneers in the Provincetown Playhouse, played one of the butterflies. Vinton Freedley, later an important producer and one of the two builders of the Alvin Theatre, played a male cricket. And Jasper Deeter, founder of the Hedgerow Theatre near Philadelphia a few years later, played a parasite.

In 1922 it was possible for two writers in the new state of Czechoslovakia to lay about them facetiously, ridicule totalitarianism and jeer at the complacencies of civilization. Fifty years later they were gone and Czechoslovakia was a captive state of Soviet totalitarianism, while Americans were fighting an imperialistic war, defending their ferocity by using dialogue similar to the sanctimonious buncombe of the Dictator in the Čapek caper of 1922.

The theatre makes more sense than life.

o o o o o o o o o o o o o o o o o o o o o o o o o o o o o o o o o o o o o o o o o

Elmer Rice

THE ADDING MACHINE

o o o o o o o o o o o o o o o o o o o o o o o o o o o o o o o o o o o o o o o o o
.

Elmer Rice's *The Adding Machine* is the classic expressionistic American drama. In a bizarre style that is close to caricature it dramatizes the crushing banality of the life of a clerk in a big-business institution. It looks and sounds coldly objective; it is almost destitute of emotional facts or statements. But it portrays a devastating tragedy in the life of **Mr. Zero**, who is the victim of an inhuman economic system. It is a grisly morality play.

When he was twenty-two years of age and a rather sullen, disgruntled young attorney, Rice astonished himself and Broadway by writing a melodrama that earned about $100,000 in royalties and naturally changed the whole course of his life. The only distinction of that melodrama—*On Trial,* produced in 1914—was its craftsmanship. It introduced into a court drama the technique of telling parts of the story backward—"the flashback," as the device came to be known.

During the next nine years none of Rice's plays were either artistic or box-office successes. While he was working on another play in the summer of 1922, the whole story of *The Adding Machine,* including its characters, the title, and some of the dialogue, inexplicably popped into his head. For the next seventeen days he put on paper what he had imagined that summer evening. In those days the Theatre Guild was one of the very few producing organizations with enough imagination and enterprise to produce an original play with a critical point of view toward the economic system. Nobody thought of *The Adding Machine* as an "audience play."

The Guild also had, or had access to, actors able to cope with an adventuresome script. Dudley Digges, a remarkable unhackneyed Irish actor who had defected to Broadway, played Mr. Zero. Helen Westley, a woman with a very forceful personality and derisive sense of humor, played Mr. Zero's contemptuous wife. Edward G. Robinson, then known only as a promising young actor, played one of Mr. Zero's acquaintances—Mr. Zero had no friends. Settings by Lee Simonson, a bold, inventive, contentious designer; music by Deems Taylor, a modish music critic and composer; staging by Philip Moeller, a cosmopolitan man of the theatre—the production represented the enthusiasm and inventiveness of some of Broadway's finest people, and *The Adding Machine* opened with a blast of intellectual defiance at the Garrick Theatre on March 19, 1923.

Some of the older critics were scornful of the expressionistic technique, which they regarded as an insufferable pose on the part of a young American writer. An anonymous writer on *The New York Times* denounced the fifth scene as "coldly and gratuitously vulgar," and seemed to feel that the whole enterprise was subversive. In those days there was a grumbling minority that did not want the theatre to become a criticism of life. But the Guild subscribers, who were the most intelligent theatregoers in town, and the general public gave *The Adding Machine* a comfortable run of nine weeks, which spelled success in 1923.

Apart from his technical skills, Rice was a political activist. He was a Socialist, which sounded then as menacing as Communist did some years later. *The Adding Machine* expressed Rice's hatred of capitalistic business organization. Of the seven scenes two are monologues that reveal the lurid fantasies, the callow defiances, the monotony, the desperation, and finally the anguish of small people caught in the routines of big business. Everything about the early scenes is corrosive—the hateful home life, the office routine, and the intolerable dullness and emptiness of social meetings. But Rice had something more imaginative to contribute to this epitaph on a loser. After Mr. Zero has been found guilty of the murder of his employer he goes to the sublime Elysian Fields where he meets the young woman office worker to whom he was timidly attracted when they were both alive. For the first time they have the freedom to acknowledge their mutual attraction.

Rice was too realistic to think that *The Adding Machine* could have a happy ending. Mr. Zero, who objects to the presence of so many drunkards, thieves, adulterers and blasphemers in the Elysian Fields, is condemned to reincarnation; and in the last scene the superintendent of the Elysian Fields tells Mr. Zero the facts of life: "You're a failure, Zero, a failure. A waste product. A slave to a contraption of steel and iron. The animal's instincts, but not his strength and skill. The animal's appetites, but not his unashamed indulgence of them. True, you move and eat and digest and excrete and reproduce. But any microscopic organism can do as much. Well—time's up! Back you go—back to your sunless grove—the raw material of slums and wars—the ready prey of the first jingo or demagogue or political adventurer who takes the trouble to play upon your ignorance and credulity and provincialism. You poor, spineless, brainless boob—I'm sorry for you."

In 1923 *The Adding Machine* had special relevance. The industrial system that is now called "the assembly line," but known then as "the endless belt," symbolized the degradation of human beings in the service of large corporations. This is commonplace now, and for the most

Dudley Digges in THE ADDING MACHINE

part accepted. But it provoked the hostility of Elmer Rice and social thinkers like him who looked at corporate success suspiciously.

The Adding Machine provoked in turn the hostility of H. Z. Torres of the *New York Commercial,* who wrote:

"*The Adding Machine* is another integral added to that speedily growing number of morbid plays, possessing neither dramatic form nor literary merit, singularly devoid of beauty, debasing in context and repellent in language, destructive of national sanity and which must inevitably corrode the moral fiber. If this so-called 'expressionism,' with its profanation of the dead, its profanity, its mockery of patriotism, and its intimate revelations of the tactics of a prostitute which are vouchsafed in *Roger Bloomer* and *The Adding Machine* are really as claimed 'the theatre of tomorrow,' then let those of us who respect dramatic literature and who love the beauty of the theatre clamor for censorship which will save to posterity the 'theatre of yesterday.' "

Too late. The theatre of yesterday was gone for good.

o o o o o o o o o o o o o o o o o o o o o o o o o o o o o o o o o o o o o o o o o o o o o o

George Kelly

THE SHOW-OFF

o o o o o o o o o o o o o o o o o o o o o o o o o o o o o o o o o o o o o o o o o o o o o

It was a time when American society was thought to be unbearably crude and bumptious. Many young intellectuals escaped to Paris to find people worthy of their cultural standards. Warren Gamaliel Harding, the most orotund and hackneyed of men, had been President from

Louis John Bartels in THE SHOW OFF

1921 to 1923. Sinclair Lewis' *Main Street* had made America self-conscious about the emptiness and bombast of middle-class life. When
George Kelly's *The Show-Off* opened at the Playhouse on February 4,
1924, the audience was ready for it. Having been wounded by the
anger of *The Hairy Ape* and the bitterness of *The Adding Machine,*

the audience was grateful for Mr. Kelly's sense of humor. He had been a vaudeville actor and a writer of vaudeville sketches; and, accordingly, he had an instinct for the line that exploded with laughter and for situations that were compact and vivid. Also, he wrote meticulous stage directions, as if he were coaching a vaudeville actor.

The subtitle was "A Transcript of Life in Three Acts." That may have sounded a little pretentious for a vaudeville actor. But it did not overstate that truth. For Kelly knew his characters intimately—lower middle class in a Philadelphia suburb, commonplace and unimaginative, absorbed in the dreary details of housekeeping in the day of coal furnaces and kerosene lamps, obsessed with the latest styles in women's fashions, preoccupied with money, destitute of ideas. Still, Kelly did not patronize them. They emerged from his script as people of scruple. Their instincts are admirable. They are loyal to one another, despite minor clashes of temperament, and they despise petty fraud, bombast and crude behavior.

Aubrey Piper, the protagonist, is a cheap bore and a blowhard. Although he is a $32.50-a-week clerk in the freight office of the Pennsylvania Railroad, he has delusions of grandeur and imagines himself a potential tycoon. He has inventive ideas. He is vain. He wears snappy clothes and invariably has a carnation in his buttonhole. "Carnation Charlie," his skeptical comrades call him. He is loud. He ends his braggart declarations with bromides like "sign on the dotted line," and laughs uproariously at his own jokes. He is in love with a romantic young lady who loves him, perhaps because he is more interesting than the somber members of her family; and she believes implicitly everything he says. The rest of the family detests him. They treat him as civilly as possible, but they believe nothing he says and try to avoid associating with him.

All this was pertinent, or was thought to be pertinent, to everyday life in the early twenties when America was getting giddy and young egotists were bellowing against the social usages of their country and were drinking illegal booze out of hip flasks. Stocks were going up sensationally. Clever people were making a lot of money and the political leadership of the country was dull and complacent. Automobiles were swarming all over the country. Radios for the general public were becoming numerous and people were listening to national radio programs of no value. The silent screen reeked with glamour. Aubrey Piper was a detestable character, but he illustrated one aspect of American life in the middle twenties, and theatregoers were conditioned by the times to recognize him. In the original production he was played by Louis John Bartels, a vaudeville actor, whose loud laugh rang through the whole play—boring and tedious, but somehow amusing and a little ingratiating. During the run of *The Show-Off* Bartels was a sensationally popular actor. One of the other parts was played by Lee Tracy, who was just moving into the theatre. Although Bartels' hearty and complacent laugh dominated Forty-eighth Street during the play's 575 performances, he never had another success in the theatre. His dramatic career came to an end when *The Show-Off* reached its last performance—a cruel though familiar situation in show business.

The Show-Off is one of the Broadway plays that discussed contemporary America with originality and insight. But when it burst on the town nearly everyone was disappointed by its mechanical ending. In the last scene the routine happy ending of the old theatre folklore destroys the truth of the characterizations. After having been a bluff, bore and blowhard, Aubrey has a big financial success just before the last curtain. He has outwitted the people who distrust and dislike him and brought good fortune not only to himself but to them. He turns out to be a benefactor. This bogus happy ending mars a comedy that is otherwise perceptive and scrupulous. It puts a vaudeville climax to Kelly's transcript of life in the twenties. Business strategy had dictated the insipid conclusion. When *The Show-Off* was on the road the apprehensive producer is said to have demanded that Kelly write a happy ending. No one knows what ending Kelly had in the original script.

But his comedy still has validity. A half century later the Phoenix-APA company revived it with Helen Hayes, a guest member of the company, playing the mother of the family. The revival was a great success. To aid the company, which was, as usual, in serious financial trouble, Miss Hayes took the play on the road the next season and turned a profit of $250,000 over to the New York company. Everything about *The Show-Off* seems destined to have a happy ending.

o o o o o o o o o o o o o o o o o o o o o o o o o o o o o o o o o o o o o o o o

Laurence Stallings and Maxwell Anderson

WHAT PRICE GLORY?

o o o o o o o o o o o o o o o o o o o o o o o o o o o o o o o o o o o o o o o o

Even if *What Price Glory?* (September 3, 1924) had not been such an exuberant play it would have been notable for an ideological reason. It eliminated the jingoism common to war plays. It was able to cope with war without saluting the flag.

Laurence Stallings, a former Marine, and Maxwell Anderson, an inflexible pacifist, wrote it in the evenings after they had finished their day's work on the staff of the *New York World*. Although World War I had deprived Stallings of one leg it did not deprive him of his sense of humor nor moderate his natural gusto. In *What Price Glory?* the principal war on the western front is not between the Germans and the Allies but between a hard-drinking Marine captain and a venomous sergeant over a French bar girl who is accessible to both.

In the twenties this was a casual way of looking at such a colossal event as a world war, and many respectable people were shocked by it. Admiral Charles P. Plunkett, commander of the Brooklyn Navy Yard, denounced it as a libel on the patriotic American armed forces, and appealed to the New York License Commissioner to stop it. There were other vigorous complaints. The raffish captain and the sergeant

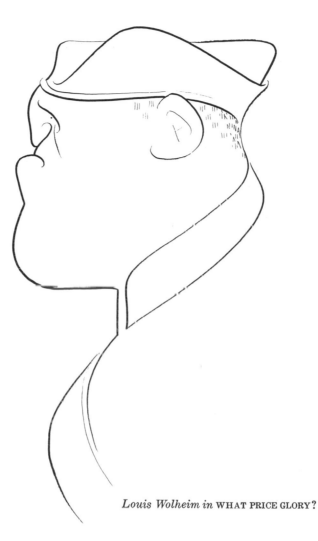

Louis Wolheim in WHAT PRICE GLORY?

talked an explosive language seldom, if ever, heard on the stage. "Sea-going son-of-a-bitch" is one of the most notable expletives used in the play. It would have blown the hats off the heads of the audience if their hats had not already been tucked into the hat racks which in those days were fastened under all theater seats. "God damn every son-of-a-bitch who isn't here!" one of the Marines yells during the grisly scene in the trenches.

People talked like that at the front and on the streets of New York, but they did not talk that way on the stage. In 1924 the city administration was not of a high moral character. Jimmy Walker, known popularly as the Night Mayor because of his addiction to night clubs, set the standards for public morals, which were not high. But the city could not ignore protests by people known to have political influence. The police accordingly sent a cavalcade of patrol wagons to arrest the cast after one performance. It was a noble gesture by a baffled administration. But Arthur Hopkins, the director and producer, instructed the cast to keep the dialogue clean that evening, and the crisis passed. The military vernacular went back into the dialogue as soon as the Black Marias returned to the police garage.

Is *What Price Glory?* realism? It seemed realistic in its day. Instead of paying tribute to the grandeur of war in honor of a nation that had just helped win one, it ignored heroism and bravery. It reduced war to a secondary status by laying principal emphasis on the wrangle between Captain Flagg and Sergeant Quirt over their common whore. In the play the captain and the sergeant have been in the Marines for years and have scuffled in many places. In their view, war is not a glorious cause but a business. The young drafted men and the young officers fresh from training camps may be idealistic, but they seem contemptible to the old professionals. Everybody does his duty. In the one scene laid in the trenches *What Price Glory?* tears an ugly page out of the obscene book of war—noise, confusion, hunger, weariness, pain, death, pigheadedness, futility. If *What Price Glory?* were an exposé of war this one shattering scene would be more effective than a polemic by an intellectual. It reduces war to the status of a silly afterthought.

Whatever the theme of the play, it memorializes the high spirits of two young writers who were longing to write a Broadway hit and make a lot of money. Stallings had written a successful war novel entitled *Plumes*. Throughout his career war was his basic theme. When he went to Hollywood later he wrote *The Big Parade, Old Ironsides,* and *The First World War*. Maxwell Anderson had written an unsuccessful verse tragedy called *White Desert*. Stallings and Anderson had seen other young writers with no experience strike it suddenly rich on

Broadway, and they saw no reason why they should not do the same.

Although they avoided the fervent set pieces of most war plays they could not help being romantic themselves. *What Price Glory?* ends with one of the most romantic curtain lines of any theatre piece. While the captain and the sergeant are fighting each other, the company is suddenly ordered back to the front for emergency duty. The captain starts off obediently if wearily. But the sergeant has just been slightly wounded (probably intentionally) and is in a victorious situation. He can now have the little French whore all to himself. But after all his years as a professional soldier his instinct is to go to the front with his outfit. "Hey, Flagg, wait for baby!" he yells as he starts hitching off to battle. It is a great curtain line. It is also romantic.

In the next to the last line of the play Quirt exclaims: "What a lot of goddamn fools it takes to make a war!" That's probably the intended theme. And the people who suspected that *What Price Glory?* was pacifist propaganda ignored the patriotic bravura of the last scene.

The performance under Arthur Hopkins' direction was superb— a blast of energy and acid humor. Louis Wolheim, whose broken nose and animal ferocity had made him so effective in *The Hairy Ape*, was triumphant as Captain Flagg; and William Boyd played Sergeant Quirt with canny humor and agility that balanced the captain's cruder style. *What Price Glory?* was a great show in 1924. It overwhelmed audiences. It also undermined the traditional respect for war.

o o o o o o o o o o o o o o o o o o o o o o o o o o o o o o o o o o o o o o o o o o

John Howard Lawson

PROCESSIONAL

o o o o o o o o o o o o o o o o o o o o o o o o o o o o o o o o o o o o o o o o o o

Both the story and the form of *Processional* were audacious in 1925. John Howard Lawson was a serious champion of "class-conscious workers." In his narrative of a coal strike in West Virginia he took their side against their traditional enemies—the owners, the strike-breakers, the soldiers sent in to keep order by the Federal Government, the Ku Klux Klan. Mr. Lawson was not the only playwright concerned with the political and social dilemmas of labor, but he wrote with the moral rectitude of a partisan: his political divisions were black and white. *Processional* was the prototype of the left-wing political plays that flourished in the next decade. In the organization of the "proletariat"—a resonant word at the time—Mr. Lawson saw "a new sun rising." As a matter of fact, there never has been a proletariat in America. Even those entitled to membership would consider a proletariat un-American.

To many theatregoers *Processional* was exciting for another reason. Mr. Lawson was conducting a revolution against theatrical form. He felt that the American theatre lacked warmth and richness. Realism and expressionism he dismissed as beside the point. He thought vaudeville was the form closest to the American scene, and he called *Processional* "a Jazz Symphony of American Life." The play begins on

George Abbott and June Walker in PROCESSIONAL

July 4 with an impromptu band playing the "Yankee Doodle Blues" and then it proceeds to tap dance through a village inhabited by immigrants and native Americans, most of whom resent the immigrants.

Processional opened at the Garrick Theatre on January 12, 1925, and again the Theatre Guild was both host and creator. To many people the performance was a memorable experience, whether or not they shared Mr. Lawson's convictions. Stark Young, critic for *The New York Times,* dismissed the political premise as ugly and willful. But he found the performance "exciting, sometimes violently original, and sometimes moving to an immense degree." Heywood Broun called it the "scratch paper of a great American play." Gilbert Gabriel described it as "a rhapsody in red." Burns Mantle observed that "the more excitable modernists" believed that it represented "a gorgeous new form in the theatre." Conservatives, however, insisted that it was formless, incoherent and ugly. It had 96 performances before the conservatives made their point.

Processional has no literary distinction and perhaps was never intended to have. The dialogue consists of a few perfunctory words, generally spoken between two characters. A half century after the original performance, its point of view lacks freshness and pertinence. Not all labor men today are the heroic victims of an evil Establishment. But amid its dull phrases and its melodramatic story line *Processional* does establish some human relationships that are moving and admirable.

The original cast was like a prep school of the modern theatre. George Abbott, now a solid member of the Establishment and competent golf player, acted Dynamite Jim with great force and left-wing piety. June Walker, who became one of Broadway's first actresses, played the rebellious daughter of a Jewish storekeeper. Ben Grauer, who became a celebrated radio and television announcer, played a rural newsboy. Lee Strasberg, the holy father of the Actors Studio, played the "First Soldier." Among the extras were Sanford Meisner, who became an enterprising director and teacher; Arthur Sircom, who became a producer of plays of quality; and Alvah Bessie, who went to Hollywood. Donald Macdonald, leading man in many plays for the

Guild in the next two decades, played the worldly-minded newspaper correspondent who drifted into honesty when the circumstances made honesty plausible. Who was the crafty Jewish storekeeper?—Philip Loeb, who came into the theatre as a comedian but had a tragic experience when his left-wing convictions wiped the comedy off his face and left him vulnerable to right-wing insurgents.

Today *Processional* and its cast look rather ingenuous—a revolutionary prank on an outdated theme, played by eager young people who could not imagine what life had in store for them. It was alive with hope and conviction when it was new. It is now part of the lost innocence of America.

o o o o o o o o o o o o o o o o o o o o o o o o o o o o o o o o o o o o o o o o o o o o o

Eugene O'Neill

DESIRE UNDER THE ELMS

o o o o o o o o o o o o o o o o o o o o o o o o o o o o o o o o o o o o o o o o o o o o o

If Eugene O'Neill had been a hack the fury with which he wrote new plays would not be surprising. When he wrote *Desire Under the Elms* in 1924 he had already written three other plays that had not been produced: *The Fountain,* a diffuse play about Ponce de Leon; *Welded,* an overwrought play about the conflicts of marriage (his second marriage, in fact), and *All God's Chillun Got Wings,* a grim play about the marriage of a white woman to a black man. The theatre could not keep up with the torrent of his new plays—bad plays as well as good. For he could be carried away with theatrical ideas that he had not yet organized in his mind. He had accumulated random ideas during the years when he was not a recognized playwright. Once he was recognized, the theatre accepted his new plays without much discrimination.

Three of his plays were produced in the year of 1924—*Welded,* at the Thirty-ninth Street Theatre on March 17; *All God's Chillun Got Wings* at the Provincetown Playhouse on May 15, and *Desire Under the Elms* at the Greenwich Village Theatre on November 11. *All God's Chillun Got Wings* had created a sensation when it was rumored that a black man would kiss a white woman on the stage. The city license commissioner and district attorney felt uneasy about it and threatened to take action against it. *Desire Under the Elms* also created a sensation. District Attorney Joab Banton brought a charge of obscenity against it, although a jury of citizens voted "Nay." Other people of conservative tastes resented the play. George C. D. Odell, a professor at Columbia, complained that O'Neill was debasing the stage, increasing the use of profanity on the stage, and writing too many portraits of insane characters. No doubt the scandal was, as usual, good for the box office. After a successful engagement at the Greenwich Village Theatre *Desire Under the Elms* moved uptown to the Earl Carroll Theatre and then to the George M. Cohan Theatre, where it closed on October 17, 1925.

But there was another reason for the long run of *Desire Under the Elms.* It is an American classic. Since O'Neill wrote other great plays, like *Mourning Becomes Electra* and *Long Day's Journey Into Night,* it would be difficult to argue that *Desire Under the Elms* is his finest work. But if he had never again written a play of such caliber, and if his career had come to an end in 1925 he would still have the rank of the greatest American dramatist. *Desire Under the Elms* would be the climax of a career that included the sea plays, *The Emperor Jones, The Hairy Ape, Beyond the Horizon,* and *Anna Christie.*

Everything about *Desire Under the Elms* is of top quality. The play is compact; one setting serves every scene. The movement of the story is inevitable and the pressure constantly increases. O'Neill often wrote diffusely; the texture of some of his plays is loose and careless.

Walter Huston in DESIRE UNDER THE ELMS

But there is not a superfluous word in *Desire Under the Elms*. Once the story has begun, it builds to its logical and shattering climax. *Mourning Becomes Electra* and *Long Day's Journey Into Night* are looser than *Desire Under the Elms*, which is a model of good craftsmanship.

The play is a classic basically because it exploits a fundamental theme. It is concerned, not with individual people, but with the universalities of lust and greed. It is not a dramatization out of Mr. O'Neill's past experience or concerned with milieus that he knew personally, as was the case of *Anna Christie* and *The Hairy Ape*. The characters are not recognizable people. Mr. O'Neill's view is that of an outsider. His Yankee dialect is an amateur attempt to mimic a style that he knew little about. The play is impersonal. Mr. O'Neill's description of the setting portrays the tragic mood more vividly than his description of the characters: "Two enormous elms are on each side of the house. They bend their trailing branches down over the roof. They appear to protect and at the same time subdue. There is a sinister maternity in their aspect, a crushing, jealous absorption. They have developed from their intimate contact with the life of man in the house an appealing humanness. They brood oppressively over the house. They are like exhausted women resting their sagging breasts and hands and hair on its roof, and when it rains their tears trickle down monotonously and rot on the shingles."

All the characters are hard people, consumed with hatred. Ephraim Cabot, the old man, owns everyone and everything; his pious view of himself is cruel and destructive. His three sons fear and hate him. So does his third wife, Abbie, whom he brings into the play after the introductory scenes. Eben, his youngest son, hates her and she hates him. Lust of the flesh is synonymous with lust for gold. Getting a son by her stepson Eben and passing it off as Ephraim's is Abbie's scheme for getting possession of the farm after Cabot dies.

What gives the play its tragic dimension is the transformation of lust into love between Abbie and Eben. Their motives have been as rapacious as those of all the characters until the climax of the play, when Abbie kills their infant son to prove that her love for Eben is genuine. After the terrible tumult of the play, Abbie and Eben go quietly off to jail and the sheriff speaks the last line: "It's a jim-dandy farm, no denyin'. Wished I owned it!"—a highly dramatic last line because it is irrelevant and opens to the rest of the world a play stifled by malevolence.

The original performance was superb. Following O'Neill's instructions Cleon Throckmorton designed a powerful production that turned the elms into shadows of evil. Walter Huston as old man Cabot gave a self-confident, pitiless, heroic performance of evil and piety; and Mary Morris as Abbie was equally powerful—a tigress in the opening scenes, a gallant woman at the end. Although *Desire Under the Elms* began as a farm play with all the familiar trappings, it grew in size and significance as it progressed. It made all the other American farm plays—*Way Down East, The Old Homestead, The Country Fair, Icebound*—look childish. Mr. O'Neill had written a masterpiece.

o o o o o o o o o o o o o o o o o o o o o o o o o o o o o o o o o o o o o o o o o o

Sidney Howard

THEY KNEW WHAT THEY WANTED

o o o o o o o o o o o o o o o o o o o o o o o o o o o o o o o o o o o o o o o o o o o

The people Sidney Howard portrayed in *They Knew What They Wanted* are about as far from Broadway as any characters can be. They are Italian wine-makers in Napa Valley, California, not far north of Oakland, where Mr. Howard was born in 1891. By American standards they are naïve people; they do not organize their lives efficiently

Richard Bennett and Pauline Lord
in THEY KNEW WHAT THEY WANTED

in terms of the American credo. They live by their emotions. But they suited Mr. Howard perfectly since he was basically a humanist with a wide knowledge of the temperament of different people. Before the United States declared war on Germany in 1917 he had served as a volunteer ambulance driver in France; he became an officer in the U.S. Army Air Corps when America joined the Allies. After being discharged from the service he joined the editorial staff of the original

Life magazine, and was its literary editor for three years. He also worked as an investigative reporter for the *New Republic* in labor matters and with Robert Dunn wrote an expository book called *Labor Spy*.

Although the Italian wine-growers were an obscure group of people in the twenties with no political significance and were unlike the people Mr. Howard had been associating with for ten years, he had vast respect for their spontaneity and benevolent impulsiveness. In his exuberant drama they do indeed know what they want. They want a loving family life. They want intimate friends. They want joyous neighborhood associations. The simple characters of *They Knew What They Wanted* are the exact opposite of the worldly people Mr. Howard had been associated with in France and in New York City. They were refreshing people to meet in the Broadway theatre in 1924.

Pauline Lord had a good deal to do with the hospitable reception the play received when the Theatre Guild put it on at the Garrick Theatre on November 24, 1924. The part of Amy, the mail-order bride, suited Miss Lord perfectly. It was a gentler version of the earthy Anna Christie she had played in 1921. Since Pauline Lord was an actress without the protection of technique, she was particularly poignant in the part of the defenseless Amy. The opposite part, that of the wine-maker, was played by Richard Bennett, an excellent actor with formidable technique, and the part of Joe, the unwitting interloper, was played by Glenn Anders, who was just beginning his stage career.

There is a plot in *They Knew What They Wanted*. Mr. Howard declared that his play was a dramatization of the Paolo and Francesca legend. Because he wrote it when he was living in Venice in 1923 he was working in a congenial atmosphere. The play tells the touching story of a San Francisco waitress who has been beguiled into agreeing to marry an aging Italian wine-maker from reading letters that were actually written, not by the prospective groom but for him, by Joe, the manager of the vineyard; and by a photograph of Joe inserted in one of the letters. She has been flagrantly deceived. In the excitement of the shattering confrontation in the first act she has an impulsive love affair with Joe and becomes pregnant. But Amy, Joe and Tony are not egotists who grab everything in sight and cunningly put their own interests first. They all make a final adjustment that recognizes the realities and restores everyone's self-respect—unlike Dante's version of the medieval legend.

If the characterizations were not so attractive and penetrating, the plot might tend to reduce the artistic stature of the play. The plot has many of the characteristics of the melodramas of the old American theatre when playwrights invented their plots first and then improvised characters to make the plots work. In all his plays Mr. Howard portrayed living characters—in *Lucky Sam McCarver,* which was all character and no play, *Ned McCobb's Daughter, The Silver Cord, Alien Corn* and in his dramatization of Sinclair Lewis' *Dodsworth.* People, the problems of people, the dilemmas of people were his chief interest and distinguished him from other playwrights who were primarily interested in moral or political ideas.

In less compassionate hands the emotional muddles of Tony Patucci, R.F.D., Napa, Cal., would have been comic sentimentality. A less sympathetic writer could hardly have avoided establishing his superiority by making fun of a simple man. But Mr. Howard took all his characters at their own value. Tony's explosions of excitement and his childish fears about marriage seem reasonable in Mr. Howard's view. Amy's succession of moods—good will, suspicion, alarm, hatred, forgiveness, reconciliation—are varying aspects of a well-meaning young lady, and they also demonstrate the virtuosity of Mr. Howard's understanding of people. Joe's worldly cynicism, softened by his devotion to Tony, makes for a valid combination of characteristics. (Incidentally, Joe's belief in the IWW—Industrial Workers of the World—was typical of the folklore of the twenties. The IWW was the standard symbol of labor insurgency. Note that it also appears in *The Hairy Ape* and *Processional.*) The irritable doctor, the bigoted but friendly priest, the neighborly R.F.D. driver, and the Chinese cook who is faithful to his employer but at the same time a separate person —all are individuals. They are products of Mr. Howard's instinct for the truth of other people and of his own modesty. He did not impose himself on his characters.

They Knew What They Wanted won the Pulitzer Prize for the 1924-25 theatrical season. None of its predecessors had had anything like as much warmth, faith and independence. It brought some of the richness of California into the harsh world of Broadway.

o o o o o o o o o o o o o o o o o o o o o o o o o o o o o o o o o o o o o o o o o o o

Sidney Howard

LUCKY SAM McCARVER

o o o o o o o o o o o o o o o o o o o o o o o o o o o o o o o o o o o o o o o o o o o o

In 1925 the fashionable speakeasy was more democratic than the traditional saloon for a basic reason: It brought the upper classes into contact with the normal drunks. Prohibition had made drinking popular. Therefore the speakeasy seemed romantic because it combined lawlessness with the drinking of whisky smuggled in from enlightened nations.

In the year after Sidney Howard won the Pulitzer Prize for *They Knew What They Wanted* he wrote a speakeasy drama called *Lucky Sam McCarver,* which opened at the Playhouse on October 21, 1925. Although he was a celebrity at the time and although the play was extremely well acted by Clare Eames (his wife) as an upper-class barfly and John Cromwell as the proprietor of a speakeasy, it had only twenty-nine performances. The spectacular failure was the result of Mr. Howard's independent craftsmanship. The play had no plot, and it had no hero or heroine in the usual meaning of those words. In a preface written at the time, when the failure was most painful, Mr. Howard said, "I am quite clear that is an unusually good play and that it has been remarkably well produced and acted." But it failed, he thought, because the public would not accept a play without the conventional melodramatic staples, including the happy ending.

In the technical sense the play does have a hero and a heroine— that is, they are the central characters. The play is included in this volume because, like everything Mr. Howard wrote, it is more interested in people than in the theatre and it does portray the life of its time. Mr. Howard was a liberal. (And it might be remarked here, incidentally, that with the magnanimity of the liberal he referred to Jews as *Hebrews*. To the liberal *goyim* the noun *Jew* was disparaging.)

Lucky Sam McCarver opens in the Club Tuileries at 11:30 P.M. on "a dry New Year's Eve," during the middle years of the noble experiment of Prohibition. The neighborhood police sergeant and a member of the police Prohibition Unit are ceremoniously drinking to the "dry New Year" and collecting their regular graft. Everything in the club is amiably fraudulent. Among the playing guests is Carlotta Ashe, a member of the Establishment, and some of her decadent cronies. She fascinates Sam McCarver. In the course of the evening one member of her party is murdered. In order to avoid a terrible scandal Sam McCarver falsifies the evidence, takes the blame and convinces the police that he has murdered the guest in self-defense.

That tense first act with its violent incident is an excellent portrait of the depraved mood of the Twenties—graphic, extravagant, reckless, dissipated; also corrupt on a colossal scale from top to bottom. Prohibition had made a lawbreaker of everyone who had any self-respect.

But Mr. Howard was not primarily interested in the sinister glamour of the speakeasy. He was interested in the hopeless clash between two people from the extremes of society—the upper-class girl who has no sense of responsibility and lives on her friends from moment to moment, and the social upstart whose sense of responsibility consists in running over or knocking down or using anyone who stands in his way to financial success. He cannot recognize the bitchery of the goddess of success because he is part of it. Both of these characters are ruthless egotists. Neither is capable of sustained fidelity to any ethical code. One is as contemptible as the other.

During the Twenties there were inevitably many plays set in speak-easies, the most spectacular being *Broadway* by George Abbott and Philip Dunning. But Mr. Howard was the only dramatist who regarded the speakeasy as a symbol of the moral degeneration of the entire nation in the Twenties. He knew that it was not just a lot of fun.

John Cromwell in LUCKY SAM MC CARVER

o o o o o o o o o o o o o o o o o o o o o o o o o o o o o o o o o o o o o o o o o o o o

Sidney Howard

THE SILVER CORD

o o o o o o o o o o o o o o o o o o o o o o o o o o o o o o o o o o o o o o o o o o o

During the course of his research into sex, Sigmund Freud concluded that mother love is, or can be, evil. It was the most subversive thought in the years before some other Germans started firing bullets at the Allies in World War I. In the middle of the next decade Sidney Howard made the same point decisively in a turbulent play called *The Silver Cord,* which opened in the John Golden Theatre on December 20, 1926.

No one was expecting an attack on mother love at that moment. Calvin Coolidge was President. U.S. Steel was quoted at $261. Babe Ruth was batting .378. But the author of the lovely, forgiving *They Knew What They Wanted* upset the American way of life by exposing the sinister side of mother love in a belligerent play. Frank Vreeland, critic for the *Telegram,* ironically dubbed it "She Knew What She Wanted." She is Mrs. Phelps, a wealthy widow who conforms to all the rules of good citizenship in "one of the more mature residential developments of an eastern American city"—in other words, Westchester County. She is proud to be a churchgoer. *The Little Flowers of St. Francis* rests on her bedside table. She is a philanthropist. She is a patron of the library. She supports the hospital.

She has devoted her life to the education and well-being of her two sons. "Motherhood," she says, "is her profession."

When the play opens, her older son, David, is just returning from two years in Europe with his new wife, Christina. Mrs. Phelps receives him joyously and the new wife courteously. She does all the talking, much of it consisting of pretentious nonsense.

Throughout the first act *The Silver Cord* is so subtly written and organized that the theatregoer can hardly imagine that Mrs. Phelps is going to turn out to be not a beneficent mother but a bitch. Her implacable possessiveness comes to the surface when she assigns David and Christina to separate bedrooms. Then the trouble begins. And Mr. Howard, who has begun the play so politely, becomes increasingly caught up in its new morality and concludes by writing with the Jovian ferocity of Ibsen. David has not married a clinging vine. Christina is a professional biologist. She knows the facts of life. She has an appointment with the Rockefeller Institute in New York. David, an architect, and Christina expect to live in New York. Mrs. Phelps believes that by living in New York Christina is sacrificing his career for hers. That is the breaking point.

There is also a younger son, Robert, engaged to a more conventional girl, Hester. When Mrs. Phelps and Robert are alone that evening she urges him to break his engagement to a girl who, she says, is not worthy of him. He does and Hester tries to commit suicide by throwing herself into the family lake.

The rest of *The Silver Cord* is a noisy, tumultuous conflict between the two young women and Mrs. Phelps. Christina has the candor of the new woman of 1926 and puts the conflict in dramatic terms. She has to find out, she tells Mrs. Phelps, "whether David is going on from this point as your son or my husband." She tells David that his mother "still wants to suckle you at her breast." Speaking to Mrs. Phelps she shouts: "You belong to a type that is very common in this country, Mrs. Phelps—a type of self-centered, self-pitying, son-devouring tigress, with unmentionable proclivities suppressed on the side." The play has an old-fashioned melodramatic conclusion: after wavering between his wife and his mother, David

Earle Larrimore and Margola Gilmore
in THE SILVER CORD

leaves his mother's house with Christina. But Robert stays with his mother and lets Hester go. He is going to revert to the dipsomania of a county dilettante.

No one was bored by *The Silver Cord,* although some people were frightened. The Theatre Guild production was superb. Laura Hope Crews, a famous comedienne, had acquired enough girth by 1926 to play Mrs. Phelps triumphantly, and she did, scaring the living daylights out of proper people in the audience. The cast included some excellent actors—Margalo Gillmore, Elizabeth Risdon, Elliot Cabot, Earle Larimore.

But *The Silver Cord* needed no favors from anyone. In 1926 it was a sensational assault on a sacred American institution. Today, Mr. Howard's melodramatic curtains for Acts Two and Three would seem too savage for such a civilized theme. But if you were attacking motherhood in 1926 you had to be sure to kill your opposition. To many respectable people Sigmund Freud was still a poltroon.

o o o o o o o o o o o o o o o o o o o o o o o o o o o o o o o o o o o o o o o o o

Paul Green

IN ABRAHAM'S BOSOM

o o o o o o o o o o o o o o o o o o o o o o o o o o o o o o o o o o o o o o o o o

In Abraham's Bosom was the first play written by a white man who understood the intricacies of the life of the black people of the South. Paul Green wrote it out of personal experience and moral conviction. The play had no predecessors. Eugene O'Neill's *The Emperor Jones,* produced in 1920, was a theatrical fantasy; his *All God's Chillun Got Wings,* produce in 1924, was a polemic. For many years in the Broadway theatre, Negro performers had been dancing and singing in styles that white playgoers imagined were expressions of the childlike exuberance of the Negro race. The performers were appreciated. But even such a gifted comedian as Bert Williams lived a virtually segregated life in the theatre. Mixed casts were not accepted for a long time. When Bert Williams was starred in the *Ziegfeld Follies of 1911* many people were scandalized. The public was not prepared to accept black performers on the basis of their talents. *In Abraham's Bosom* did not generate much excitement when it opened at the Provincetown Playhouse in Greenwich Village on December 30, 1926, and it was never a real success, even after it won the Pulitzer Prize in 1927. But it was the first play in which a white man who had lived all his life among blacks was able to write about them as human beings afflicted with unique problems.

Paul Green was born on a farm near Lillington, North Carolina. One day when he was a youth he went to the adjoining town of Angier for a load of fertilizer. While he was there he hung around the railroad station to enjoy the excitement of seeing a train. The wood-burning locomotive thrilled him. When the train came to a stop a well-dressed, friendly Negro schoolteacher strolled along the station platform, greeting people cordially. For no apparent reason except bad temper the engineer, who had stepped down to the platform, snatched a cane from a man in the crowd and struck the Negro in the face. The act was totally barbaric. Mr. Green never forgot it—and especially the Negro's terrible loss of dignity. Mr. Green's reactions were not political, but human. He had been present on an inhuman occasion in a rural town of North Carolina.

When Paul Green wrote *In Abraham's Bosom* many years later he had not forgotten the incident, but his theme was more general. His play is the tragedy of a black field hand, Abraham McCranie, who is trying to get an education and teach school and help raise the level of his black contemporaries. Abe is the son of a white plantation owner and a black field hand. Abe's father is rather proud

Rose McClendon and Frank Wilson
in ABRAHAM'S BOSOM

of him. He, Abe, Abe's wife Goldie, and Abe's aunt Muh Mack have moments of real comradeship when they are by themselves. On one of these occasions the white father takes Abe's side against the blacks who oppose his attempts to educate himself. "Let him keep his books," the white father says. "He's the only nigger in the whole county worth a durn."

In Abraham's Bosom is not a melodrama. Mr. Green knows that the problems it raises are too numerous and subtle for melodramatic treatment. For the blacks are as much opposed to Abe's aspirations as the whites. They resent what they regard as his arrogance. "Abe talks too much to white folks," a fellow turpentine worker observes. Although the blacks talk like revolutionaries when they are by themselves, they are meek and and servile when whites are present. They are resigned to the comfort and security of having no trouble with the whites. "White and black make bad mixtry," one field hand says. "Give a nigger a book and just as well shoot him. All de white folks tell you dat."

Abe has no real friends. His ambition isolates him from the blacks as well as the whites. His father horsewhips him when Abe resists the abusive language of his white half-brother Although his father takes pride in Abe he cannot tolerate infraction of the code of white supremacy. The white man's hand is against Abe in everything. The board of education closes the school he is teaching in when he writes an idealistic speech about Negro education. He then goes to Durham to get away from his enemies. But he is driven from his job in an electric generating plant when he talks back to an abusive white man. *In Abraham's Bosom* ends tragically. Abe accepts the fact that he is a failure. "I end here where I began," he says in the last scene, when he realizes that the blacks do not want what he could have given them: "They're asleep, asleep, and I can't wake them." In the violent last scene he is killed by a mob of white men, and the last word is spoken by an unseen white man: "It's the only way to have peace, peace. Peace, by God."

The Twenties were the heyday of the folk play, which somehow was regarded as a purer form than most plays. *In Abraham's Bosom* was looked upon as a folk play. It is loose in form; it lacks tension and tempo and it is wordy. It includes folk songs and hymns—which were standard parts of the folk play. It reflects some of the beliefs and enthusiasm of Professor Fred Koch who taught drama at the University of North Carolina where Mr. Green was also a teacher. Professor Koch was a man of faith, energy and tolerance.

But Mr. Green's combination of reality and idealism gives *In Abraham's Bosom* greater distinction than any other play about Negroes at the time. It was acted with moving simplicity at the Provincetown Playhouse—and later at the Garrick Theatre—by black actors who seldom had the opportunity of appearing in a serious play about their own people. Jules Bledsoe, Frank Wilson, L. Rufus Hill, and Rose McClendon were talented and winning actors who understood the problems of the play. They gave a modest glowing performance that filled the theatre with tenderness and compassion. The technical shortcomings of the script of *In Abraham's Bosom*, and Mr. Green's complicated, almost incomprehensible version of the black vernacular in his dialogue probably accounted for the lack of box-office success.

o o o o o o o o o o o o o o o o o o o o o o o o o o o o o o o o o o o o o o o

Dorothy and DuBose Heyward

PORGY

o o o o o o o o o o o o o o o o o o o o o o o o o o o o o o o o o o o o o o o

When *Porgy* opened at the Guild Theatre on October 10, 1927 it looked like an inspired Negro show—a little loose and ponderous perhaps, because it was not all in one style, but full of friendly insights, neighborhood humor, and a kind of lumbering vitality. Ten years later it was famous throughout the world as the libretto for George Gershwin's sweeping opera, *Porgy and Bess*.

Only a year before *Porgy* opened, Paul Green had taken a stand against Negro discrimination in his *In Abraham's Bosom*. *Porgy* does not have a partisan point of view. It is a rambling lithograph of life

Frank Wilson in PORGY

in a Negro neighborhood called Catfish Row in Charleston, South
Carolina. Dorothy and DuBose Heyward, the authors, were citizens
of Charleston and familiar with such communities. There is no political point of view in their play. It accepts the realities of its time.
A creative work of art by two professional writers from the South,
it eliminates the familiar stereotypes of Negro life in the Twenties
and substitutes the taste, awareness and literary skill of two artists.
The brutal values of the life of the time are implicit in *Porgy* but
they are not stated or specifically opposed.

In all cases except one the appearance of white men in Catfish
Row is bad news. The exception is a benevolent aristocrat who manages to get one of the Catfish Row people out of jail. But all the other
white intrusions are hostile and malevolent. Two policemen, one de-
tective, one coroner (all completely alien in Catfish Row) resort to
power since they lack understanding. They threaten and bully everyone indiscriminately. When a white man comes through the gate into
the dingy courtyard the residents vanish instantly. The shutters on
the windows bang. The doors are slammed shut. You would think
that nobody had ever lived there.

But when they are left to themselves the residents live with
boldness and style. Their Catfish Row is a busy community—gambling, drinking, drug-taking, whoring and fighting on the one hand;
but also storekeeping, fishing for market, washing clothes, sewing
and peddling on the other. "Here comes the honey man," says the
Honey Man in the most musical of the street cries. *"Yo' gots honey?*
Yes, ma'am, I gots honey. *Yo' gots honey in de comb?* Yes, ma'am,
I gots honey in de comb. *Yo' gots honey cheap?* Yes, ma'am, my honey
cheap."

Most of the people in Catfish Row are respectable God-fearing
citizens—believers, charitable, tolerant. Although they are overwhelmed by the violence they are not crushed by it. Most of them
live decent lives in the midst of poverty and prejudice.

Amid all the distractions of *Porgy* there is a plot. Crown, a powerful bully, and his woman, Bess, dominate it. During a quarrel over
gambling Crown accidentally kills a neighbor. He flees into the wilds

of Kittiwah Island to elude the police. While he is away, Porgy, a cripple and a professional beggar, takes Bess into his room and cares for her. The story concerns the attempts by Crown and Sporting Life to take Bess away from Porgy.

Porgy is not so much an organized play as a rambling, episodic evocation of Negro civilization in a poor quarter of the town. The inhabitants are, among many other things, superstitious people. The shadow of a buzzard flying overhead frightens them. A hurricane terrifies them. In times of dread and danger they join in the singing of spirituals, which are the soul of the play. One of them goes:

> *Ain't it hahd to be a nigger!*
> *Ain't it hahd to be a nigger!*
> *Ain't it hahd to be a nigger!*
> *Cause yo' can't git yo' rights when yo' do.*
> *I was sleepin' on a pile ob lumbah*
> *When a w'ite man woke me from my slumbah*
> *An' he say, "Yo' gots fo' work now cause yo' free."*

The Theatre Guild production was memorably spectacular, directed with flair and thunder by Rouben Mamoulian. In the Twenties there were so few experienced Negro actors that white actors in blackface often played Negro parts, but all the Negro parts in *Porgy* were played by Negroes. The original cast included the best Negro actors of the day: Georgette Harvey, Wesley Hill, Rose McClendon, Frank Wilson, Jack Carter, Leigh Whipper, Evelyn Ellis, Percy Verwayne. On Broadway they were almost like a repertory company. Whenever Negro parts were available they were there. They brought beauty and dignity as well as humor and vitality to the epic of Catfish Row. In the Twenties they were known as colored people or, less frequently, as Negroes. The word *black* was thought to be humiliating.

o o o o o o o o o o o o o o o o o o o o o o o o o o o o o o o o o o o o o o

Eugene O'Neill

STRANGE INTERLUDE

o o o o o o o o o o o o o o o o o o o o o o o o o o o o o o o o o o o o o o

On January 30, 1928, Eugene O'Neill upset the normal routine of Broadway with a drama that took five hours to play. The curtain for *Strange Interlude* at the John Golden Theatre rose at five-thirty, descended at seven for a dinner interlude of eighty minutes; then the performance resumed and continued until after eleven o'clock. That was a sensational schedule and one which the public found exciting. It raised cozy problems about the proper dress. Should a well-bred play-goer appear in evening dress at five-thirty? Most members of the opening-night performance did not. But they noted with considerable awe and respect that Otto Kahn, the banker and patron of the arts, appeared in street dress at five-thirty but changed into evening dress for the second part of the performance.

Mr. O'Neill always enjoyed the epochal. *Mourning Becomes Electra* in 1931 also was five hours long; so was *The Iceman Cometh* in 1946 and *Long Day's Journey Into Night* in 1956. Long plays suited him. They are dramatic. Toward the end of his career Mr. O'Neill worked on a cycle of nine plays about a New England family, although he could never finish it.

There was a legitimate reason, however, to turn *Strange Interlude* into a long play. In the novels of the nineteen twenties—in

Lynn Fontanne and Helen Westley
in STRANGE INTERLUDE

James Joyce's *Ulysses* specifically—the stream-of-consciousness method of character exposition made it possible for an author to get behind the surface of a character into his interior thoughts and motivations. Although the old-fashioned "aside" in the theatre was obsolete Mr. O'Neill thought it could be used again to adapt the stream-of-consciousness method to the stage. This had been done at least once before. In 1915 Alice Gerstenberg's one-act play *Overtones* had made provocative use of the method in which a character spoke his private thoughts to the audience in an aside, in addition to his direct conversation with other characters. Mr. O'Neill proposed to use the stream of consciousness method in a serious probe into the shapelessness of the lives of characters who do not believe in God— his endemic theme.

There was one other contemporary factor. Although Freudianism, with its insistence on sexuality, had been available as a system since 1908 (when the International Psychological Association was formed) it was purely avant-garde on Broadway. People were delighted to be told that sex was important as well as enjoyable and that their most popular hobby had a respectable epistemology. Not that Freudianism was completely new on the stage. Sidney Howard's *The Silver Cord* in 1926 dramatized the Oedipus complex by exhibiting mother love as a monstrous evil. And there was another precedent. In 1912 Arthur Hopkins had produced Eleanor Gates' *The Poor Little Rich Girl* because he thought it was an interesting play. After it opened a doctor pointed out that it was pure Freudianism— a revelation that delighted both the author and the producer. Like Shakespeare, they had not realized that they were qualified analysts.

Freudianism permeates Mr. O'Neill's *Strange Interlude*. All the characters analyze themselves and one another by expressing their interior thoughts in asides. Dr. Edmund Darrell uses Freudian vocabulary to diagnose the mental ailments of the protagonist, Nina Leeds. Nina is a self-centered only child. She blames everything she doesn't like on the malice or stupidity of other people. As a result of her father's machinations, she did not marry and never had sexual relations with a glamorous young man whom she loved and who was killed in World War I. According to Mr. O'Neill, this frustrated love affair poisons her character for the rest of her life. She marries a weakling whom she can dominate. When his mother tells her that there is insanity in his family she has a secret abortion. She then has a clandestine amour with Dr. Darrell, who gives her a baby she has confidence in. She also accepts the platonic love of a novelist who has been a friend ever since they were both young.

In her search for emotional fulfillment and escape from the pain of her existence Nina uses men. She has more strength of character than they have. At the end of the sixth act there is a vivid scene in which she is seated with the three men most important in her life.

It is the climax of her struggle for contentment, and she speaks her thoughts about them in the most cogent aside in the play: "My three men!... I feel their desires converge in me!... to form one complete beautiful male desire which I absorb... and am whole.... They dissolve in me... their life is my life... I am pregnant with the three!... husband!... lover!... father!... and the fourth man! [the baby]... little man!... little Gordon... he is mine, too!... that makes it perfect!" (Neither she nor Mr. O'Neill could imagine that the baby might turn out to be a girl.)

Since Lynn Fontanne played Nina with power, concentrated aggression and magnetism, and since the three men were played with ardor and constancy by Glenn Anders, Tom Powers and Earle Larimore, this was the most memorable scene in the first production. It dramatized the situation boldly. The remaining three acts serve the purpose of completing Mr. O'Neill's theme, expressed in the last act: "Strange interlude! Yes, our lives are merely strange dark interludes in the electrical display of God the Father."

Strange Interlude demonstrates more than any other of Mr. O'Neill's full-length plays the close ties between his idea of theatre and the romantic, melodramatic theatre of his father, James O'Neill, the perennial star of *The Count of Monte Cristo*. *Strange Interlude* is full of melodramatic devices and assumptions. No one dismisses Nina as a bitch; she is deferred to as a privileged woman in need of understanding. In the last act the hackneyed device of the will turns up to complicate the conclusion. The dialogue is full of clichés: Nina's comment on her promiscuous amours is straight out of the old theatre—"giving my clean body to men with hot hands and greedy eyes." Her mother-in-law refers to the family insanity as "the curse of the Evanses." The craftsmanship of *Strange Interlude* is more visible than the creativity.

Strange Interlude had a long run in New York, and a traveling company headed by Pauline Lord, who was too diffuse for the part of a demoniac woman, had a long run throughout the country. For the play does have power on the stage. No matter how contrived the story, characters and dialogue, there is the beat of doom in Nina's unrelenting torment of her three men. There is "that feeling of death again," in the words of one of the characters. *Strange Interlude* is a potboiler—but an oversized potboiler consistent with the stature of the man who wrote it. It brought Mr. O'Neill his third Pulitzer Prize in eight years. In the Twenties no other American dramatist could compare with him.

o o o o o o o o o o o o o o o o o o o o o o o o o o o o o o o o o o o o o o o o o o

Charles MacArthur and Ben Hecht

THE FRONT PAGE

o o o o o o o o o o o o o o o o o o o o o o o o o o o o o o o o o o o o o o o o o o

Out of admiration for their impertinent style of juvenile delinquency, Ben Hecht and Charles MacArthur were labeled the "Katzenjammer Kids" when their *The Front Page* opened at the Times Square Theatre on August 14, 1928. They gave the newspaper business the raspberry in that lusty melodrama. They also violated some of the theatre's most hallowed canons of taste.

The Front Page is a pell-mell melodrama. It differs from the conventional melodrama in one significant respect. It has no hero, unless you except the minor character of a two-bit street-walker who does not waver in her loyalty to a convict she admires. Nor does it have a happy ending. Nobody emerges with honor from this outbreak of bedlam in the police reporters' room in the Criminal Courts building in Chicago. The noblest virtue of any of the characters is naïveté. The others are either political crooks or police reporters who, in the words of one of them, are "a cross between a bootlegger and a whore."

There is a basic situation around which the melodrama whirls. A meek, idealistic anarchist is about to be hanged for being a Communist ("Reform the Reds with a rope" is the political slogan). While the play is going on, the gallows is being tested by dropping sandbags which land with a grisly thump that shakes the police reporters' room. "They are fixing up a pain in the neck for somebody," one of the reporters remarks with a leer.

Meanwhile, the reporters are playing poker, answering calls from their city rooms or telephoning in trivial stories, while keeping up a steady stream of profane and filthy conversation on a cynical level. One of the Chicago newspapers is trying to persuade the sheriff to advance the hanging from seven o'clock to five o'clock for the benefit of its early edition. Nothing could be lower from any point of view—moral, political or professional—than the derisive melodrama Mr. Hecht and Mr. MacArthur wrote. Nothing could be more exciting or entertaining.

Both men had served as reporters on Chicago newspapers. The vicious managing editor who dominates the last act of their play is based on the character of a city editor of the Chicago *Herald-Examiner*—a fabulous egotist, bully and scoundrel. After graduating from crime reporting to playwriting the authors do not feel romantic about journalism. In addition to their humorously venomous portraits of police reporters, some of their stage directions express their contempt: Their managing editor, for example, is "that product of thoughtless, pointless, nerve-drumming unmorality that is the Boss Journalist."

After *The Front Page* had opened with a large bang, some New York editors and publishers were distressed by its portrait of iniquity; certain noble rejoinders appeared in the press later on. The *New York Times* critic, who enjoyed the play as a whole, blanched at the "Rabelaisian vernacular unprecedented for its uphill and downdale blasphemy." But no one who had ever worked in a police headquarters could deny that the tone of the language and the behavior

Osgood Perkins in THE FRONT PAGE

of the characters there were on the level Mr. Hecht and Mr. Mac-
Arthur indicated, and no one with any experience in city hall regarded politicians as sublime.

Nor could anyone deny that the melodramatic craftsmanship of
The Front Page was brilliant. The play is a constant uproar. Its
situations are in a state of continual flux; tensions are constantly
tightening and loosening as the different characters come and go,
and as their dialogue is segued into the main story. Most of the humor is outrageous; it snarls and snaps at everything. The last line
is famous. The treacherous managing editor has been trying to sab-
otage the wedding plans of his best reporter, Hildy Johnson. Just
before Hildy and his fiancée start out for the railroad station to take
the train to New York, the managing editor gives Hildy his watch
with a profuse speech of gratitude, affection and good wishes. But

as soon as Hildy and his girl are out of earshot the managing editor instructs his office to notify the police in La Porte, Indiana, to board the train, arrest Hildy Johnson and return him to Chicago: "The son of a bitch stole my watch!" the managing editor exclaims.

The original performance, staged by the legendary George S. Kaufman, was one of Broadway's greatest accomplishments—taut and crackling and loud. The two chief parts were played by Lee Tracy, who was just becoming a star, and Osgood Perkins, a much admired and prized actor who died a few years later while rehearsing in another play. In 1928 *The Front Page* shocked not only the newspaper business but theatre audiences, who were elated to hear on the stage some of the earthy language they used at home. But the play is certainly not a period piece. It has been frequently revived; it was successfully presented in 1969 with Robert Ryan and John McGiver in a series at the ANTA Theatre in New York; in 1972 it was acted in London by the National Theatre Company. It had become respectable at last.

o o o o o o o o o o o o o o o o o o o o o o o o o o o o o o o o o o o o o o o

Sophie Treadwell

MACHINAL

o o o o o o o o o o o o o o o o o o o o o o o o o o o o o o o o o o o o o o o

By 1928 expressionism was no longer a novel technique which had startled audiences with Georg Kaiser's *From Morn to Midnight* in 1922 and Elmer Rice's *The Adding Machine* in 1923. In both of these plays the attitude toward the characters was harsh. They were the wretched victims of an indifferent universe. The "Young Woman," who is the chief character in Sophie Treadwell's *Machinal,* is also the victim of an indifferent universe which whirls around her savagely and eliminates her from the vast organism of human life. But some of the later scenes affecting the "Young Woman" are written simply, in the vernacular of daily life, which gives her a personality. Miss Treadwell describes her as "a soft, tender woman in a hard, mechanized society." She is not the usual statistic of the expressionistic drama. She is a human being and the author has a compassionate feeling toward her. The author knows that being the victim of an indifferent universe is not all contemptible but is also pathetic and desolating.

Machinal, put on at the Plymouth Theatre on September 7, 1928, was suggested by the sensational murder case of Ruth Snyder and Judd Gray a year or two before. Secret lovers Ruth Snyder and Judd Gray murdered her husband in the expectation of living together on his life insurance. The case involved not professional criminals but obscure, rather stupid middle-class people and it started Miss Treadwell on a philosophical speculation about what effect the harsh environment of a modern city might have on a young woman too weak to cope with it.

The expressionistic portions of *Machinal* adumbrate the inhuman bedlam and pace of a modern city. The background voices of office workers and the mechanical noises of riveting machines, typewriters, telephones, and office buzzers create a modern city in sound. The dialogue is terse and shrill—composed, as it is, of the stinging speeches of hard-driving, self-preoccupied, shallow people on the make. The "Young Woman," a gentler person, is the secretary of an executive who falls in love with her and wants to marry her. She is terrified by the physical aspects of marriage and the formalities of homemaking, but she marries him to escape the torments of trying to earn a living. Some of her random thoughts are as follows: "Wants to marry me—Mrs. George H. Jones—Do you take this man to be your wedded husband—I do—to love honor and to love—kisses—no—I

can't—George H. Jones—straight—thin—bald—don't touch me—
George H. Jones—money—no work—no worry—free!" and so on.
But the marriage is a failure. George H. Jones is a businessman who
epitomizes all the things in the city that repel her.

Two or three years later she does have a moment of ecstasy with
an amorous man who is passing through the city. For the first time
in her life she is joyously happy. Then, in a moment of revulsion, she
kills her husband as Ruth Snyder did. In the last scenes she is convicted of murder, part of the evidence against her coming from the
man she has loved. That is the inhuman city's final rejection of the
"Young Woman." On the way to the electric chair she is still a sol-
itary lost soul: "Am I never to be left alone! Never to have peace!
When I'm dead, won't I have peace?" she cries. Her last words in the
electric chair are: "Somebody! Somebod——"

The story is sordid from the beginning. The environment is cold.
The characters are callous. The relationship between characters is
selfish and sullen. Not that the "Young Woman" is any better; she
too is weak and mean.

Although tragic things happen, *Machinal* is not a tragic play,
because the "Young Woman" is a nonentity. She has no positive
qualities. She brings nothing to society except lovely hands that everyone admires and a disarming personality. Her weakness—or
"softness" and "tenderness" in Miss Treadwell's words—amounts to
cruelty to anyone who has a right to expect anything from her—her
mother, her husband, her child.

Yet *Machinal* glows with wistful beauty. In some elusive way it
touches the hearts of the audience and stirs their sympathy. In the
original performance, which was staged by Arthur Hopkins, the acting of Zita Johann as the "Young Woman" was as incandescent as
anything Miss Treadwell had written. Miss Johann's frail, lonely,
faltering characterization poured a strange illumination into the play
and could not be ignored or rejected. It was Miss Johann's high point
in the theatre; she never had another success. An obscure actor
named Clark Gable played the lover with the same ardent clarity that
later made him one of Hollywood's most memorable actors.

Clark Gable and Zita Johann in MACHINAL

By mixing realism with expressionism Miss Treadwell touched a live nerve in the deadened city she was writing about, and found the one weak point in the technique of expressionism—total objectivity and detachment. Everything that happens in *Machinal* is cruel or contemptible. But Miss Treadwell, being on the side of the damned, made a rueful, touching play out of forbidding materials.

o o o o o o o o o o o o o o o o o o o o o o o o o o o o o o o o o o o o o o o

Elmer Rice

STREET SCENE

o o o o o o o o o o o o o o o o o o o o o o o o o o o o o o o o o o o o o o o

Originally Elmer Rice intended to call his play *Landscape With Figures*. He loved and collected art; perhaps he even saw his stage play in terms of a lithograph. But *Landscape With Figures* would have been a pretentious title for a remarkably realistic play about a polyglot handful of New York citizens living in a seedy tenement. **Mr. Rice** knew such neighborhoods intimately in his boyhood. What he had to contribute years later when *Street Scene* opened at the Playhouse on January 19, 1929, was the compassion and wistful hopes of an enlightened Socialist. "Why must people always be hurting and injuring each other?" one of the characters inquires. "Why can't they live together in peace?" Mr. Rice put that thought in terms of a question. He was too much a realist to believe that it could be answered affirmatively in the New York city of his day.

At the time he was writing *Street Scene* Elmer Rice was known

*Millicent Green, Horace Braham and
Erin O'Brien Moore in* STREET SCENE

on Broadway as the author, when he was a skinny, bespectacled youth, of a machine-made play called *On Trial* that had made a lot of money and an expressionistic drama called *The Adding Machine* which was admired but was not a fabulous success. Still, his reputation did not help him. Just about every producer who read it rejected *Street Scene*. It looked to them in manuscript diffuse and formless and seemed to have no theme. Finally, William Brady, a producer with the instincts of a promoter, accepted it without enthusiasm. George Cukor, the director Mr. Brady and Mr. Rice agreed on, was so bewildered by the manuscript that he deserted the rehearsals after two days and Mr. Rice, with no previous experience, faced the emergency by directing it himself. He directed it ably. In the next spring it received the Pulitzer Prize. What Mr. Rice had seen in his forty-one commonplace characters emerged on the stage and convinced audiences that the play had not only literal truth but also spiritual understanding.

The materials of the play are shabby. The action takes place on a baking summer day in an ugly old brownstone that has become a walk-up tenement in a mean section of Manhattan. Jo Mielziner, who designed the vivid setting, found the model at 25 West 65th Street. Like the play, the setting looked literal but was softened by the artist's personal empathy. Although the facts were shabby, the setting was beautiful.

And that is Mr. Rice's point of view. The characters who gossip on the front stoop or lean out of the windows or walk along the street are subsistence people in the days when public relief was niggardly and cautious. Their national origins are American, Irish, Swedish, German, Italian, Polish, Jewish—all trapped in the same economic dilemma. They are compulsive talkers. They have reactionary ideas. They do not trust boys with long hair or girls with short dresses. They are full of racial prejudices. They are bigots by inertia, most of them being incapable of independent thought. Although they try not to offend one another they repeat the stereotypes of racial distrust. In 1929, before the Nazi massacres, their anti-Semitism was uninhibited—seemingly plausible then, unbelievable today. Mr. Rice's characters include a doctrinaire Jewish intellectual full of political cant, his daughter, a schoolteacher, and his son, a college student. They are as full of racial hostility as their neighbors. When the schoolteacher is trying to persuade her younger brother not to fall in love with a Gentile girl, he replies: "I've told you a thousand times that Jews are no better than anyone else."

The story of *Street Scene* is as banal as the dialogue. Mrs. Maurrant, married to a bitter-tongued, drunken stagehand, is having an affair with the man who collects payments for the milk company. Mr. Maurrant surprises them together in his apartment and kills both of them in a scene of passion familiar to readers of tabloids. The murder and the search for the murderer supply the only real tension in the play. Everything else is a record of mediocrity.

But the characters and their monotonous lives are not stereotypes, because Mr. Rice believes in them. To him they are real people in a depressing environment. He does not romanticize them; his respect for them is not sentimental. He respects the variety of their experiences. As the play drifts along, Rose Maurrant, the Maurrants' daughter who is a young secretary, becomes the catalyst. She provides some standards of humanity. She knows that the environment in which they are all living is evil. She has a vision of a kinder world. When Sam, her neighbor and admirer, in a fit of pessimism, asks her what there is in life to compensate for the pain of living she replies: "There's a lot. Just being alive—breathing and walking around. Just looking at the faces of people you like and hearing them laugh. And seeing the pretty things in the store windows. . . And—oh, I don't know —listening to a good band and dancing." By being aware, Rose saves *Street Scene* from the sterility of the naturalistic method.

The play was shrewdly cast and beautifully directed. A lovely young actress with a perceptive mind—Erin O'Brien Moore—played Rose Maurrant with a kind of restless vision of a better world. All the leading parts were played by excellent actors—Mary Servoss as the passionate Mrs. Maurrant, Beulah Bondi as a lethal gossip, Leo Bulgakov, late of the Moscow Art Theatre, as the Jewish political insurgent, Horace Braham as the Jewish student, Anna Kostant as his sister, Robert Kelly as the violent Mr. Maurrant. They were the principal instrumentalists in an orchestrated performance.

Someone called *Street Scene* a tone poem. That was a prophetic description of a drama and performance that had rhythm and melody. For, in 1947, Kurt Weill, the composer, and Langston Hughes, the Harlem poet, transmuted *Street Scene* into a lovely opera that captured the music of New York City and is sung and acted repeatedly.

1930-1940

○ ○

George Gershwin, Ira Gershwin, George S. Kaufman and Morrie Ryskind

OF THEE I SING

○ ○

In 1931 *Of Thee I Sing* in the Music Box Theatre was the opposite of the depression throughout the country. The national mood was dark and apprehensive. There were ten million jobless Americans—destitute, in fact, for there was no unemployment insurance at that time. Then, on the evening of December 26, a jubilant marching song blasted out of the orchestra pit and a procession of actors marched across the stage with jeering political slogans. The song was *Wintergreen for President* and the two most audible lines were refreshingly flippant:

> *"He's the man the people choose—*
> *Loves the Irish and the Jews."*

In the depths of the depression this witty satire on politics and government found a very sympathetic audience among New York playgoers able to pay six dollars for a ticket. They found it a relief to laugh at a political system that helped banks but not people. But the permanent distinction of *Of Thee I Sing* lies in the devastating effect it had on standard musical comedy—on the bogus romance of the Sig-

mund Romberg and Rudolf Friml operettas and on the adolescent
story line of musical comedies like *No, No, Nanette* and *Irene.* Although Jerome Kern's flowing melodies had given *Show Boat* great
distinction in 1927, the romantic book was hardly more than the framework for its songs. Incidentally, 1927 was the year in which George
S. Kaufman and the Gershwins tried to break away from the old formula with a musical show called *Strike Up the Band.* It was too savage
and cynical for the public; it concluded with preparation for war
against Soviet Russia—a horrifying thought. Three years later the
book was revised and *Strike Up the Band* succeeded. But *Of Thee I
Sing* made the departure from the old banalities decisive. After this
play was produced, it became increasingly difficult for librettists to
write like imbeciles.

Some formidable wits pooled their talents in the composition of
Of Thee I Sing. George S. Kaufman and Morrie Ryskind wrote the
book, Ira Gershwin wrote the lyrics, and George Gershwin composed
the score. As Broadway showmen they had no real confidence in anything in life except a hit song and an explosive wisecrack. Although
they changed the nature of musical comedy by turning it into a criticism of life they retained the old structure. John P. Wintergreen has
been elected President on a platform of love. In the second act he is
about to be impeached for breach of promise in a suit brought by a
Southern hellcat. He is saved in the smashing last scene by the an-
nouncement of his wife's pregnancy. The legality of this conclusion is
shaky. But it provided the big scene that customarily concluded musical comedies. *Of Thee I Sing* did not create a new form.

The pace is brisk, however, and the nonsentimental mood is stimulating. Masters of the wisecrack, the authors destroy whatever they
mention. The political slogans on the signs carried in the opening scene
are both plausible and annihilating: "Vote For Prosperity and See
What You Get," "Turn the Reformers Out," "He Kept Us Out of Jail,"
"The Full Dinner Jacket." The authors reduce everything to the level
of Broadway. The one word "baby" in a lyric written by Ira Gershwin
makes a torch song out of a national hymn: *Of Thee I Sing, Baby.*
The criticism of government and politics is contemptuous; and amid

Victor Moore in OF THEE I SING

the explosion of gags potshots are taken at prohibition, radio announcing, Roxy, Mae West, Rudy Vallee, baseball, and anything else accept-
able to the public. Except for the conventional framework of the show
it is anarchy.

For all the wit and contempt for fraudulence *Of Thee I Sing* would
never have been the sensational box-office success it was without the
appealing personality of Victor Moore as Vice President Alexander
Throttlebottom. He brought personal warmth into an essentially heartless show. The authors' concept of the office of Vice President as a
ludicrous superfluity, in view of the nonentities who had been Vice
President, is both hilarious and plausible.

In the first act, the political hacks want Throttlebottom out of the
way. "No, no," one of them exclaims when the candidate for Vice

President offers to make some campaign speeches. "You know Vice Presidents don't usually go around in public. They are not supposed to be seen."

Victor Moore, a vaudeville comedian, knew how to make something funny out of a nobody. His wobbly-headed walk, his tear-choked apologetic voice were fabulously comic and likable. He was not the technical star—William Gaxton as Wintergreen and Lois Moran as his wife had the leading parts. But Victor Moore made the empty office of Vice President the star part in a bitter cartoon.

In May of 1932 the judges of the Pulitzer Prize confirmed the cynicism of the play. They gave the prize to the two authors of the book and to the writer of the lyrics, but omitted George Gershwin, who had composed the music. Since the terms for awarding the Pulitzer Prize included writers of words but not writers of music, they passed over in sanctimonious silence the top genius of the show. After that ceremonious gaffe the cynicism in *Of Thee I Sing* seemed like good citizenship. Nobody was surprised when the text of the play was published in book form as stage literature.

o o o o o o o o o o o o o o o o o o o o o o o o o o o o o o o o o o o o o o o o

Maxwell Anderson

BOTH YOUR HOUSES

o o o o o o o o o o o o o o o o o o o o o o o o o o o o o o o o o o o o o o o o

Two days after Franklin D. Roosevelt had been inaugurated as President, a character in Maxwell Anderson's *Both Your Houses* made this morbid comment: "God, what a government! It's bad enough to have it, but imagine having to pay for it!" This devastating remark, and a great many others, had been written during the last days of the Hoover Administration and was not directed specifically at the New Deal. *Both Your Houses*, which opened at the Royale Theatre on March 6, 1933, was a furious blast at the dishonesty of all government and in the last act predicted a revolution. Alan McClean, the former school-teacher who represents idealism in the play, threatens the old pros: "It takes about a hundred years to tire this country of trickery—and we're fifty years overdue right now. That's my warning. And I'd feel pretty damn pitiful and lonely saying it to you if I didn't believe there are a hundred million people who are with me, a hundred million people who are disgusted enough to turn from you to something else. Anything else but this."

Exhilarated by the acclaim and success of *What Price Glory?* in 1924, Mr. Anderson had become an exceedingly prolific playwright with high standards of intent. He had written or collaborated in the writing of *First Flight*, an unsuccessful play about the early life of Andrew Jackson, *The Buccaneer*, a play about Captain Harry Morgan's plundering of Panama City, *Outside Looking In*, a dramatization of Jim Tully's book about his career as a tramp, *Saturday's Children* and *Gypsy*, plays about contemporary manners, *Night Over Taos*, a play about the history of the West, *Gods of the Lightning*, a play about the Sacco-Vanzetti case, and *Elizabeth the Queen*, a play about Queen Elizabeth and the Earl of Essex, written in verse. That schedule represents a play a year by a dramatist with high resolve. Most of them were failures. None of them lacked intelligence.

Both Your Houses is a polemic, written with anger and disgust in the old-fashioned style of the contrived melodrama. The plot is imposed on the characters, most of whom lack individuality. Alan McClean (named before Procter & Gamble gave birth to their sanitizing Mr. Clean), is a freshman member of the House of Representatives from Nevada. New to politics, he is shocked to discover that the financing of the local campaign that elected him was tinged with corruption. Now a member of the Appropriations Committee he is outraged to discover that the deficiency bill on which the committee is working is a colossal pork barrel designed to re-elect the committee members and to win enough support from the House to get it passed. The ingratiating scoundrel on the committee, Solomon Fitzmaurice, describes the situation to his chairman as follows: "Why, damn it, Simeon, you've let 'em pile odds and ends of boodle onto this last forty million until you've run it up to two hundred and seventy-five—and still going strong! There isn't a lobby in Washington that hasn't got a section all to itself!"

When Mr. McClean realizes that he cannot block the bill he de-

Walter C. Kelly, Mary Phillips and
Sheppard Strudwick in BOTH OUR HOUSES

cides to use the technique of the old hacks and make the bill untenable by filling the barrel with every piece of pork he can lay hands on. But the old hacks outwit him. They get the bill passed with a margin large enough to override a Presidential veto. In the last scene McClean accepts defeat, but threatens the other members of the committee with revolution.

Both Your Houses lacks the reckless gusto of *What Price Glory?* and the literary distinction of *Elizabeth the Queen*. It is standard playwriting of the old school. But it happened to open at the moment when the new Administration of Roosevelt looked as if it might be the revolution that McClean threatened his colleagues with in the last scene. Roosevelt had already declared the bank holiday, and the "100 days" of reform and innovation were just beginning. It is interesting to speculate on the reception the play might have had if it had opened earlier in the depression when the Hoover Administration was paralyzed.

The play had still another advantage. The production, staged by Worthington Minor, included a number of uncommonly talented actors, and their performance was exciting. Genial Walter C. Kelly, who had long been famous in vaudeville as "the Virginia Judge," was the most colorful actor. He invested the orotund part of Solomon Fitzmaurice with the warmth and drollery of his vaudeville acting; he made the part hilarious and delightful. Sheppard Strudwick, a lean, curly-haired young man with a modest style and a good voice, played the part of Alan McClean. The cast included other excellent actors—Morris Carnovsky, J. Edward Bromberg, Mary Phillips, Jane Seymour, Russell Collins, Oscar Polk, Joseph Sweeney—all favorites at the time. Amid the gloom and hopelessness of the depression *Both Your Houses* made the theatre seem pertinent and constructive and it won the Pulitzer Prize of 1932–33.

Although Mr. Anderson was no revolutionary, he was like Alan McClean in one respect: he had been a Middle Western schoolteacher (in North Dakota) and he shared the point of view of many Americans in small towns. On the evening of October 24, 1928 he had demonstrated the depths of his political convictions by collaborating with Harold Hickerson on a play about the Sacco-Vanzetti case—*Gods of the Lightning* at the Little Theatre. Nicola Sacco and Bartolomeo Vanzetti, two aliens and professed anarchists, had been convicted of murdering a factory paymaster and a guard in 1920 in Braintree, Massachusetts. Thousands of people all over the world believed that they were innocent of the murders and that they were convicted by a jury and judge biased because of their radical political ideas. The night on which they were electrocuted in Boston, August 22, 1927, was a night of vigil everywhere, particularly in New York. Two months later the play was an angry elegy on a lost cause. It put Mr. Anderson and Mr. Hickerson on record, and the cast also included a number of excellent actors who were willing to go on record against what they believed to be an instance of cruel injustice—Sylvia Sidney, Leo Bulgakov, Horace Braham, Charles Bickford. The Broadway theatre was part of the conscience of America.

o o o o o o o o o o o o o o o o o o o o o o o o o o o o o o o o o o o o o o o o o

Jack Kirkland

TOBACCO ROAD

o o o o o o o o o o o o o o o o o o o o o o o o o o o o o o o o o o o o o o o o o

Tobacco Road opened at the Masque Theatre on December 4, 1933; it did not close until it had played 3,180 performances. In later years *Life With Father* played 3,244 performances and *Fiddler on the Roof* had 3,242. But those are the only Broadway productions that have had longer careers.

Since *Tobacco Road* was a clumsy dramatization by Jack Kirkland of Erskine Caldwell's novel, why did it have such a long run? Possibly because of the scandal it contained. It was more profane than any play up to that time. "By God and by Jesus" is Jeeter Lester's consistent expletive, repeated many times throughout the play. There is one particularly bawdy scene. Standing on a chopping block at a window outside his shack Jeeter happily watches his son Dude, and Dude's new wife, Bessie, consummate their marriage on a bed inside. In 1933 profanity and voyeurism were in short supply on the stage.

But there is something more positive than scandal in *Tobacco Road*. The play is a devastating portrait of human degradation. It is a horrifying segment of social truth. Jeeter Lester is a Georgia cracker living on land exhausted from too many years of tobacco and cotton cropping. Starved, dirty, tired, shiftless, he lives on a barren farm with a bitter wife, a feeble mother, a hare-lipped daughter, and an ornery son. They live on the lowest scale of civilized values.

Nevertheless the misery of their lives does not make them creatures that once were men. It is the genius of *Tobacco Road* to make them interesting people. Jeeter cannot cope with the disasters of his life. He cannot stir out of inertia long enough to cart firewood to town where he could sell it, nor can he solve the problems that make it impossible for him to plant a crop. But Jeeter has a tireless tongue and a lively mind. He is cunning and pious at the same time. He steals food. He is a schemer. Religion rattles around inside his empty head: "The Lord sends me every misery He can think of just to try my soul. He must be aiming to do something powerful big for me because He sure tests me hard. I reckon He figures if I can put up with my own people I can stand to fight back at the devil."

Although he is a derelict, he still has pride. Faced with eviction from the crumbling shack where he lives he still adheres to the code of family. He was born on the land, he says, and is going to stay there until he dies and he will not work in the mills for wages: "God made the land but you don't see him building no durn cotton mills."

There is a certain ebullience of invention in *Tobacco Road*. The characters do not lead dull lives. They are not prudent. They act on impulse. Dude, the sullen teenager, does not want to marry Sister

Bessie Rice, a recent widow and a fake evangelist. But when she says she will buy a new automobile with the $800 her late husband left in life insurance, Dude agrees to marry her instantly, and off they go to Augusta and buy a shining car with all the cash Bessie has. An ignorant and irresponsible driver, Dude starts to wreck the car the first day he drives it.

The callousness of the characters is so primitive that it becomes funny. Lov, Jeeter's son-in-law, tries to make his taciturn wife talk by pouring water over her and "chunking" sticks and rocks at her. Killing a Negro with his car does not seem to be a matter of importance

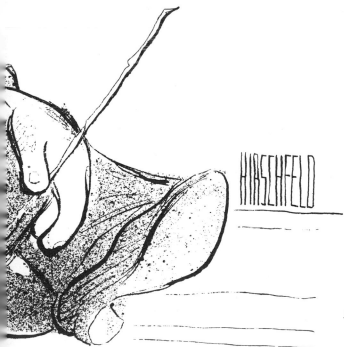

Henry Hull in TOBACCO ROAD

to Dude. "Niggers will get killed," Jeeter comments. "Looks like there just ain't no way to stop it." When Jeeter's mother disappears, everyone concludes that she must have died in the broom sedge set on fire to clear the fields. "I'll go and look around for her one of these days," Jeeter says. When Dude accidentally runs over his mother, who dies soon afterwards, Jeeter is dazed. The death of his wife does affect him, but neither he nor any of the characters of *Tobacco Road* have the energy or the emotion to feel sympathy or remorse for anything.

There is a lot more than scandal in *Tobacco Road,* although scandal is valid theatre. There are human beings living with spirit in a spiritless environment. "Gallant" is too magnanimous a word to apply to a piece of trash like Jeeter Lester. But note that he never abases himself. He is a man. "My concern is with the living," he tells his dying wife fatuously. *Tobacco Road* shows him doing the best he can in hopeless circumstances. If it were not for his vitality and independence, and the author's many insights, *Tobacco Road* would be a boring or a depressing play.

o o o o o o o o o o o o o o o o o o o o o o o o o o o o o o o o o o o o o o

John Wexley

THEY SHALL NOT DIE

o o o o o o o o o o o o o o o o o o o o o o o o o o o o o o o o o o o o o o

When *They Shall Not Die* was put on at the Royale Theatre on February 21, 1934, the author, John Wexley, denied that he was writing about the notorious Scottsboro Case against nine Negroes in Alabama.

That was his escape clause. In real life the leader of the nine Negroes was Hayward Patterson. In the play the leader was Heywood Parsons. And no one who was stirred by Mr. Wexley's play doubted for a moment that he was attacking the barbaric miscarriage of justice in Scottsboro.

There were three notable propaganda plays in that season: an antiwar play, *Peace on Earth,* by George Sklar and Albert Maltz; a good play about a dock strike in New Orleans, *Stevedore,* by George Sklar and Paul Peter, and Mr. Wexley's play. His roaring attack on legal bigotry in the South was by all odds the ablest. His title turned out to be prophetic. It took fifteen long, costly years to clear the Negroes who were maliciously charged with raping two white girls, but all except one were ultimately released; and the one who was not, Hayward Patterson, broke out of jail in 1948 and escaped to Michigan, which refused to extradite him to Alabama. Northern propaganda like Mr. Wexley's saved the lives of nine Southern Negroes.

The play is a concentrated and violent sketch of what actually happened in 1931. The Negroes were charged with having raped two white girls in a gondola car in a freight train they were riding through Alabama to Memphis, Tennessee. The two white girls were whores; one of them recanted her testimony against the Negroes in a retrial. Those were the basic facts in the actual case. Everything is in black and white in the play—figuratively and literally. Both of the girls initially deny that any of the Negroes has touched them. But brutal sheriffs and district attorneys bribe or threaten them into testifying that they have been raped. "I don't keer if they are whores," says the sheriff, "they are white women! You think I'm gonna let them stinkin' nigger lice get away from me? Like hell I am! They're gonna git whut's comin' to em' long as I'm the law round heah!"

The play includes savage beating of the black prisoners by the police and finally by the National Guard called out to prevent a lynching. In the second act there is an unbelievable sentimental interlude in which one of the girls recants her testimony under the protection of the only one of her clients she loves. The last act consists of a tense trial scene in which the two opposing points of view are bluntly stated.

Claude Rains and Ruth Gordon
in THEY SHALL NOT DIE

Referring to a New York lawyer who has come to Alabama to represent the Negroes, the state's attorney instructs the jury: "Gentlemen of the jury, tell 'em, tell 'em that Southern justice cannot be bought an' sold with Jew money from New York." And at the end, when it is clear that the jury is going to convict the Negroes again, the lawyer from New York says: "I'll go to the Supreme Court up in Washington and back again ... if I have to do it in a wheelchair ... and if I do nothing else in my life, I'll make the fair name of this state stink to high heaven with its lynch justice.... These boys, they shall not die!"

They Shall Not Die is a propaganda play that does not pretend to be a work of art. The Scottsboro Case is the theme, and the theme is a cause, and the cause is vividly stated and defended.

It was vividly acted in the theatre by people caught up in the moral issue. From the financial point of view *They Shall Not Die* was hopeless. It included sixty-four speaking parts and twenty-four extras. But no one was niggardly about the production. The Theatre Guild (which was producing Maxwell Anderson's *Mary of Scotland* and Eugene O'Neill's *Ah, Wilderness* and *Days Without End* that season) produced *They Shall Not Die* with its best director, Philip Moeller, and its best scene designer, Lee Simonson. The actors for this militant polemic included many who were famous or were to be famous later on—Claude Rains, Tom Ewell, Helen Westley, Linda Watkins, Ruth Gordon, Frank Wilson, Dean Jagger—and many of Broadway's most reliable players—Hugh Rennie, Ralph Theadore, St. Clair Bayfield, Ben Smith, C. Ellsworth Smith, Ralph Sanford, Thurston Hall. Among the extras was Angus Duncan, who later became executive secretary of Actors Equity, and a very important man in the theatre.

The production of *They Shall Not Die* demonstrated the theatre's congenital interest in the life of America and in justice and a humane state. The theatre was not cautious, prudent or frugal. It was part of the American democratic tradition and it was not afraid of being called Communist by respectable bondholders and fogies.

o o o o o o o o o o o o o o o o o o o o o o o o o o o o o o o o o o o o o o o o

S. N. Behrman

RAIN FROM HEAVEN

o o o o o o o o o o o o o o o o o o o o o o o o o o o o o o o o o o o o o o o o

After enjoying the wit and comforts of rich worldlings for seven happy theatre years S. N. Behrman yielded to reality in *Rain From Heaven,* which the Theatre Guild put on at the Golden Theatre on December 24, 1934. He had been shocked by the calamities of Alfred Kerr, Berlin's finest drama critic. A Jew, Mr. Kerr had had to go into exile because of the anti-Semitic ferocity of the Nazis. Furthermore, Gerhart Hauptmann, Germany's most famous dramatist, had severed personal relations with Mr. Kerr for the same reason, despite the fact that Mr. Kerr had been Mr. Hauptmann's staunchest advocate for years. The intrusion of hatred and viciousness into the civilized world of literature shocked Mr. Behrman. Although he was a mild man he was the first Broadway playwright to protest the Nazi program of exterminating the Jews.

Not that Mr. Behrman abandoned the iridescent world of the rich in order to denounce the Nazis. The introductory stage directions set *Rain From Heaven* in the living room of an English country house which shows "the knack of combining an air of improvisation with solid comfort which appears to be a special attribute of the British country house." Since Mr. Behrman was brought up in a poor family in Worcester, Massachusetts, he always enjoyed the grandeur of the

Jane Cowl in RAIN FROM HEAVEN

rich. *Rain From Heaven* is not a propaganda play. It is a sagacious analysis of characters. Its rich people include Lady Lael Wyngate, a creative liberal, and Hobart Eldridge, an incipient American fascist. Hobart believes that "democracy is passé." Lady Wyngate believes "that in the main people are reasonable and corrigible and sweet-fragments of God."

Rain From Heaven includes the traditional bloodless romances common to plays about the rich. But Mr. Behrman managed to arrange them to illustrate the differences in character that constitute his play. Lady Wyngate is in love with, and is loved by, a heroic American explorer who hasn't the least notion of politics. He is illiterate in everything involving the mind. She knows she cannot marry him because he cannot believe that her active liberalism is genuine. He regards it as a social gambit. He is, she tells his brother, "a symbol of simplicity, courage and directness," living in "a world of cruelty and chicanery."

In *Rain From Heaven* the drama critic whose experience instigated the play is a music critic, Hugo Willens. He has been in a concentration camp because he wrote a satirical pamphlet called "The Last Jew." The pamphlet said that without Jews the Nazi party would have no political program and would have to reserve and reward the last Jew in order to continue its political existence. Although the dialogue of *Rain From Heaven* is urbane and amusing, Mr. Behrman manages to comment on anti-Semitism incisively. Jews are a luxury item, Hugo Willens observes: "Our science and our art are tolerated and even praised while the economic level is high. Once the golden stream is damned and constriction sets in we are the first to be squeezed."

In the glamorous, heady environment of an English country home, which is isolated from the realities, Mr. Behrman manages to define the political point of view that seasoned the bland life of the international set in 1934. Lady Wyngate, the most attractive character of the play, defines the mood of the day as follows: "The truth is there's a pest all over all the world just now, an epidemic of hatred and intolerance that engulfs us all. . . . People have suffered too much during the last twenty years—they can't stand any more, that's all. In one way or another they are letting off steam." She seems to think it may be temporary. Hugo Willens, the exiled music critic with Jewish blood in his veins, proposes to return to Germany because he wants to view the world "completely without illusion." Now we know that a return to Germany by a Jew in 1934 would have been not a spiritual excursion but suicide.

In the play it makes the savagery of the Nazi seem temporary. But Lady Wyngate puts everything in the right perspective in her concluding remarks to Willens: "Our enemies will beat against us and find that we have a strength beyond their clamor, beyond their forces." It was a near thing when the inevitable war broke out with terrible virulence in 1939. But in 1945 the conclusion was as Lady Wyngate and Mr. Behrman had imagined in 1934. The liberal rich and the liberal gentry and the liberal Mr. Behrman had more strength than the Nazis, and democracy was not passé and *Rain From Heaven* was a good deed in a naughty world.

o o o o o o o o o o o o o o o o o o o o o o o o o o o o o o o o o o o o o o o o o o

Clifford Odets

WAITING FOR LEFTY

o o o o o o o o o o o o o o o o o o o o o o o o o o o o o o o o o o o o o o o o o o

After reading the script of Clifford Odets' *Waiting for Lefty,* Luther Adler, one of the actors in the Group Theatre, remarked to Harold Clurman, one of the directors: "Harold, the Group has produced the finest revolutionary playwright in America." On January 5, 1935, theatregoers confirmed that opinion when *Waiting for Lefty* was produced at a benefit performance for the *New Theatre Magazine* at the Civic Repertory Theatre in Fourteenth Street. The play concerned the revolt of the members of a taxi union against their corrupt officers. At the end of the play one of the members shouted: "Hello, America! Hello, we're storm birds of the working class. Workers of the world.

... Our bones and blood.... Well, what's the answer." "Strike" the actors seated in the audience yelled. "Strike, strike, strike!!!" The audience joined in this ringing uproar, and went home in a jubilant daze after having seen an overwhelming play.

Up to this time Odets had been a minor actor in the Group Theatre company. He had written a full-length play that he called *I Got the Blues,* and that some members of the management did not like. At this time the New Theatre League, a leftist organization, asked Mr. Odets to write a simple play that union members could stage anywhere without scenery. Mr. Odets wrote *Waiting for Lefty* in three evenings. His story was based on a taxi union strike of the year before. In his play six or seven members of the union committee sat on the stage in a circle of chairs. The audience, among whom a few actors were seated, represented the members of the union. When the secretary of the union addressed the members from the stage he was also addressing the audience. The confrontation between stage and audience was direct and personal.

The secretary was suspected of being a stooge of the bosses, and, in fact, he was. His advice to the members against striking was received with hostility. To illustrate the need for some action that would increase the income of the members Mr. Odets then staged five miniature plays in a circle of light in the midst of the committee on the stage. The miniature plays were intimate, blunt and factual—a driver's wife giving him the desperate economic facts of their family life; a strikebreaker unmasked; two lovers who could not marry because they could not earn enough money, and so on. There were several references to Lefty, the popular chairman of the committee who was mysteriously absent. At the end of the play it appeared that he was not present because he had been murdered—presumably by the union officers or the taxi owners. That's when the members of the union and the audience yelled, "Strike, strike, strike!"

In Soviet terminology *Waiting for Lefty* was an agitprop play, designed to arouse the workers against the tyranny of the bosses. Mr. Odets believed in militant plays about social and political situations: "We are living in a time when new works of art should shoot bul-

Clifford Odets and Elia Kazan in WAITING FOR LEFTY

lets," he said ferociously. A member of an organization that was living at the bottom of the economic scale, he wanted to dramatize the national situation. Throughout the country unemployment was massive. Although the Roosevelt Administration in 1935 had radically altered the balance of government responsibility, welfare was not on the modern scale, privation was widespread, and the prospects were gloomy. When Mr. Odets joined the working class in this one-act polemic he was joining a genuine movement; and the admiring attitude some of his characters had toward the Soviet Union was shared by many anxious Americans.

But Mr. Odets was no revolutionary. He was a romantic, unsophisticated young man whose experience in life had been meager. He knew poor people intimately because he had been one of them, although not one of the desperate. He wanted to join a movement that would broaden his life. "Just once before I die," he told his friend Harold Clurman, "I want to write a fine revolutionary play." As it turned out, he had excellent qualifications for such a task; an instinctive sense of theatre and an extraordinary gift for pungent dialogue that contained flashy figures of speech and that came off the streets and out of the alleys. It gave his plays excitement. After *Waiting for Lefty* was produced, Mr. Odets became the hero of political insurgents and added his rhetoric to theirs. But a few years later it turned out that he was really interested in cultural things like music and painting and other pursuits of the bourgeoisie. In later years the more successful he was on Broadway and in Hollywood the less interested he was in the revolution.

Waiting for Lefty was a headlong play. In March, 1935, it was put on at the Longacre Theatre for the general public along with another short Odets play. Tickets were sold for fifty cents to a dollar and a half. Whatever its ideology may have been, it provided a memorable theatre experience. The dialogue was fiery. The plot and structure were dynamic. Having cast the audience as members of the union, Mr. Odets was in an almost impregnable position. The characters on both sides—villains as well as heroes—had strong convictions. "Hell," exclaimed one of the union members, "Some of us boys ain't even gotta shirt to our backs. What's the boss class trying to do—make a nudist colony out of us?" Subsequently, *Waiting for Lefty* was acted all over the country. Some of the actors in other productions were sent to jail, charged with subversive activity.

Today, *Waiting for Lefty* seems sophomoric. America is not so ignorant or inhuman as Mr. Odets believed it was in 1935, and the Soviet Union is not so enlightened or benevolent. It is amusing now to recollect that one of the actors who yelled "Hello, America! We're storm birds of the working class," was Elia Kazan, then at the beginning of his career. Since 1935 he has succeeded spectacularly in the theatre, the movies, and in fiction. He has not been leading any revolutions for years.

o o o o o o o o o o o o o o o o o o o o o o o o o o o o o o o o o o o o o o o o o

Clifford Odets

AWAKE AND SING

o o o o o o o o o o o o o o o o o o o o o o o o o o o o o o o o o o o o o o o o o

Clifford Odets' *Awake and Sing* was produced in the Belasco Theatre on February 19, 1935. The year of 1935 was Mr. Odets' big year. After *Waiting for Lefty* aroused sensational enthusiasm at a special performance on January 5, 1935, Mr. Odets became the theatre's man of the year. Some of the directors of the Group Theatre had not liked a full-length play he had been working on for months and which he called *I've Got the Blues*. But the success of *Waiting for Lefty* provoked second thoughts. The Group Theatre put on the full-

Morris Carnovsky, Stella Adler and
John Garfield in AWAKE AND SING

length play under the title of *Awake and Sing* six weeks after *Waiting for Lefty* exploded, and the new play was eagerly received. There were two more Odets plays that year: *Till the Day I Die,* an anti-Nazi play, was put on at the Longacre Theatre on March 26 in a double bill, and *Paradise Lost,* a further examination of the middle class, was put on in the same theatre on December 9.

In a preface to his published plays Mr. Odets remarked: "If you have acquired by now the distressing sense that I am situating myself historically, correct! Talent should be respected." He could hardly believe that he was as talented as his success in 1935 indicated, and he proudly accepted his new status as a celebrity.

Awake and Sing is a reflection of personal experience. Clifford Odets was born into a Jewish family in Philadelphia in 1906. Although the Bergers in the play live in an apartment in the Bronx their problems are the common ones of similar people in Eastern cities. "All of the characters," Mr. Odets noted in the program, "share a fundamental activity: a struggle for life amid petty conditions." They are concerned with survival in a period of privation and anxiety. The public mood was gloomy about the future as well as the past.

Although *Awake and Sing* dramatizes the plight of the middle class, it might also be looked on as a drama about the Jewish matriarch. She is Bessie Berger, the overpowering wife of a mild business man, the tyrannical mother of two teen-age children, the scornful daughter of an unsuccessful barber and the sister of a braggart clothing manufacturer. Bessie is inexhaustible; she has brought up her family in middle-class respectability and she is determined that her daughter and her son will have families and raise their children the same way. Bessie is an unselfish, protective monster. She has a big heart and a ruthless personality.

All the characters are individualists. They live close together in a state of continuous acrimony. There is a streak of mutual respect and affection between Jacob, the Marxist barber, and his grandson, Ralph, who is the kind of imaginative young man Mr. Odets must have been. At the end of the first scene in the second act, Jacob sympathetically takes Ralph in his arms. That is the only spontaneous expression of affection in the play. Although the Bergers represent family solidarity they live in hostility. They have murderous wit but no humor. The Odets dialogue is colorful and fantastically capricious; it veers off situations like a string of firecrackers. It abounds in embarrassed irrelevancies. After Ralph has made a big romantic declaration of his hopes for the future, his realistic grandfather, the old barber, makes a flat reply: "Electric clippers never do a job like by hand."

In the last act there are some headlong clashes between characters that change the dramatic situation radically. But most of the play is composed of indirect clashes in which the characters bounce off the subject with sardonic remarks in bitter overtones; "I'm *so* nervous—look, two times I weighed myself in the subway," says the son-in-law, who has just learned that he is not the father of his wife's child.

Harold Clurman said, "Mr. Odets is a poet of the decaying middle class with revolutionary yearnings and convictions." The incandescent dialogue is the poetry—some of it very self-conscious. In the play the revolution is personified in old Jacob, the tenement intellectual who dreams of Russia as the promised land. "Charity, a bone for the dog," he says scornfully of the American system. "But in Russia an old man don't take charity so his eyes turn black in his head. In Russia they got Marx." "Who's Marx?" his irritated son-in-law puts in ironically. "An outfielder for the Yankees," says a cynical visitor. The revolution does not get much respect in *Awake and Sing*. Ralph has a traditional American dream that better suits the other members of the family: "Get teams together all over. Spit on your hands and get to work. And with enough teams together maybe we'll get steam in the warehouse so our fingers don't freeze oil. Maybe we'll fix it so life won't be printed on dollar bills."

Awake and Sing just suited the actors of the Group Theatre. The wry phrases came to their lips naturally. When the directors finally decided to produce the play the actors cheered. The play was in their bones. Jules Garfield (later John Garfield) played the part of the uncorrupted Ralph with a kind of purity of spirit. But the whole cast today reads like a role of honor with actors who have since had notable careers—Morris Carnovsky, Stella Adler, Luther Adler, Sanford Meisner, J. Edward Bromberg, Art Smith, Phoebe Brand. They told the passionate story of the Berger family inside a Boris Aronson set that illustrated dinginess and poverty.

Since *Awake and Sing* is a discursive play it has been frequently compared to Chekhov. The comparison makes a literary virtue out of a young writer's lack of discipline. The play lacks the wistful tenderness and the detached perspective of the great Russian. But in 1935 when people were confused, bitter and apprehensive *Awake and Sing* was a stimulating statement of some homely truths.

"Awake and sing, ye who dwell in dust," the prophet Isaiah said long before the terrible depression of the 1930's. The song Mr. Odets sang is like an elegy. But there is no doubt that the characters are awake.

o o o o o o o o o o o o o o o o o o o o o o o o o o o o o o o o o o o o o o o o

Maxwell Anderson

WINTERSET

o o o o o o o o o o o o o o o o o o o o o o o o o o o o o o o o o o o o o o o o

Maxwell Anderson's *Winterset* seemed more significant on the stage of the Martin Beck Theatre on September 25, 1935 than it does in book form today. In the first place, the Sacco-Vanzetti case was then a sensitive political issue. In the second place, poetic drama was an aesthetic cause. Many people hoped that poetic drama would restore literary distinction to the theatre.

Justice is the theme of *Winterset*. To secure justice is to defy the state, said Mr. Anderson in the best liberal tradition of the time. "And for justice who has once seen it done?" one of the characters dolefully remarks. The story of *Winterset* is both theatrical and high-minded. The characters are sharply drawn. Mio, the hero, is a footloose young man committed to clearing his father's name of the charge of murder. The father had been executed by the state. Marianne is a tenement girl whose brother was a witness to the murder. Judge Gaunt, the presiding judge, is now trying to convince himself that his verdict was just. There are several gangsters, street people, and police in the play, engaged in violence or the repression of violence. *Winterset* is an underworld melodrama on a high ethical plane worthy of the author of *Gods of the Lightning* and *Both Your Houses*.

Mr. Anderson's first drama *White Desert,* produced in 1923, was written in verse because, in his own words, he enjoyed writing verse. Two of his most successful dramas, *Elizabeth the Queen* (1930) and *Mary of Scotland* (1933) were also in verse. In those two plays the mystique of royalty made the use of verse seem appropriate. In *Winterset* Mr. Anderson used verse to tell a story of contemporary life with characters who, except in two instances, represented primitive society. To read *Winterset* now is to realize that Mr. Anderson was writing very much in the Shakespearean tradition. The Sacco-Vanzetti case may have been the immediate provocation of *Winterset,* but there are several echoes of Shakespeare. The startling speed with which Mio and Marianne fall in love and their instantaneous ardor—baffling in terms of a modern street setting—are an echo of *Romeo and Juliet;* and Judge Gaunt, with his senile mind and his singing of quatrains, is King Lear. Also, *Winterset* follows Shakespeare's formula of alternating prose and poetry.

In all his plays Mr. Anderson has a remarkable gift for words. His dialogue is vigorous, colorful and militant, and his figures of speech come out of the vernacular without self-consciousness. His prose is especially notable for spontaneity and force. In *Winterset* his verse is for the most part a wordy form of prose. It takes many words to say things that he could say bluntly in prose and with greater pith and lucidity. The figures of speech are academically plausible, but they are deliberate and their thought is formal. The cosmic speculations that turn up are abstract imitations of the Shakespeare style; they lack the flavor of human beings. And the verse does not heighten the drama or widen the significance of *Winterset.*

Margo, Burgess Meredith and Richard Bennett in WINTERSET

Instead, it blunts and diffuses the drama. It smells of the study more than of the dark and dingy streets of New York in the Brooklyn Bridge district. It lacks the recklessness and the virtuosity of Shakespeare.

Although the style of *Winterset* is self-conscious the spirit is admirable. It faces the grisly facts of life without equivocation. Although the epilogue lacks the earthy power of Shakespeare's conclusions, it states a point of view with candor and conviction:

> Mio, my son—know this where you lie.
> This is the glory of earth-born men and
> women, not to cringe, never to yield, but
> standing, take defeat implacable and defiant,
> die unsubmitting. . . .

On the stage *Winterset* had the support of masterly scenery by Jo Mielziner—massive and ominous; and a dark, swirling performance staged by Guthrie McClintic. Richard Bennett, the gallant old pro who had appeared in O'Neill's *Beyond the Horizon* and Howard's *They Knew What They Wanted,* played the tragic part of Judge Gaunt. Two uncommonly talented young actors played Mio and Marianne—Burgess Meredith and Margo (who did not use a surname in the theatre). Although the verse—especially when it drifted off into pompous abstractions—gave most of the actors trouble (and almost all of the audience) the performance was both impressive and aspiring.

Winterset won the first Critics Circle award in 1936 with fourteen votes out of the membership of seventeen. It also won considerable professional commendation, although Percy Hammond, speaking for the dissenters on a radio program, adapted to the occasion a popular epithet from the *New Yorker*: "I say it's spinach and I say to hell with it."

o o o o o o o o o o o o o o o o o o o o o o o o o o o o o o o o o o o o o o o o

Sidney Kingsley

DEAD END

o o o o o o o o o o o o o o o o o o o o o o o o o o o o o o o o o o o o o o o o

There were forty-five actors in the sprawling cast of Sidney Kingsley's *Dead End* when it opened in the Belasco Theatre on October
28, 1935. Some of them were grouped anonymously as "small boys"
(among them little Sidney Lumet, now an illustrious film director)
or "G-Men" (among them Edward Goodnow, now a big Florida operator) or "policemen" or "ambulance drivers" or "inhabitants of an
East River terrace." Anonymity was the essence of *Dead End*. For
the massive city of New York was the star actor. Callous, imperious,
hostile, contemptuous, complex, it overwhelmed all the human actors
and also Mr. Kingsley's play.

His theme was the importance of environment on the future of
native boys and girls. "The place you live in is awfully important,"
says Gimpty, the unemployed young architect who grew up in the
neighborhood slums. "When I was in school they used to teach us
that evolution made men out of animals. What they forgot to tell us
is that it can also make animals out of men."

Dead End demonstrates the implacability with which a slum
environment makes a potential gangster out of an attractive street
urchin who is trying to find a place in the world. In the concluding
scene there is a suggestion that his sister and the jobless young ar-

Joseph Dowling and Sheila Trent and
The Dead End Kids in DEAD END

chitect may keep him out of reform school by interceding for him with the police. But Tommy (none of the boys has a last name) is the adolescent prototype of "Babyface" Martin, a murderer and gangster of national notoriety who grew up in the same environment.

That is the text. But New York City is the actual drama. Tommy, "Babyface" Martin, the architect, and all the other characters are victims of the city. Nobody wins anything. Even the few well-to-do people who saunter around the edges of the play win nothing except a walled-in refuge from the unlimited ruthlessness of the city. Norman Bel Geddes was primarily responsible for the impression *Dead End* gave when it was originally produced. A scene designer afflicted with giganticism, he crowded the Belasco stage with a colossal setting that contrasted a new luxury apartment house on one side with an ancient, crumbling tenement on the other, and somewhere found room enough for an ugly sand hopper and the top of a steam shovel. The forestage represented the pierhead of a cross street that ended at the East River; the audience sat where the East River would be if the setting were real. The slum boys who were diving into or climbing out of the river were actually using the orchestra pit. The setting graphically represented the economic and cultural differences that keep New York from being a community.

Mr. Kingsley (who had won the Pulitzer Prize two years previously with his hospital play, *Men in White*) is a naturalistic writer. Reporting what he sees is his basic technique. *Dead End* reports in explicit detail the contrast between the sheltered life of a few rich apartment dwellers and the wild, rootless lives of slum boys who run around pounding and pushing one another and talking in what Mr. Kingsley describes as "a shocking jargon that would put a truckdriver to shame." Actually, their jargon is less shocking than the foul language used in many routine plays of the 1970s.

When the curtain goes up, a fat, greasy woman is leaning out of the tenement window, peeling an orange and throwing the peels into the street. "Babyface" Martin, whose facial appearance has been radically changed by surgery, strolls out on the pier. After having been on the lam for seven years he hopes to see his mother and his old girl friend again. Since he is on the "wanted list" he has to avoid the police. The jobless architect knew him when they were both boys in this decaying neighborhood and recognizes him. Tempted by the reward of $4200, he informs on Martin to the police. The police ambush Martin and kill him on the pier. In the third act the police pick up Tommy, a Martin admirer, for using his knife on the father of a rich boy whose watch he has stolen. A pitiless environment has given birth to another gangster.

Dead End was a conspicuous success in 1935. It made a sensational impression and ran for 268 performances. Aside from its vivid naturalism it speculated on the social causes of crime. But now the gutter jargon seems artificial and clumsy and the functional story seems like a TV crime show in need of the benevolent services of Joe Mannix or Matt Dillon.

Under that towering setting by Norman Bel Geddes *Dead End* vehemently dramatized the inhumanity of a city that is crowded with human beings.

o o o o o o o o o o o o o o o o o o o o o o o o o o o o o o o o o o o o o o o o o o

S. N. Behrman

END OF SUMMER

o o o o o o o o o o o o o o o o o o o o o o o o o o o o o o o o o o o o o o o o o o

Nothing important was ever mentioned in the witty drawing-room comedies of Somerset Maugham and Frederick Lonsdale. Polished tedium has always been one of the theatre delights from Farquhar and Congreve to Oscar Wilde and Noël Coward. In the thirties S. N. Behrman brought some ominous echoes of the somber outside world into the comedies of manners for which he had unique talent. *Rain From Heaven* in 1934 was the first. Two years later—on February 17, 1936, to be precise—he seasoned the felicities of *End of Summer* with some unpleasant realities.

Mr. Behrman is not a political activist. He is an amiable playwright who enjoys the rich and the cultivated and makes them look livelier on the stage than they are in real life. He has more character than the characters in his plays. But as a man of conscience he does not ignore the world. *End of Summer* illustrates not only his talent but also his sense of values. The play is dominated by an impetuous lady who has good impulses but no common sense—primarily because that is the kind of character Ina Claire could play brilliantly. She had already endowed Mr. Behrman's *Biography* with crackling speech and radiant vitality. In *End of Summer* she headed a brilliant cast that included Osgood Perkins, Mildred Natwick, Van Heflin, Tom Powers, Shepperd Strudwick, and Doris Dudley—all superb actors and all of whom made *End of Summer* a sparkling delight.

The play includes the standard romantic dilemmas that keep drawing-room comedies in motion. There is one divorce—of course, a friendly one—and several amours of a more tentative kind. But 1936 was midway through a depression in which more than twelve million Americans were out of work, and the difference between the rich and the poor was not so much tragic as brutal. The essential conflict in Mr. Behrman's light comedy is between the rich and the jobless. In the Twenties the dissident young people were flappers and revelers who did not challenge anything. But in *End of Summer* the young people are the protagonists, and they are realists. They are inclined to despise the rich; and since they are articulate, they have plausible reasons.

End of Summer is not a propaganda play and Mr. Behrman does not carry the conflict to the point of revolution. But the two young men in his play who are fresh out of college and ominously unemployed bring some of the bitter tang of the outside world. One of them is genuinely in love with the daughter of a rich family, but he has ethical scruples against marrying her and living on her money. Marrying a rich woman is to him like going on the dole (called "welfare" today). The daughter is an amateur radical because she does not want to be a Sunday supplement heiress. She marches in picket lines. She petitions Congress for peace.

The other young man is a militant radical with a glib and wounding tongue. While he is unemployed and looking for a job he cannot accept the hospitality of a rich family for ethical reasons: "When we are in New York doing nothing, we belong to the most respectable vested group going," he tells his wealthy hostess. "The unemployed. As such we have status, position, authority. But if we stay here doing nothing—what are we? Low-down parasites."

In the course of the play Mr. Behrman also takes a sideswipe at psychoanalysis, which was still an exciting novelty. His psychoanalyst

Osgood Perkins and Ina Claire
in END OF SUMMER

is omniscient, greedy and unscrupulous. "I can't stand him—not from the moment I saw him," says one of the young men. "Because he's incapable of disinterestedness himself, he can't imagine it in others. He's the kind of sneering, cynical—he's a marauder. The adventurer with the cure-all. This is just the moment for him. And this is just the place!"

All drawing-room comedies have to end happily. By the last act in *End of Summer* the charlatan psychoanalyst and a predatory Russian count have been exposed as impostors and are eliminated. The older rich and the young dissidents make a sort of peace that fulfills the necessities of the final curtain. Although *End of Summer* is not a play of protest, Mr. Behrman in 1936 did not close the door of his studio to the sick world outside. By recognizing the existence of, and the political causes of, inequality he broke out of the silken world of Somerset Maugham and Frederick Lonsdale and threatened himself with technological unemployment. For how can you introduce serious thought into drawing-room comedy?

o o o o o o o o o o o o o o o o o o o o o o o o o o o o o o o o o o o o o o o o o o o o o

Robert E. Sherwood

IDIOT'S DELIGHT

o o o o o o o o o o o o o o o o o o o o o o o o o o o o o o o o o o o o o o o o o o o o

Robert E. Sherwood was a high-minded citizen who loved a good time. In *Idiot's Delight*, which opened at the Shubert Theatre on March 29, 1936, he had the best of both worlds. It was an antiwar play, written by a respected veteran of World War I, and it was a rousing good show with plenty of music-hall mischief. It also gave Alfred Lunt the chance to play a song-and-dance man—just the least bit of caricature in his characterization—and it also presented him as the impresario of six empty-headed show girls whose sleazy glamour kept the audience's mind off serious subjects.

The title of the play refers to war. "Idiot's Delight. The game that never means anything and never wins," as one of the characters defines it. In a bitter postscript to the printed text Mr. Sherwood pointed out that in 1936 the Italians had just invaded Ethiopia, the Germans were occupying the Rhineland, and Anthony Eden, British Foreign Secretary, had just told the House of Commons that the current situation "is dreadfully similar to 1914."

Disillusioned by the corrupt and blundering decade that followed the Administration of Warren Harding (for whom Mr. Sherwood voted in 1920), the author had become a crusader against war. *Idiot's Delight* is both a cry of warning and a declaration of faith in the decency of the average human being. Mr. Sherwood could not believe that the world would go to war again. He believed that by refusing to become Fascists "we may achieve the enjoyment of peaceful life on earth rather than degraded death in a cellar." It was the hopeful view of the world of a young man who had already once supported his convictions by risking his life. Mr. Sherwood was not only a genial person but also a man of honor in the old tradition.

Although *Idiot's Delight* is fundamentally a propaganda play, enjoyment keeps breaking in. A clever young man, Harry Van, enters a hotel in the Italian Alps that has a magnificent view of Switzerland. But the serenity of the environment is shattered by a military airfield nearby where pilots are practicing war maneuvers. The Italian Government is detaining travelers bound for Switzerland. The guests who accumulate at the hotel include a German scientist, a recently married British couple, a labor leader, a mysterious munitions manufacturer and Irene, his young mistress, Harry Van, six show girls, and a number of Italian military officers.

In the course of the play war does break out, the Italian planes

The Lunts in IDIOT'S DELIGHT

bomb Paris, and the labor leader is executed for making subversive remarks. All the other guests are belatedly permitted to travel on to Switzerland except the manufacturer's mistress. Harry Van decides to stay with her. *Idiot's Delight* is a romantic melodrama, lively and sophisticated on the surface, but the background is barbaric. In the last scene while Harry and Irene are seated at the piano, war breaks out and bombs go off with a roar and with flashes of light through the windows. The curtain falls while Harry and Irene sing "Onward, Christian soldiers!"

In the middle of the Thirties America and England were full of young men who swore they would never go to war again. They were militant pacifists; they defied their respective governments with furious manifestations. They had also convinced themselves that wars are made not by governments but by munition manufacturers to promote business. Mr. Sherwood was one of the pacifist generation. Amid all the show-business extravaganza, *Idiot's Delight* gave him a forum for several ringing declarations. Nobody in the play actually believes that there will be a war. The labor leader says: "This is not 1914, remember! Since then some new voices have been heard in the world—loud voices. I need mention only one of them— Lenin—Nikolai Lenin." The munitions manufacturer says there will be no war: "They are all much too well prepared for it." The British couple agree: "No matter how stupid and blundering our government may be, our people simply won't stand for it." Harry Van, whose opinions coincide with some of Mr. Sherwood's assertions in the postscript, says: "I've remained an optimist. . . . Above everything else I've found Faith. Faith in peace on earth and good will to men." Mr. Sherwood remarked in his postscript that he thought calmness, courage and ridicule "will remove the threat of war, which is the Fascist's last gesture of self-justification." He was wrong.

The conclusion of the play does not follow Mr. Sherwood's optimism in his postscript: War breaks out; and three years later history itself validates the shattering conclusion of the play instead of Mr. Sherwood's benign faith.

Idiot's Delight was a vastly entertaining play in 1936 because it expressed not only the author's concern and faith but also his personal exuberance. Mr. Sherwood's craftsmanship was superb; the play flowed rapidly and spontaneously and dug deeper as it went along. The tone was lighthearted; the dialogue was quick and gay. The play gave Lynn Fontanne and Alfred Lunt another holiday, like the one they had enjoyed in Mr. Sherwood's *Reunion in Vienna* in 1931. Miss Fontanne's cool, condescending, ornate trollop and Mr. Lunt's breezy night-club comic contributed to a jubilant performance that captivated Broadway at a time when war seemed likely but no one could really believe it.

Idiot's Delight won the Pulitzer Prize for 1936.

o o o o o o o o o o o o o o o o o o o o o o o o o o o o o o o o o o o o o o o o o o

Irwin Shaw

BURY THE DEAD

o o o o o o o o o o o o o o o o o o o o o o o o o o o o o o o o o o o o o o o o o o

In 1936 a Brooklyn man twenty-three years of age wrote a harrowing antiwar drama, *Bury the Dead,* put on at the Ethel Barrymore Theatre on April 18. He was Irwin Shaw, since then the author of several plays and many novels. Inasmuch as World War I ended when he was five years of age he had had no experience on the battlefield. But he was not alone in his hatred of war. There were many antiwar crusaders in the Thirties, although most of them took part in World War II and many of them were killed in the service of their countries.

Bury the Dead may have been influenced by Hans Chlumberg's *Miracle at Verdun,* produced in New York in 1931. In that play the soldiers buried at Verdun rose from their graves and set out to find out what effects the war that killed them had had on the world that survived. *Bury the Dead* is concerned with the after-death experience of six American soldiers killed in "the second year of the war that is to begin tomorrow night." The scene is a desolate battlefield. When the play begins, a squad of American soldiers are digging graves for the cadavers piled up to one side. The comments of the gravediggers are macabre: "I don't like the way they smell, that's all," one soldier complains. "File 'em in alphabetical order, boys," the sergeant orders. "We may need to refer to them later." "You'd think the rats'd at least wait until the stiffs were underground," another digger muses. "Did you ever see such a fat rat in your whole life?" his buddy remarks. "I bet he ate like a horse, this one." Another comrade then goes on, "Ah, sergeant ... this rat's a fine pedigreed animal— fed only on the choicest young men the United State's turned out in the last twenty years."

Bury the Dead reminds the audiences of the physical horrors and obscenities of war. In real life the desolate fact of stinking death is concealed under the pompous ceremonies of guards of honor and solemn rifle salutes and the sounding of taps at the graveside. Mr. Shaw describes dead soldiers not as fallen heroes, but as filthy corpses.

Not many of the living characters in the play protest the depravity of war. But the dead soldiers do. That is the point of the play. They rise from their graves. They propose to spread out over the world and warn the people against the gruesome futility of war. An older soldier, looking at them, remarks to a comrade: "What are they—a parcel of kids. Kids shouldn't be dead, Charley ... What the hell are they doin' dead? Did they get anything out of it?"

There are many touches of mischievous irony in the last scenes of *Bury the Dead.* For the generals are completely confused and inadequate. Men who refuse to be buried violate army regulations, one of the generals complains. One of them becomes pious: "We are a civilized race. We bury our dead. Lie down!" he shouts at them.

Will Geer in BURY THE DEAD

Trying to enlist the support of the soldiers' women, another general takes a patriotic stand: "We are fighting this war to protect the foundations of the homes of America! These foundations will crumble utterly if these men of yours come back from the dead. I shudder to think of the consequences of such an act. Our entire system will be mortally struck. Our banks will close, our buildings collapse.... Wars can be fought and won only when the dead are buried and forgotten."

In *Bury the Dead* the situation becomes static. After the dead have risen and resist all attempts to shame them into lying back once again in their graves, the play ends on a weak note. It lacks a conclusion as provocative as the scenes at the graveside. But in 1936, when war seemed a remote insanity, a young Brooklyn author portrayed war as sterile, ghastly and loathsome. In imagination he dealt with the realities more bluntly than many writers who had been at the front.

Note that his war "that begins tomorrow night" is a war that nobody wants and the public does not support. That kind of war poisoned the life of America in Vietnam thirty years later. *Bury the Dead* was more prophetic than anyone realized at the time.

o o o o o o o o o o o o o o o o o o o o o o o o o o o o o o o o o o o o o o o o o o o o o o

Marc Blitzstein

THE CRADLE WILL ROCK

o o o o o o o o o o o o o o o o o o o o o o o o o o o o o o o o o o o o o o o o o o o o o o

When the Federal Theatre was established by the Works Progress Administration in 1935 to give employment to jobless theatre people the benevolent government assumed that they would be grateful and docile. But they were unemployed citizens and far from being docile. By early summer of 1937 many of them had dedicated their talents to a militant revolutionary play that divided America into the iniquitous exploiters and the virtuous exploited and that urged the virtuous exploited ones to revolt instantly. It was Marc Blitzstein's

The Cradle Will Rock, a "Play in Music," as he described it, and the most triumphant proletarian play ever done in America.

By June 1937 Orson Welles and John Houseman had been rehearsing *The Cradle Will Rock* for nine weeks at the dainty Maxine Elliott Theatre. Fourteen thousand tickets had already been sold, and it seemed to the enthusiastic mutineers that capitalism would collapse as soon as the opening-night curtain came down. Faced with the responsibility of subsidizing sedition the Federal Theatre Administration in Washington was in a panic. Two hours before the curtain was to go up on the last preview and when Thirty-ninth Street was beginning to fill up with ticketholders the Federal Theatre Administration in Washington ordered all Federal Theatre productions to close temporarily pending a reorganization.

This act of desperation was the best thing that ever happened to *The Cradle Will Rock.* Nobody accepted the order with docility. John Houseman, on the telephone, managed to get the Venice Theatre uptown to open that evening and had a piano delivered there on a truck. Everyone, including the restless audience, moved uptown to the Venice Theatre. The composer, sitting in his shirt sleeves at the piano on the rim of the stage, and Orson Welles, in a chair on stage as master of ceremonies, conducted an impromptu performance. The actors and singers performed their parts from seats in the audience. It was exciting. But it was also creative. For by force of circumstances it had jettisoned the scenery, the costumes, and the orchestra. In street clothes the actors looked like the impoverished victims of a tyrannical and ruthless society, and Mr. Blitzstein looked more like a persecuted agent of the dispossessed than he would have if he had been leader of the orchestra.

In its successive productions in 1938, 1947, and 1964 *The Cradle Will Rock* has always been performed as if it represented the worthy poor. By separating the play from its scenery and décor the Federal Theatre did more in 1937 for *The Cradle Will Rock* than a conventional production could ever have done.

The title of the play refers to the time when unionized labor with a closed shop will blow the Establishment away. The story be-

gins in "Steeltown, U.S.A." where the laborers in a steel foundry are
holding a union drive for a closed shop. As their leader points out,
in an open shop the boilermaker can be kicked around, demoted and
fired. But in a closed shop every boilermaker is protected by 50,000
other boilermakers.

The villain is Mr. Mister who owns steel mills and newspapers,
controls universities and churches, and is the boss of the entire com-

Howard Da Silva, Bert Weston, Olive Stanton,
Blanche Collins and Marc Blitzstein
in THE CRADLE WILL ROCK

munity. He has a Liberty Committee (a tart jab at the Liberty League of reactionaries in the Thirties) composed of a minister, a college president, a physician, an artist, a musician, and a football coach. They represent Mr. Mister in the streets and help him fight unionism: "We don't want a union in Steeltown," they shout.

The play is composed of ten scenes, most of which reveal Mr. Mister's technique in organizing and directing citizen opposition to unions. Some of the scenes are set in nightcourt where the victims of society are on trial for breaking laws. The play itself is written in an ironic doggerel. In the concluding scene the labor leader warns Mr. Mister of the coming victory of closed shop unionism:

> Well, you can't climb down and you can't sit still;
> That's a storm that's going to last until
> The final wind blows . . . and when the wind blows
> The cradle will rock.
> (*Music, bugles, drums and fifes.*)

CURTAIN

Mr. Blitzstein was less a dramatist than a composer. The glory of *The Cradle Will Rock* derives less from his trite story than the virtuosity and power of his music. If Bert Brecht and Kurt Weill were the strongest influences on Mr. Blitzstein's work, Kurt Weill was the more important and creative of the two. *The Cradle Will Rock* is a stirring march song that ridicules the enemy and canonizes the pure in heart. Some of the arias are exalting. The climaxes roar with fury.

Some very talented theatre people have been members of the cast in the original and succeeding productions—Will Geer, Howard da Silva, Alfred Drake, Hiram Sherman, Vivian Vance, Muriel Smith, Jack Albertson. Leonard Bernstein played the tiny part of a petulant court clerk in the production that opened on December 27, 1947— the day, incidentally, when more snow fell on New York than ever before or since. On the streets New York looked deserted; it was silent, empty and ghoulish. But the Mansfield Theatre, where *The*

Cradle Will Rock opened, was bright and warm and bursting with people and enthusiasm. Theatre people know what is irrelevant and what is important. The show—not the weather—is invariably the important thing.

∘ ∘

Arthur Arent

ONE THIRD OF A NATION

∘ ∘

The "Living Newspaper" was the Federal Theatre Project's most creative accomplishment, and the most creative edition of the "Living Newspaper" was *One Third of a Nation*. It opened at the Adelphi Theatre on January 11, 1938. The "Living Newspapers" were documentaries or teaching plays on current social problems. *One Third of a Nation* documented part of an assertion President Franklin Delano Roosevelt made in his second inaugural address: that one third of the American nation was "ill housed, ill clad and ill nourished."

One Third of a Nation, written by Arthur Arent, illustrated the shameful history of the housing problem in New York City. The concluding scenes argued the political thesis that the profit motive was responsible for the barbarism of tenement facilities and that the United States Government would have to build public housing fit for human beings.

The text consisted of facts. But the genius of *One Third of a Nation* was its overwhelming scenic and polemic theatricalism. For

the original production Howard Bay constructed on stage the skele-
tonized forms of a four-story tenement with crumbling stairways,
rusted fire escapes, and a street overflowing with garbage cans and
ugly masses of junk. In the sensational first act the tenement caught
fire and the tenants ran down the stairs to the street. Moe Hack's
terrifying lighting plot with its explosion of flames and billows of
smoke made this introductory scene a triumphant statement of an
agonizing social problem. Like everything else in this edition of the
"Living Newspaper," the introductory scene was meticulously documented by footnotes in the text and in this case by references to
recent tenement fires in Manhattan, Brooklyn, and Long Island City.

The second scene showed building inspectors looking for the
cause of the fire. They concluded that it resulted from violations of
the old tenement code. Although the then current building code reg-
ulated the construction of new tenements, it had left unrevised the
code for buildings put up before 1901. Having stated this premise,
One Third of a Nation then searched the historical background of
New York City housing from the Colonial days of huge land grants
to the twentieth century when landowners consistently exploited the
people who had "to have a place to live"—the recurrent theme. The
author of the play pointed out that the landowners contributed nothing to the city which had made them rich, and that the people who
paid well for such rickety flats were the ones who had developed the
city with their intelligence, labor, industry, enterprise and commerce.

One Third of a Nation was fundamentally a social survey composed of abstract facts arranged in a political order. But on the stage
it was impetuously theatrical because the author, the director, the actors, and the craftsmen found ways of visualizing the documentary
material. It showed how in the eighteenth century the first tenant
leased a plot of land that he could inhabit comfortably because there
was lots of room. Throughout the following scenes, set in later
periods, this plot kept shrinking, and finally the last tenants had
hardly room enough to shave, read the newspaper or tie their shoe-
laces. More and more actors occupying the same plot of land and
pushing against one another more and more aggressively illustrated

the social point. Among the heartless exploiters, the play noted Trinity Church and the Astor and Wendell estates.

Since the Federal Theatre had been originally designed to give employment to jobless theatre people, the sweeping form of *One Third of a Nation* had one practical use: It employed a lot of people. Apart from the huge staff and crew, it employed about eighty actors—thirty of whom had to make ninety-three fast costume changes in seventy minutes. From the audience's point of view it was also a success. In New York the play had 273 performances at a ticket scale of fifty cents to one dollar.

The play made some members of Congress uneasy, however, for it advocated socialism in the administration of public housing and denounced lazy and corrupt politicians. It pointed out that during the previous four years Congress had spent $3,125,000,000 on the Army and Navy—more than enough to clean up all the slums in New York. Advocating more money for housing, the play argued that it was just as important to keep a man alive as to kill him.

Apart from being exciting theatre *One Third of a Nation* was a terse exposé of public inertia. Congress thus found itself subsidizing not only theatre people but also economic logic, public welfare and freedom of speech. That was too much. Congress killed the Federal Theatre Project in June of 1939 with a sigh of relief. The brilliance and success of *One Third of a Nation* had contributed substantially to the trauma of a frightened Congress.

o o o o o o o o o o o o o o o o o o o o o o o o o o o o o o o o o o o o o o

Clifford Odets

GOLDEN BOY

o o o o o o o o o o o o o o o o o o o o o o o o o o o o o o o o o o o o o o

Two and one-half years after *Awake and Sing* was produced, Clifford Odets' *Golden Boy* was put on at the Belasco Theatre on November 4, 1937. The play fairly vibrated with energy. It was a dynamic play—better organized and more specific and conclusive than *Awake and Sing*. It also communicated the mind of a different Odets. Having accepted an extravagant Hollywood contract, he was no longer "a piece of the decaying middle-class with revolutionary yearnings and convictions." He was a big-shot screen writer who was afraid he was losing his soul.

In the original draft Mr. Odets called his play "a modern allegory." In it Joe Bonaparte, son of a fond and simple Italian peddler in a tenement district, has genuine talent for playing the violin. To his father playing the violin is a satisfying way of life. "Don't expect for Joe to be a millionaire," the father tells a skeptical neighbor. "He don't need be a millionaire. A good life sa possible." But Joe dreams of a sensational worldly success. He is a good amateur boxer. In the course of the play he becomes a sensationally successful professional boxer—famous, extravagant and admired. He is "out for fame and fortune," he says, "not to be different or artistic." But boxing breaks his hands. He can no longer play the violin with distinction. In the

Luther Adler and Morris Carnovsky in GOLDEN BOY

last act he accidentally kills his opponent, and in a rush of remorse and self-hatred he drives off recklessly with his girl friend and is killed in an accident.

Purely as theatre, *Golden Boy* is superb. The characters are vivid. The dialogue is lively and earthy in the prizefighting world as well as in the tender world of Joe's father and family. The fundamental philosophical ideas are stated bluntly. Joe's father is a disarming character whose use of English is primitive but whose standards of conduct are enlightened. Arguing with the same skeptical neighbor he says: "You make me laugh, Mr. Carp. You say life sa bad. No, life sa good. Siggie and Anna fight—good! They love—good! The streets, winter an' summer—trees, cats—I love-a them all. The gooda boys and girls, they who sing and whistle—very good! The eating and sleeping, drinking wine—very good! I gone around on my wagon and talk to many people—nice!"

The fight manager, his rootless girl friend, and an inhuman racketeer who is promoting Joe's fighting career are all sharply-portrayed individuals, and they say perceptive things. When Joe is at the peak of his boxing career the coach puts his finger on Joe's essential instability: "Your heart ain't in fighting . . . your hate is. But a man with hate and nothing else . . . he's half a man . . . and half a man . . . is no man. Find something to love, or someone."

Golden Boy has two other theatrical distinctions. The pace is fast and inevitable. Once Joe starts promoting himself as a professional prizefighter the story rushes along logically and the scenes of contrast between the sleazy world of the ring and the loving world of Joe's father are pertinent and graphic. Moreover, *Golden Boy* is a homely play. The images are solid: a violin, a taxi, boxing gloves, a gymnasium, a glamorous automobile, expensive clothes.

But it was written by a kindly, brooding young man who once doubted the political system, but now doubts himself. The distinctions he makes between wordly success and human fulfillment are passionately felt and openly stated: "With music I'm never alone when I'm alone. . . . When I play music, nothing is closed to me. I'm not afraid of people and what they say. There's no war in music." When his father visits Joe just before a fight he makes the same distinction: "Now I know it's too late for music. The men must be free and happy for music—not like you." In Hollywood Mr. Odets had found success barren and bewildering.

Golden Boy was brilliantly staged by Harold Clurman, and the settings by Mordecai Gorelik were memorable designs in chiaroscuro. The Group Theatre actors were never better. Luther Adler gave a headlong performance as Joe. Frances Farmer acted the girl friend with appealing doubts and sympathies. Morris Carnovsky, who had played the troubled father in *Awake and Sing,* lovingly played the father whose spirit is broken by his son. Elia Kazan played the ruthless and alert gangster. The cast included other actors who later became famous—Art Smith, Lee Cobb, Jules (John) Garfield, Robert Lewis, Martin Ritt, Howard da Silva, and Karl Malden.

Golden Boy was a real event on Broadway. It proved that Mr. Odets was not a revolutionary playwright, but a gifted middle-class writer afflicted with self-doubts and spiritual uncertainty, and thoroughly modest in the privacy of his soul.

o o o o o o o o o o o o o o o o o o o o o o o o o o o o o o o o o o o o o o o

John Steinbeck

OF MICE AND MEN

o o o o o o o o o o o o o o o o o o o o o o o o o o o o o o o o o o o o o o o

What happens in *Of Mice and Men* is horrifying and melodramatic. Lennie, an ignorant, feeble-minded ranch hand—"bindle stiff" is the proper term—kills a hooker and is in turn killed by his pal. Lennie is a psychoneurotic case; he is not responsible for the seizures of violence that frequently take possession of him. *Of Mice and Men* is not an imaginative tragedy on a lofty plane. But it has one supreme virtue. It was written by a great humanist. John Steinbeck, who wrote it, created a fresh, breathing world of simple men whom he knew and respected. They are ignorant, shiftless ranch hands who wander from bunkhouse to bunkhouse in Salina County, California, where Mr. Steinbeck once lived. Although they are not enlightened men they try to live as honorably as they can within the boundaries of their experience. They are driven onward by some pathetically imagined dream of peace and comfort on a farm of their own. George, who is Lennie's pal, makes this observation: "Guys like us got no families. They get a little stake and then they blow it. They ain't got nobody in the world that gives a hoot in hell about 'em."

They are loners. But they have impossible dreams of a glorious day, not of success, but of independence: "We'd have a little house.... If we don't like a guy we can say: 'Get to hell out,' and, by God, he'd have to do it. An' if a friend come along, why, we'd have an extra bunk. Know what we'd say? We'd say, why don't you spend the night. And, by God, he would."

If it were not for Mr. Steinbeck's emotional commitment to the characters, *Of Mice and Men* might be an ordinary suspense melodrama. An air of irrational death hangs over it from the beginning. In the first scene beside the road Lennie is strangely simpleminded and his talk is infantile. But his buddy, George, is kindly and protective. Although George is frequently impatient over Lennie's imbecilities, he is loyal. They are escaping from a ranch where Lennie has unintentionally provoked an uprising. The other hands on the ranch where they find employment in the next scene are hospitable—a little wary perhaps, because Lennie is obviously a strange person, but they are all decent men. They live outdoors in a world of hard physical labor, but their minds keep running off into pleasant fantasies. Even the hooker, recently married to the boss's son, relies on fantasies to sustain her: "I'll go in the night an' thumb a ride to Hollywood," she says. "Gonna get in the movies an' have nice clothes—all them nice clothes like they wear. An' I'll set in the big hotels and they'll take pitchers of me. When they have them openings I'll go an' talk in the radio—an' it won't cost me nothin'—'cause I'm in the pitcher."

Everything physical about *Of Mice and Men* is battered and mean. But a kind of somber beauty hangs over it because Mr. Steinbeck has been there and understands and loves it. The psychotic murder that provokes the last act and the reluctant murder of Lennie by his despairing buddy are bizarre and unique and meaningless.

Of Mice and Men does not have the universality of Eugene O'Neill's *Desire Under the Elms*, but it is a profoundly moving human drama. When produced at the Music Box on November 23, 1937

Art Lund and Jo Sullivan in OF MICE AND MEN

it represented a triumph of the commercial theatre. Under the generous management of Sam Harris, a former boxing manager and sports operator, the play re-created the warm, open, parched beauty of Southern California and portrayed native characters sympathetically. The setting and the characters were as far from Broadway as it was possible to be, but the businessmen of Broadway captured it with admiration and affection. It introduced Broadway audiences to a race of remote, lonely men who had character. It had 207 performances and won the Critics Circle Award in the spring of 1938.

o o o o o o o o o o o o o o o o o o o o o o o o o o o o o o o o o o o o o o o

Thornton Wilder

OUR TOWN

o o o o o o o o o o o o o o o o o o o o o o o o o o o o o o o o o o o o o o o

In the gloom of the Depression Thornton Wilder wrote a heartening play. *Our Town* was produced in Henry Miller's Theatre in New York on February 4, 1938. Set in the year of 1901 in a mythical Grover's Corners, New Hampshire (a mythical Peterborough, actually), it said nothing about the Depression that had afflicted Americans since 1929, nor could it comment on the tense European situation that exploded into World War II the next year. Even if Mr. Wilder had been trying to write a tract for his era, those two disasters lay outside the time sequence of *Our Town*. But his play was both beautiful and reassuring. The wide scope of his story and his quiet humanism reminded his audiences that the events of the day may not be decisive, that the human race is in the long run invincible, that it adheres to social customs that also sustain it and that individuals are only the raw material of something that is grander. In the introduction to Act Three the ruminative Stage Manager says: "There's something way down deep that's eternal about every human being." Heartening words to hear at any time, but especially in 1938.

Mr. Wilder was obsessed with destiny, which he trusted; he was an optimist because he could not believe the worst. Speaking of Grover's Corners he said: "I have set the village against the largest dimension of time and space." Everything that happened to the characters and everything they said is a literary metaphor of the long experience of mankind. The time sequence is eternal.

The method of *Our Town* cannot be separated from the theme. There is no curtain, and very little scenery. Everything appears to be impromptu. And the pivotal character inevitably becomes the Stage Manager who is really chairman of the program. He opens the play with some factual material about the author, the locale, the date, the people and their institutions, the characters and their backgrounds. If the various scenes of *Our Town* were played inside the conventional naturalistic scenery with curtain and props and all the other theatrical devices for fabricating illusion, the action would seem trite and the dialogue boring. For what the characters say is deliberately prosy. They are not trying to be brilliant people. They are speaking the colloquialisms of daily life. What they represent has size and relevance because they represent Everyman. And what they say is the litany of the human race.

The three acts portray the homely essentials—daily life, love and marriage, death—this last, Mr. Wilder says, after the manner of Dante's Purgatory. The play is moving because of Mr. Wilder's unfailing compassion. The last act, set in the Grover's Corners cemetery on a windy hilltop, would be unbearable if he were not hovering over it like an anxious *conférencier*. After Emily, wife of George, both of whom are leading characters, has died and has settled back in her lonely grave among the other dead, she makes one especially poignant remark: "O earth," she exclaims wistfully, "you're too wonderful for

Frank Craven in OUR TOWN

anybody to realize you," and then she continues, "Do any human beings ever realize life while they live it—every, every minute?" The Stage Manager takes the liberty of answering her: "The saints and poets maybe—some," he casually remarks. We can now add: "Some dramatists, too."

Now that *Our Town* is a standard work all over the world it is

interesting to recall that it had an unpromising beginning. Business
was so bad in Boston during the preliminary tour that the production
was withdrawn after the first week. Bostonians found it dull. In New
York two weeks later the reception was mixed. Many theatergoers
thought the simplicity of form was perverse pretentiousness. After it
received the Pulitzer Prize in May, audiences began to come and
continued to come for 336 performances, as they would continue to
come year after year all over the world. The Critics Circle, eluding
immortality as successfully as possible, gave its prize to John Steinbeck's *Of Mice and Men*—a good play but not a great one.

○ ○

Robert E. Sherwood

ABE LINCOLN IN ILLINOIS

○ ○

In the course of the three acts of Robert E. Sherwood's *Abe Lincoln
in Illinois* Lincoln passes through a crisis of conscience and emerges
as a man of resolved principles. During the early scenes he tries to
avoid making responsible decisions. Events overcome his reluctance.
In the last scene, after he has been elected President, he goes off to
Washington resigned to the realities of his mission "not knowing when
or whether ever I may return."

Two and one-half years before *Abe Lincoln in Illinois* was produced, Mr. Sherwood had written an antiwar play, *Idiot's Delight* in
a flamboyant, breezy, theatrical style; and he had said in his post-

script that he did not believe another war would break out. The difference in tone between *Idiot's Delight* and *Abe Lincoln in Illinois* is remarkable. The plays might have been written by different people. One can only conclude that Mr. Sherwood also was going through a crisis of conscience. In *Abe Lincoln in Illinois* the character of Lincoln matures. Also the character of Robert Sherwood.

Mr. Sherwood was not vain enough to identify himself with Lincoln. But at the moment he was interested in the character of Lincoln because he also was facing intellectual and moral problems. Lincoln hated war, but set out for Washington at a time when war was inevitable. Mr. Sherwood hated war, but at the time of the Lincoln play war looked inevitable. In fact, war broke out about eleven months after the play opened in the Plymouth Theatre on October 15, 1938. The somber Lincoln play marked the conclusion of Mr. Sherwood's jovial career as author of good-natured comedies.

The Lincoln of the play is the heroic figure of American mythology. He is studying grammar like a schoolboy in the first scene. He is President-elect in the last scene. In between, the play chronicles the story that all Americans know. There is a minimum of dramatic invention and there are many gaps in the story, for the author did not feel obliged to tell it literally. Nor is the dialogue remarkable. There are no rhetorical declarations. The prayer for the life of a boy on the prairie is prosaic, although it marks a fundamental change in Lincoln's character, and even the farewell speech from the Springfield, Illinois railroad station is undistinguished. Throughout, the tone is deliberately conversational. But since the play is part of American mythology the audience does not have to be instructed or convinced. It supplies out of its own heritage the moral grandeur that Mr. Sherwood leaves out and that would probably have sounded pompous if he had tried to find words for it.

"Underwritten" is the word for the play. But it is deeply moving because it is about the sacred principles of America. In 1938 Hitler was assassinating freedom, and step by step making war inevitable. Perhaps freedom had a deeper meaning in America then than it does in normal times. Many people had in the back of their minds the

Raymond Massey in ABE LINCOLN IN ILLINOIS

awful thought that the American ideals of liberty and equality might be "decadent and doomed," as Lincoln says when he is leaving Springfield.

But *Abe Lincoln in Illinois* would be a moving play in any period of American history. It is a play about a man who was committed to principle, written by a man of the same nature. Mr. Sherwood shared the old dream that America could preserve "the intellectual and moral world that is within us, so that we may secure an individual, social and political prosperity, whose course shall be forward, and which, while the earth endures, shall not pass away." Not inspiring rhetoric, but a statement of American hopes by a man who cherished them.

The play is an elegy by a man whose experience gave him special insight into the character of Lincoln. It is a celebration of American beliefs. On the stage it needed—and always needs—an actor who does not diffuse the image of Lincoln that every American has in the back of his mind. Raymond Massey was the man. He made the play believable, not only because he had a rough resemblance to the traditional portraits of Lincoln but also because of the mild tempo, the personal modesty and the homeliness of his acting. His success in the role ruined his career as an actor. The public could never accept him in less exalted parts.

Abe Lincoln in Illinois won the Pulitzer Prize in 1939, but the cranky individualists of the Critics Circle could not make up their minds. They gave no prize that year, thus sparing themselves the unbearable ordeal of having to talk and dine together on the evening when an award would normally be given.

o o o o o o o o o o o o o o o o o o o o o o o o o o o o o o o o o o o o o o o o o o

Philip Barry

THE PHILADELPHIA STORY

o o o o o o o o o o o o o o o o o o o o o o o o o o o o o o o o o o o o o o o o o o

In the last years of the Depression and only a few months before World War II broke out, Philip Barry wrote his most successful drawing-room comedy, *The Philadelphia Story*, which opened at the Shubert Theatre on March 28, 1939. Drawing-room comedies were his most congenial medium. The rich and the elite fascinated him as figures of comedy, and he had an instinct for conventional dramatic crafts-manship along with a knack for subtly malicious dialogue: "It's astonishing what money can do for people, don't you agree, Mr. Cannon? Not too much, you know,—just more than enough. Particularly for girls," one of his rich characters remarks dryly.

But Mr. Barry was no dilettante. He was a devotedly religious man; he had a conscience. He wanted to write about the essence of life, and he did write a few philosophical plays, *White Wings, Hotel Universe, Here Come the Clowns*, that failed at the box office—a painful experience for him. Thanks in large part to the acting and the leaping popularity of Katharine Hepburn, *The Philadelphia Story* was a conspicuously successful play. Everyone was delighted with its glamorous story, the relaxed luxury of the life of the rich, and the tolerance and easy sophistication of rich people. Having inherited wealth and social position the Lord family accepts life with equanim-ity in this play.

Katharine Hepburn in THE PHILADELPHIA STORY

But people like the affluent Lords who lived on a great estate near Philadelphia were not universally popular at the end of the Depression. Too many people had suffered to feel magnanimous about the rich. Today it is interesting to observe the skill with which Mr. Barry introduces the bitterness of the outside world without impairing the immaculate grace of drawing-room comedy.

Tracy Lord, the chief character, has divorced one husband and is about to marry a second. The Lord mansion, with its lavish staff of servants, is bustling with gala preparations. Everything is gay except for the puzzling presence of a writer and a photographer from an aggressive magazine called *Destiny*. *Destiny* is Mr. Barry's stand-in for *Fortune* which in 1939 was, like *Time* and *Life*, pioneering in a new form of magazine writing that was not exactly yellow but that invaded privacy and made arbitrary social judgments with smug self-righteousness.

Mike, the magazine writer, and Liz, the photographer, are hostile observers of the rich social set. They have come to write an "in-depth" article about the wedding. On both sides their presence is a confrontation. After looking the place over, Mike says to Liz: "Answer me honestly, Liz; what right has a girl like Tracy Lord to exist? . . . What place has she got in the world today? Comes the revolution, she'll be the first to go." In 1939 reference to a Communist revolution was not just a figure of speech. But the Lords can be as glib as he is. When Mike, who has declared himself a Jeffersonian democrat, comments with distaste on the grandeur of the Lords' country place, Tracy's brother replies: "Have you ever seen his [Jefferson's] house at Monticello? It's quite a place, too." ("Home team—one; Visitors—nothing." Liz remarks sardonically.) Eventually Mike and Tracy clash. It is class warfare. When Mike protests Tracy's vilification of him as a snob she goes on: "You're the worst kind there is: an intellectual snob. . . . You're a mass of prejudices, aren't you? You're so much thought and so little feeling."

Since the journalist and the photographer are minor characters, they influence the story but do not control it and get out of it nothing for themselves. Mr. Barry obediently fulfills his obligations as author of a comedy about the beautiful people, and *The Philadelphia Story* ends happily. Tracy does not marry the fascist prig to whom she is engaged and who thinks that *Destiny* is a magazine that fills a definite place in the system. She remarries her first husband whose greatest achievement is his skill as a yachtsman. There is an entertaining irony in the conclusion.

The original cast of *The Philadelphia Story* included, in addition to Miss Hepburn, some exceptionally gifted actors who went on to conspicuous careers—Shirley Booth, Van Heflin, Joseph Cotton, and a talented teen-age harpy, Lenore Lonergan. The play had ninety-six performances before it took to the road, which was awaiting it.

The Drama Critics Circle did not give an award that year.

o o o o o o o o o o o o o o o o o o o o o o o o o o o o o o o o o o o o o o o o o o o o o o o

S. N. Behrman

NO TIME FOR COMEDY

o o o o o o o o o o o o o o o o o o o o o o o o o o o o o o o o o o o o o o o o o o o o o o o

When S. N. Behrman wrote his first comedy—*The Second Man*—in 1927 the future looked bright and gay. Life looked like an eternal comedy, and follies and vanities and cleverness and epigrams looked like good theatrical investments. Life seemed to be not a jungle but, instead, a pleasant meadow.

Although drawing-room comedy is Mr. Behrman's natural medium, he has the conscience of a citizen. The style is light but the mind is full of grave concern. In 1939 Mr. Behrman wrote his best play—

Laurence Olivier and Katharine Cornell
in NO TIME FOR COMEDY

No Time for Comedy, which was put on at the Ethel Barrymore Theatre on April 17, 1939. In its description of the dilemma of a clever
playwright in a barbaric world it has serious motivation. "All over
the world people are being murdered and tortured and humiliated,"
the playwright remarks to his wife, an actress. "Death is rained from
the sky on whole populations.... And you expect me to sit in my
room contriving stage situations for you to be witty in.... I tell you
it's all an irrelevance, an anachronism, a callous acquiescence."

That is the dilemma of the play. It was Mr. Behrman's personal
dilemma in 1939, and he resolved it brilliantly. In drawing-room comedy the plot can be trivial and the craftsmanship elementary. Style is
the only thing that counts. *No Time for Comedy* begins with the standard device of a comic Negro servant talking on the telephone and
supplying essential exposition and entertainment simultaneously.

Mr. Behrman gets to the main point briskly. Gay, the playwright,
is married to Linda, the actress. He is in a slump because he has no
comic ideas. She is in a slump because he has not written anything
for her to play. During this dismal interlude he meets a married
woman, Amanda, who fancies herself as an uplifter. By appealing to
Gay's vanity she urges him to put off his antic way and write a
serious play that contains the bitterness and challenge of the times.
He writes a play on immortality and calls it *Dilemma.* Since *No Time
for Comedy* is a standard drawing-room comedy the central situation
produces some of the standard conflicts—realignments of amorous
couples, outbursts of temperament, sardonic lines. "Sleep with him if
you like," Gay's wife says bitterly to her rival, "but for pity's sake
don't ruin his literary style." Mr. Behrman's play accomplishes the
ultimate goal of comedy: it makes serious people look foolish.

Since Mr. Behrman's dilemma coincides with the dilemma of Gay
in the play, *No Time for Comedy* makes some pertinent cultural
statements. Amanda tells Gay that his plays are dishonest because
they do not deal with his intellectual and professional torments. She
argues that drawing-room comedy is a form of cowardly escape from
the shattering realities of the contemporary world.

It is obvious, however, that Mr. Behrman's personal beliefs coincide with Linda's more charitable philosophy. To Gay's observation that "we are living in an era of death" Linda replies: "What if we are? ... One should keep in one's own mind a little clearing in the jungle of life. ... Is it more profound to write of death of which we know nothing than of life of which we may learn something, which we can illuminate, if only briefly, with gaiety, with understanding? ... No, the difficult thing, the admirable thing is to live."

In the end Gay decides to write a frivolous play to be called *No Time for Comedy*, and so Mr. Behrman makes his point with irony and humor. Some extremely talented theatre people helped him to make his point. The part of Linda was played with humor and a kind of magnetic sincerity by Katharine Cornell, who probably shared Mr. Behrman's point of view. The part of the playwright was played with temperamental agility by Laurence Olivier, who in 1939 was just beginning his illustrious career. His "temperamental agility" would be blandly called "virtuosity" in the reviews a few years later. Margalo Gillmore, an accomplished actress, played the part of Amanda with charm and craft and asperity. John Williams played a disdainful, laconical financier, and Robert Flemying played a philanderer. It was noted with some anger at the time that the three American men of the world were played by three British actors. "In all important matters style, not sincerity, is the essential," Oscar Wilde had remarked on a previous occasion, thus anticipating the casting problems of Sam Behrman's play.

No Time for Comedy had 185 performances on Broadway. In a collapsing world Mr. Behrman did not lose himself in the jungle but kept on cultivating his own garden. Both he and the garden are still here.

o o o o o o o o o o o o o o o o o o o o o o o o o o o o o o o o o o o o o o o o o

William Saroyan

THE TIME OF YOUR LIFE

o o o o o o o o o o o o o o o o o o o o o o o o o o o o o o o o o o o o o o o o o

There is one antiphonal line in William Saroyan's *The Time of Your Life* that is especially comic. A taciturn Arab in Nick's Pacific Street Saloon in San Francisco never joins in the general conversation but periodically mutters: "No foundation. All the way down the line." This mournful iteration, spoken out of loneliness by a commonplace barfly, expresses a universal sentiment, applicable to just about every situation, and it is invariably hilarious. It is still quoted affectionately by people who first heard it in the Booth Theatre on October 25, 1939.

This sentiment could also apply to the ragtag and bobtail saloon loungers in Mr. Saroyan's boozy caper. They are a bunch of oddballs —a race-track seer, his bewildered retainer, a prosaic young man who thinks he is a comedian and another who discovers that he is a good saloon pianist, a witless, desperate young man who thinks he is in love with a nurse who does not want to marry him, a visitor who spends most of his time punching a slot machine, a prostitute, a talkative bunco man, a vicious cop, the skeptical saloonkeeper, a newsboy, plus others too obscure to have names. None of them has much signifi-cance. None of them has a mission. They all exist from moment to moment over beer, whiskey and champagne. They have nothing in common except a need for companionship. "It's a good, low-down,

honky-tonk American place that lets people alone," Mr. Saroyan remarks in his stage directions.

And it is all very personal. *The Time of Your Life* is fundamentally an expression of Mr. Saroyan's native enthusiasm. World War
II had begun in 1939 and the future for America looked gloomy and
Mr. Saroyan was quite aware of it. "Man wages wars against himself," he said in his preface to the published text. But he could not
help having the time of his life every day. He had written a mad, cheerful novel called *The Daring Young Man on the Flying Trapeze*, which
could have been a description of himself. He had made many friends

on Broadway with a tender idyll about obscure people, *My Heart's in the Highlands,* an impulsive anecdote that was beautifully acted by a Group Theatre cast. In 1939, war and other alarms and portents could not kill Mr. Saroyan's happiness in being alive. He was not—and is not now—a literary Pollyanna. His experience has been harsh. Nor is he an evangelist. But he cannot help enjoying life.

Although the characters in *The Time of Your Life* are not humorists and do not crack jokes, Mr. Saroyan and the audience know that they are funny. Kit Carson's opening line is: "I don't suppose you ever fell in love with a midget weighing thirty-nine pounds." And there is another reflection of Mr. Saroyan's personality that makes his play delightful. The relationships between the characters are kindly. They are bums—ignorant, futile people—but they are also idealists. "This is a good world," one of the characters remarks. "It's wonderful to get up in the morning and go out for a little walk and smell the trees and see the streets and the kids going to school. . . . This is a nice world. Why are we all so lousy?"

Every now and then a piously vicious cop rushes into the saloon, yells at helpless people and roughs them up. All the saloon derelicts become tense and self-conscious when he is around. He brings out the worst in everybody. In the last scene the bunco man kills him off stage. The murder is only an incident, but it is the only direct bit of action in the play. "Then," according to Mr. Saroyan's final stage direction, the play "goes into its beautiful American routine again." Everyone again becomes boozy, friendly, slow, tolerant and kindly.

Since *The Time of Your Life* conformed to none of the familiar rules of playwriting in 1939 it gave the Theatre Guild serious trouble. The first production was scrapped; it was dull, baffling and pointless. But the second production, directed by Eddie Dowling and Mr. Saroyan, gave the diffuse script form, rhythm and reality and it delighted everybody for a long time. There were some prominent actors in the cast. But there were no stars. All the actors succumbed to the languors and sociability of Nick's Pacific Street Saloon, Restaurant and Entertainment Palace, and preserved the informality of Mr. Saroyan's prose poem in ragtime.

The Time of Your Life won both the Pulitzer Prize and the Critics Circle award in 1940. In a fit of originality Mr. Saroyan refused the Pulitzer Prize which was the one that paid money.

o o o o o o o o o o o o o o o o o o o o o o o o o o o o o o o o o o o o o o

Paul Osborn

MORNING'S AT SEVEN

o o o o o o o o o o o o o o o o o o o o o o o o o o o o o o o o o o o o o o

In certain circumstances comedy and tragedy are interchangeable. Paul Osborn's *Morning's at Seven,* which opened at the Longacre Theatre on November 30, 1939, is a case in point. Mr. Osborn willed it a comedy. But his touching portrait of old people in their second childhood, quarreling peevishly, wounding one another savagely, might logically be tragedy. The circumstances are tragic.

But Mr. Osborn's sense of proportion makes it comedy. His younger generation, for instance, consists of Homer Bolton, age 40, and his fiancée Myrtle, who keeps a hope chest. The image of a hope chest twelve years or more old is either ludicrous or pathetic. Homer and Myrtle are bloodless and prudish people of middle age. He blushes when she asks him the size of his underwear; and his mother's casual reference to a double bed embarrasses him. Homer and Myrtle have been engaged for seven years and "went together" five years before their engagement. As representatives of the younger generation in *Morning's at Seven* they are ludicrous.

And so are the petty discords and peregrinations of the old people

Dorothy Gish, Enid Markey and
Russell Collins in MORNING'S AT SEVEN

—all of them in their sixties or seventies. The three old men—Theodore, Carl and David—are married to three old sisters—Cora, Ida and Esther. An unmarried sister, Arry, has lived with Theodore and Cora all her adult life. All three families live in adjoining houses in a suburb. But the propinquity of their neighborhood life does not give their old age dignity and it has not made them happy. Old age has made them temperamental, crotchety, ingrown and dull, and has filled them with useless regrets. Their golden years are barren and irascible.

If Mr. Osborn were a romantic, this would be a tragic situation. But he is a realist and portrays it as humorous. In the opening scene Theodore is not elated because the doctor who has just examined him has not found anything seriously wrong. "Said it wasn't anything to worry about," he complains to his wife Cora. "By God, I don't know how a doctor like that gets the reputation he has!" Theodore is particularly dejected because the doctor didn't tell him to cut down on his smoking: "It stands to reason that when a man gets along in his late sixties he's got to cut down on things like that." Unreasonableness is comic in a civilized society, and Theodore could not be more unreasonable.

The essence of *Morning's at Seven* is much more intricate and absurd. Everything is at loose ends. In the second act everyone's life goes to pieces. Cora suddenly wants her husband to move with her into a new house where they can be alone for the rest of their lives. She proposes to give their old house to her sister Arry. Cora can't stand her sister any longer, and in fact suspects that years ago her husband and Arry had a romantic affair.

David is so bored with his wife and her sisters that he makes her move upstairs and leave him alone on the first floor. "You know, of course, without my telling you, how much you all depress me," he tells his wife's family most unctuously and politely. Carl wants to leave his wife and move in with David, whom he regards as some sort of prophet. Carl is a lost soul. He complains that although he has never wanted much from life, he did once want to be a dentist, "but I wasn't up to it," he adds mournfully.

After having been engaged to Homer for seven years, Myrtle

startles him and astounds her elders by reporting that she is pregnant. No one had ever suspected that such a thing could happen. Homer and Myrtle are such pale and conventional people that the idea of her unchurched pregnancy seems hilarious. "Well, well, well, well! What the hell do you know about that!" Uncle Theodore exclaims. "That's a pretty good one! Yes, sir, by God, you certainly had your uncle Thor fooled!"

But there is more to *Morning's at Seven* than that. If such a thing were possible, it is a droll elegy. An undertone of tragedy keeps creeping in. These are people whom life is pitilessly discarding. They feel forsaken and hopeless. Carl is full of regrets and anxieties. "Where am I in life?" he inquires helplessly. "I'm not where I should be at all! There's some other place in life where I should be! Now I'm sixty-eight years old and where am I?"

When Arry is being cruelly evicted by her sister, she feels dispossessed of everything: "It suddenly seemed as if all the years I've already lived didn't make much sense. I might just as well not have lived them." For comedy and tragedy are rooted in the same paradox —mortality. The immortal soul is confined in a mortal body. Mr. Osborn's compassionate salute to old people has comic proportions, and it was played as comedy by the brilliant original cast that included Dorothy Gish and Russell Collins. But it could have been played as bleak tragedy, as if the morning were not at seven and God were not in his heaven and life is merciless and old age obscene.

*Sara Allgood, Barry Fitzgerald and
Arthur Shields in* JUNO AND THE PAYCOCK

○ ○

Sean O'Casey

JUNO AND THE PAYCOCK

○ ○

Juno and the Paycock was not merely produced; it exploded. When Sean O'Casey wrote it he was supporting himself with pick and shovel, and during its two-week engagement at the Abbey Theatre in Dublin in 1924 he kept on mixing cement in a road gang. Seduced by the royalties of 25 pounds he then quit his road job and became a professional writer. *Juno and the Paycock,* a roaring drama about some bombastic tenement dwellers, startled the English-speaking theatre. In New York it was badly acted in 1926 in the tiny Mayfair Theatre (converted from an appalling cafeteria), but it was acted with great skill and relish by visiting Abbey Theatre companies in 1927, 1931, 1932, and 1940. The 1940 cast was the most uproarious because Barry Fitzgerald was the most turbulent of the Captain Boyles and Sara Allgood was the most overwhelmingly maternal of the Junos. The conflict between them was heroic.

    Juno and the Paycock could not have been more exciting if Mr. O'Casey had packed into it everything he knew about tenement life in Dublin. He had lived in a tenement for all of his forty-four years. The intimacy of his knowledge of tenement people extends to his stage directions. Of Juno: "She is forty-five years of age, and twenty

157

years ago she must have been a pretty woman; but her face has now assumed that look which ultimately settles down upon the faces of the women of the working-class: a look of listless monotony and harassed anxiety, blending with an expression of mechanical resistance." And Captain Boyle, the "Paycock": "He is a man of about sixty; stout, gray-haired and stocky. His neck is short, and his head looks like a stone ball that one sometimes sees on top of a gate-post. His cheeks, reddish-purple, are puffed out, as if he were always repressing an almost irrepressible ejaculation. On his upper lip is a crisp, tightly cropped moustache; he carries himself with the upper part of his body slightly thrown back, and his stomach slightly thrust forward. His walk is a slow, consequential strut." The characterizations are thoroughly circumstantial, as if Mr. O'Casey were describing people he knew. The dialogue has the flair and richness of words and phrases he must have heard all around him and probably used himself. It is Elizabethan in its extravagance and rhythm and directness.

Set in the year of 1922 *Juno and the Paycock* exists in the midst of labor and political troubles. The Boyle son, Jerry, has lost one arm in the rebellion against English rule. But he is a minor character. Juno, the indomitable mother, and Captain Boyle, the indolent and deceitful father, are the chief characters, and most of the story involves Juno's unsuccessful attempts to get him to work. Although the circumstances of the play lead to tragedy, the racy and pungent characterizations are the play's fundamental genius. Captain Boyle lives in a world of flamboyant conceit and fantasy. On the basis of one voyage across the Irish Sea to Britain he imagines himself a maritime hero. He is followed everywhere by a bootlicking loafer who flatters him and cadges drinks off him, sings romantic songs and talks in amusing couplets.

Mr. O'Casey was a militant unionist and a political leftist. But Juno, his most heroic character, has no patience with strikes or national revolution. As the head of the house and its only wage-earner she has no patience with disorder. She would like to conform. But eventually the Irish disorders reach into her tenement and take away her son. He is executed by his former comrades for being an informer.

This terrible family catastrophe generates the most piercing scream of anguish in modern drama. Juno says: "Mother o' God, Mother o' God, have pity on us all. Blessed Virgin, where were you when me darlin' son was riddled with bullets? Sacred Heart o' Jesus, take away our hearts o' stone, and give us hearts o' flesh! Take away this murd-herin' hate and give us Thine eternal love!"

What is the theme of *Juno and the Paycock?* Not revolution or rebellion. Not freedom. Not family unity. Not the lack of communication between the characters. The theme is the rancorous stupidity of the tenement characters. Mr. O'Casey relished the comedy of their strutting and their irresponsible behavior and their extravagant language and he shared the depth of the tragedies that engulf them. But *Juno and the Paycock* is a portrait of hopeless, passionate stupidity. The date is 1922, but the play is still pertinent a half century later. In Ulster temperament still overwhelms reason and hatreds still result in the murder of neighborhood people.

o o o o o o o o o o o o o o o o o o o o o o o o o o o o o o o o o o o o o o o

Robert E. Sherwood

THERE SHALL BE NO NIGHT

o o o o o o o o o o o o o o o o o o o o o o o o o o o o o o o o o o o o o o o

In the political context of the spring of 1940 Robert E. Sherwood's *There Shall Be No Night* was sobering and impressive. Literally it is a play about the Soviet invasion of Finland. But it was written by a public-spirited man who had been active on the Committee to Defend

America by Aiding the Allies and who had written a challenging newspaper advertisement headed "Stop Hitler Now." Nothing in the play
urges the United States to join the Allies on the battlefields of Europe.
But when the play opened on April 29, 1940 in the Alvin Theatre,
with Alfred Lunt and Lynn Fontanne in the leading parts, everyone
knew that it challenged the isolation of the United States. It was a
propaganda play. Some worried people in Washington thought it
ought to be suppressed. Many others wrote bitter letters to Mr. Sherwood; some called him a warmonger.

Even when *There Shall Be No Night* was new it seemed like a
rickety play, put together laboriously to prove a thesis. Now that the
political circumstances in which it was written have dissipated and a
third world war, though possible, is not imminent, the play seems too
contrived to be taken seriously. The heroism with which Dr. Kaarlo
Valkonen, a Finnish neurologist, abandons his convictions and goes
to his doom at the front, is in an obsolete traditions of war plays,
before *What Price Glory?* changed the holy point of view.

When the play opens, Dr. Valkonen has just won a Nobel Prize
for a recent study in the causes of mental diseases. He regards war
as a primitive aberration, but in the national crisis he behaves like
the standard patriot and grabs a weapon. Everyone in the play—the
doctor's American wife, their son and his fiancée, and the American
radio crew—is insufferably noble and fearless. As if Mr. Sherwood
suspected he was writing too sanctimoniously, the dialogue abounds
in apologetic phrases—"Oh, I know it's presumptuous of me to be
talking to you," . . . "I'm sorry I seem to be emotional about it," . . .
"Forgive me, gentlemen," and so on. To read the text today is to realize how much the anxieties and moral uncertainties of the American
position in 1940 hid the banalities of the script.

But all this ignores the worth of the man who wrote it and the
readiness of the Broadway theatre to take a moral stand on a public
issue. War was Mr. Sherwood's oldest obsession. After serving with
the Canadian Black Watch in World War I and being sent to a field
hospital for treatment of wounds, he looked on war as the supreme
fraud. The hardening of his point of view is illustrated by his shift-

Alfred Lunt and Montgomery Clift in THERE SHALL BE NO NIGHT

ing attitudes in three plays: a rather lighthearted exposure of war in *Idiot's Delight* in 1936; a reluctant acceptance of the reality of war in *Abe Lincoln in Illinois* in 1938, and a regretful call to arms in *There Shall Be No Night* in 1940.

Mr. Sherwood was a congenital optimist. What Dr. Valkonen says represents Mr. Sherwood's point of view. In the first act he points out a favorite Sherwood thesis: that although science is curing many common diseases, it cannot cure degenerative diseases like "insanity, which is degeneration of the brain—and cancer, which is degeneration of the tissues." Like Mr. Sherwood, the doctor is a congenital optimist. Even in the last act, in the midst of death, he is optimistic. When the bombs are exploding all around he says to his comrades: "Listen! What you hear now—this terrible sound that fills the earth—it is the death rattle. One may say easily and dramatically that it is the death rattle of civilization. But I choose to believe differently. I believe it is the long deferred death rattle of the primordial beast. We are conquering bestiality, not with our muscles and our swords, but with the power of the light that is in our minds." Things have not turned out that beautifully.

A worldly man who lived a sophisticated life, Mr. Sherwood was a believer all his life. During World War II he served his country as a speech writer for President Franklin D. Roosevelt and as an executive in the Office of War Information. Not the least of the valuables he sacrificed for his country was his ability to write a good play. When he returned to New York in 1945 he tried to pick up his theatre career where he had left it in 1940. But his *The Rugged Path* in 1945 was a bungled play, and the musical *Miss Liberty*, which he wrote with Moss Hart and Irving Berlin in 1949, was distressingly mediocre. He had given all he had.

His commitment of conscience was not unique. *There Shall Be No Night* was the meeting place of thoroughbreds. Mr. Lunt and Miss Fontanne acted in it as believers. They were just returning from a long, exhausting national tour of *The Taming of the Shrew* when Mr. Sherwood gave them the manuscript of his play. They quickly abandoned their plan to take a rest at their home in Genesee Depot, Wisconsin, and started work on the play. They played it more than 1600 times in America and in London during the blitz. They did not stop until a bomb hit the Aldwych Theatre.

By the normal standards of peacetime *There Shall Be No Night* is a pedestrian play—part of the fustian of the old melodramatic stage. But it still preserves the gallant spirit of a man of principle and the willingness of the Broadway theatre to respond to a public crisis.

o o o o o o o o o o o o o o o o o o o o o o o o o o o o o o o o o o o o o o o o o o

Lillian Hellman

WATCH ON THE RHINE

o o o o o o o o o o o o o o o o o o o o o o o o o o o o o o o o o o o o o o o o o o

In 1941 Lillian Hellman was the celebrated author of two skillful melodramas populated by hateful characters—*The Children's Hour* of 1934 and *The Little Foxes* of 1939. Most of the characters were monsters and Miss Hellman despised them. But her professional attitude underwent a fundamental change when Hitler's evil triumphs darkened the world. Always a concerned citizen, she became alarmed about the war. *Watch on the Rhine,* which opened at the Martin Beck Theatre on April 1, 1941, is, with one exception, composed of delightful people who Miss Hellman could admire. She chose sides in the gravest problem of the Western world while most people temporized. Not only her mind, which is formidable, but also her heart was involved in this play about the nobility of antifascism.

Watch on the Rhine is not so expertly put together as *The Children's Hour* and *The Little Foxes.* The terrible intrigues and cruelty of war constitute the theme. But nearly two-thirds of the play is familiar comedy dominated by a rich matriarch, Fanny Farrelly of Washington, who has a witty and malicious tongue. In the early scenes the play is composed of the standard elements of upper-class comedy of manners. At curtain rise the maid is looking over the family mail and commenting on the members of the family and providing the

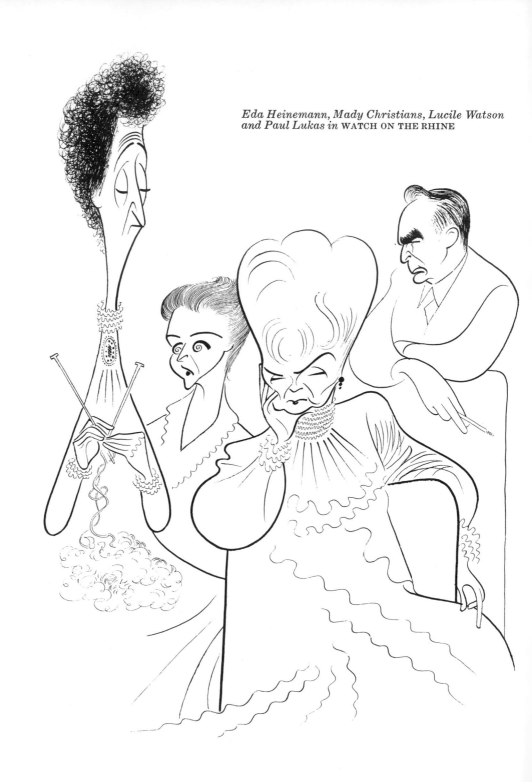

Eda Heinemann, Mady Christians, Lucile Watson and Paul Lukas in WATCH ON THE RHINE

routine exposition in the usual comic vein. A portrait of the celebrated founder of the family hangs on the wall where the characters can refer to him. The dialogue is brimming over with references to celebrated people and the personal foibles of the rich. David, the son, says "I'm going to have a drink. I have never had a drink before breakfast since the day I took my bar examination." Or Fanny: "He was fancy when she married him. Not so fancy now, I suspect, although still chic and tired. You know what I mean, the way they are in Europe." Since the part of Fanny was played with humorous composure by the expert Lucile Watson (and since all the parts were extremely well played) the first two-thirds of *Watch on the Rhine* was vastly entertaining in the original production.

But the evil of Naziism and the nobility of resisting it is the theme of *Watch on the Rhine*. In the last third of the play this overwhelms the amenities of the Farrelly family, and turns a comedy into a melodrama. Among the guests in the Farrelly home are the daughter, Sara, her German husband, Kurt Müller, and their three children. They have come to stay in the family home after a long period of wandering through Europe as German political refugees. Another guest is a Roumanian count. He discovers that Kurt is an active member of an anti-Nazi conspiracy. He threatens to denounce Kurt to the German embassy in Washington unless he is paid $10,000. In the last act Kurt Müller dispassionately kills the count and resumes his wanderings to promote the anti-Nazi conspiracy. This is the theme of the play, but it is almost an anticlimax to the comedy scenes and the exact nature of Kurt's conspiracy or occupation is never explained. It is also the part of the play written least well.

The characters are extremely well drawn—not only the uninhibited matriarch, but her son and daughter and also the Roumanian count and his countess. The characterizations of Sara, her husband and children are especially winning. Their unheralded entrance is not only good theatre but it also is touching and illuminating because it brings into urbane comedy the privations of a civilized family that has had little food and no comforts for a long time. They are the most ingratiating characters Miss Hellman ever described.

But *Watch on the Rhine,* when removed from the emotional furor of 1941, is, like Robert Sherwood's *There Shall Be No Night,* a contrived rather than an organic drama. Miss Hellman did not put it together as expertly as she composed the dramas in which her personal emotions were not involved. In 1941 Kurt Müller's callous murder of the Roumanian scoundrel was more believable than it is now—justifiable homicide, perhaps, since the Nazis were doing the same thing. And Kurt's farewell to his children seemed more heroic then. He regrets the necessity of slaughtering the count and continues: Murder is bad, no matter who commits it, "but you will live to see the day when it will not have to be. All over the world, in every place and every town, there are men who are going to make sure that it will not have to be. They want what I want, a childhood for every child. For my children, and I for theirs. In every town and every village and every mud hut in the world, there is always a man who loves children and will fight to make a good world for them. And now goodbye. Wait for me. I shall try to come back to you."

An inspiring farewell in 1941. Hackneyed rhetoric today, uncannily resembling Dr. Valkonen's resonant peroration in Sherwood's *There Shall Be No Night.* It was the heyday of the immaculate conception of the holy tomorrow.

Watch on the Rhine received the New York Drama Critics Circle award in 1941.

○ ○

Thornton Wilder

THE SKIN OF OUR TEETH

○ ○

When the curtain rose on Thornton Wilder's *The Skin of Our Teeth* at the Plymouth Theatre on November 18, 1942 the introductory remarks sounded like *Our Town*. The radio announcer says: "The sun rose this morning at 6:30 A.M. This gratifying event was first reported by Mrs. Dorothy Stetson of Freeport, Long Island, who promptly telephoned the Mayor." These opening remarks seemed to be carrying on the timeless, leisurely, bucolic simplicities of *Our Town* of 1938.

But in 1942 the American situation was much more ominous. For eleven months the United States had been at war with Japan and Germany. Sabina, the garrulous trollop of *The Skin of Our Teeth*, reminded the audience: "Don't forget that a few years ago we came through the depression by the skin of our teeth. One more squeeze like that and where will we be?" The audience knew that the squeeze was much nearer strangulation than it had ever been before. A veteran of World War I, Mr. Wilder knew what that meant. But, as in the case of *Our Town*, he was not devastated. He was not forgetting that the human race had gone through catastrophe after catastrophe and had emerged by the skin of its teeth, and he never doubted that it would survive World War II.

The Skin of Our Teeth is a beautiful testament to the indestruc-

Fredric March and Tallulah Bankhead in THE SKIN OF OUR TEETH

tibility of man and, in Mr. Wilder's opinion, the immutability of progress. Speaking on his behalf, the chief character sums up his experience and his knowledge of life on earth: "I know that every good and excellent thing in the world stands moment by moment on the razor-edge of danger and must be fought for—whether it's a field, or a home or a country. All I ask is the chance to build new worlds, and God has always given us that. . . . We've come a long ways. We've learned. We're learning. And the steps of our journey are marked for us here."

Although the subject of *The Skin of Our Teeth* is serious, the style is comedy—the comedy of mythology. The play is set in Excelsior, New Jersey, in the home of Mr. Antrobus, a composite of all the great progressives and innovators. He has invented the wheel, the alphabet, and the multiplication table. He believes in creation because he is part of it. "Antrobus" means "going forward"; he is Mr. Wilder's symbol of progress. The play opens in August on the coldest day of the year; a glacier is crawling south. A dinosaur and a mammoth are trying to get inside Mr. Antrobus' house; and hungry, frostbitten men and women are beseeching Mr. Antrobus for food and shelter. Mr. Wilder has compressed the experience of hundreds of thousands of years into one homely first act that is concerned not with abstract ideas but with such tangibles as food, shelter and warmth.

Mr. Antrobus does not know what is happening nor what to do about it. He acts on instinct. First, he turns out the dinosaur and the mammoth, thus beginning their extinction. By letting in the suffering human beings (including Moses, Homer, and three of the seven Muses), he maintains the continuity of the human race through one of its most awful catastrophes. In terms of Mr. Wilder's knowledge and literary style, this act is both amusing and reassuring; it puts one of the darkest periods of life into grand perspective.

Since Mr. Wilder does not want to be solemn and stuffy, however, he pokes fun at his play. Every now and then Sabina or the Stage Manager breaks the illusion by talking directly to the audience or by correcting the actors or by improvising something in another style—like a procession of sandwich men with pertinent quotations from Spinoza, Plato and the Bible. The quotations are too compact and literary to be absorbed in the theatre. And Mr. Wilder's little games with the form of the play are acts of self-deprecation. They violate the purity of an inspired comedy. They are an academic joke.

For Mr. Wilder does not have to apologize for his faith, which gives strength, humor and warmth to the central parts of his play. The second act is a comic fantasy about the 600,000th annual convention of the Fraternal Order of the Ancient and Honorable Order of Mammals, Subdivision Humans, only a few days before the Flood. The third act—imaginative, compassionate and logical—shows Mr. Wilder's metaphorical characters emerging from the bomb shelters after a war and starting life again. It is familiar and it is both pathetic and gallant. The whole play is full of generosity and love.

The original production, with Tallulah Bankhead as the voluptuous Sabina and Fredric March and Florence Eldridge as Mr. and Mrs. Antrobus, was vigorous and entertaining. But many theatregoers could not stand *The Skin of Our Teeth*. They found it unintelligible and they left the theatre after the first act—some of them highly audible about the play and its author. But the play had a long run before audiences who were grateful for Mr. Wilder's faith, skill and wisdom. In the last scene one of the sandwich men carries a quotation from the Bible: "And the Lord said let there be light, and there was light." Some of it spilled over into the Plymouth Theatre because Mr. Wilder could not believe that the human race was doomed.

He and Robert Sherwood in *There Shall Be No Night*, were the last of the optimists among serious theatre writers. Nothing has happened since 1940 and 1942 to substantiate their vision of a more enlightened world. Since those years the weary cynicism of Sabina has been more pertinent: "Why do we go on pretending? Some day the whole earth's going to have to turn cold anyway, and until that time all those other things will be happening again: it will be more wars and more walls of ice and floods and earthquakes."

The Skin of Our Teeth won the Pulitzer Prize in 1943.

o o o o o o o o o o o o o o o o o o o o o o o o o o o o o o o o o o o o o o o o o o

Edward Chodorov

DECISION

o o o o o o o o o o o o o o o o o o o o o o o o o o o o o o o o o o o o o o o o o o

During the years when Americans were fighting overseas in World War II Broadway kept the peace. It did not produce militant plays on political topics. But there was one conspicuous exception. Edward Chodorov did not believe that the fascism Americans were fighting was confined to Europe and Asia. He believed that fascism in American industry and politics was already a challenge to freedom at home.

Mr. Chodorov startled Broadway with *Decision,* a tempestuous play on that subject at the Belasco Theatre on February 2, 1944. It is set "in an American city at the present" where the expansion of a manufacturing plant into a war industry has brought a great many Negroes into a predominantly white community. Before the curtain goes up there has been a race riot in which several workers in the plant have been killed. A citizens committee is meeting under the chairmanship of Riggs, the superintendent of schools, to deal with the threat to the traditional peace of the town. The committee has reason to believe that the riot was deliberately provoked by U. S. Senator Dufresne and his local henchman, Masters, editor of the local newspaper. The citizens committee proposes to present the evidence to the U. S. Attorney General.

Mr. Chodorov's *Decision* is a political melodrama. His subject

Georgia Burke in DECISION

of race relations involves a bitter confrontation between Masters, the bigoted editor who thinks the New Deal is communism, and Riggs, the believer in democracy. Masters tells Riggs: "Now look, Riggs— on the level—who do you think you are? Abe Lincoln? Going to free the nigger all over again? Well, he's not going to be free—not to stand up and work as an equal with the decent white man—and certainly not to draw the same pay—not permanently—not around here—not while I'm around." In the last act *Decision* comes to a sensational conclusion. After having been fraudulently charged with raping one of his students, Riggs is arrested, confined to police headquarters and lynched during the night. The local government is totalitarian.

The cast of *Decision* includes another character who provides an outside point of view. He is Tommy Riggs, son of the school super-intendent and home on leave after having been wounded in Italy. After fighting fascism there he cannot believe that fascism is des-troying the good temper of his home town. In a discussion of the local crisis early in the play Riggs tells Tommy that the editor and others are planning "a fascist-minded future for us all. . . . I believe we are living now in the midst of a very real civil war—a war that must be decided before you come home for good—or you will come home to the ashes of the cause for which you fought."

When Tommy learns that his father has been lynched, his first impulse is to marry the girl to whom he has been engaged for some time and move away from his home town for good. But friends of his father and the support of the 15,000 workers at the plant convince him to stay and carry on his father's crusade. "Let's go!" he exclaims at the final curtain.

Since no Broadway producer would accept *Decision* Mr. Cho-dorov, Edward Choate, and some friends put it on the stage under their own management. It had 160 performances. In the midst of World War II when the mind, spirit and energy of the nation were concentrated on winning the war overseas, no one challenged Mr. Chodorov's right to charge American war profiteers with fascism. Senator Joseph McCarthy had not yet paralyzed freedom of speech in America. In 1944 a "controversial" play was not a euphemism for "treason." Broadway preserved its traditional freedom of speech.

o o o o o o o o o o o o o o o o o o o o o o o o o o o o o o o o o o o o o o o o o o o

Richard Rodgers and Oscar Hammerstein II

CAROUSEL

o o o o o o o o o o o o o o o o o o o o o o o o o o o o o o o o o o o o o o o o o o o

If it were not for the complicated character of Billy Bigelow, a bum, *Carousel* would not belong in a book of plays about people. It is the Rodgers and Hammerstein musical version of Ferenc Molnar's enthralling play called *Liliom*. *Carousel* was produced at the Majestic Theatre on April 19, 1945. Although the locale is switched from Budapest to New England in the years between 1875 and 1888, the narrative and the characters are essentially as Molnar wrote them in his play that opened in New York in 1921.

Since *Liliom* is a thoroughly original theatre work it is difficult to define accurately, and the same kind of uncertainty applies to *Carousel*. Is it a nostalgic romance? Is it a folk tale? Is it a fantasy? Whatever the definition of the whole work may be, the characterization of Billy Bigelow is a penetrating portrait of a moody, no-good drifter who is unable to express his inner feelings spontaneously. He is genuinely in love with a naïve factory worker named Julie Jordan, but his masculine pride—his *machismo*—prevents him from acknowledging it. He regards tenderness as a betrayal of manhood.

After marrying Julie and injuring his pride further by living with her as a charity guest in the home of one of her relatives, he beats her. The neighbors regard this as brutality and they despise

Jan Clayton and John Raitt in CAROUSEL

him for it. But Julie's reaction is more understanding. She regards it as an involuntary reaction to the shame he feels for his uselessness and also as a show of contempt for the neighbors. Since Billy is unhappy and quick-tempered she excuses him. In contemporary terms Billy is a schizophrenic—a schizophrenic bum, in fact.

This is a difficult character to describe on the stage without making him seem totally repellent. Molnar was able to make him interesting. But the great contribution *Carousel* makes to understanding the inner recesses of Billy's difficult character is the joyous soliloquy written by Mr. Rodgers and Mr. Hammerstein. Julie has just told Billy that she is pregnant. After having been depressed by his inadequacy as a breadwinner Billy is euphoric. His masculine pride suddenly has a reason for being. The long, impulsive, rapturous, wondering and very intimate soliloquy sung by John Raitt is a masterpiece. By now it is also a classic, for it is frequently sung as a concert piece. Looking ecstatically into the future Billy speculates on what his little boy or possibly his little girl may look like, and he resolves to be a worthy father:

> *I got to be ready before she comes,*
> *I got to make certain that she*
> *Won't be dragged up in the slums*
> *With a lot o' bums—*
> *Like me!*
>
> *She's got to be sheltered and fed and dressed*
> *In the best that money can buy!*
> *I never knew how to get money,*
> *But I'll try—*
> *By God! I'll try!*
> *I'll go out and make it*
> *Or steal it or take it*
> *Or die!*

Carousel is full of the familiar looks and glances and diversions that make musical shows enjoyable. But when Billy's exhilarating soliloquy comes along towards the end of Act One, *Carousel* has to be taken seriously as a creative work.

In the midst of World War II Mr. Rodgers and Mr. Hammerstein were in a glorious mood. They were overflowing with songs and rhymes and good feeling. They had just refreshed the formula for musical comedy by writing *Oklahoma!* They came to *Carousel* feeling triumphant. The score is Mr. Rodgers' richest. In addition to Billy's exultant soliloquy it includes the jubilant idyll called "June Is Busting Out All Over," which has the spontaneity of bird song, and a very moving hymn, "You'll Never Walk Alone."

Following the style of the original Molnar drama, *Carousel* moves from scene to scene, not like something planned, but like an improvisation. Although it cannot be defined it can be enjoyed. It does full justice to the turbulent spirit of Billy Bigelow by giving him a song that is both touching and eloquent.

o o o o o o o o o o o o o o o o o o o o o o o o o o o o o o o o o o o o o o o o o

Garson Kanin

BORN YESTERDAY

o o o o o o o o o o o o o o o o o o o o o o o o o o o o o o o o o o o o o o o o o

When World War II was over, Garson Kanin came marching home with an American morality play, *Born Yesterday*, which opened at the Lyceum Theatre on February 4, 1946. It turned out to be one of the few windfalls of peace. Not that *Born Yesterday* is a war play. The primitive racketeer who nearly dominates it has made a fortune

Judy Holliday and Paul Douglas
in BORN YESTERDAY

out of selling junk to war industries, and he wants to expand. That is the basic situation. But *Born Yesterday* demonstrates a belief in the American democratic system that service in the war induced in many men. Fascism lurks in the back of its mind as the pitfall into which democracy might easily fall.

Born Yesterday is a popular comedy on the Pygmalion theme. Billie Dawn is a dumb broad who lives with Harry Brock, a wealthy racketeer. She has never had a disinterested thought in her life. When Paul Verrall, a writer for the *New Republic*, tells her that Harry has never thought about anybody but himself she retorts: "Who does?" That makes Paul angry. "Millions of people, Billie," he shouts. "The whole damn history of the world is the story of the struggle between the selfish and the unselfish." "I can hear you," Billie replies warily. She protects her ignorance by refusing to take sides.

The story of *Born Yesterday* is conventional. Billie and Paul, a neighbor in the same hotel, fall in love. They double-cross Harry, not only by getting married but also by stealing legal papers that document his scheme for buying some useful legislation. The plot of *Born Yesterday* comes from the old theatre of magic, romance, happy endings, and wish fulfillment.

But the characterizations represent valid aspects of contemporary American life. Harry Brock is the perfect racketeer. Having begun as a petty thief in his youth he has advanced by a series of orderly steps to the hierarchy of big thief. Although he is a big shot with political power he is a monster. He knows nothing except the rackets. He is stupid egotist. His language is primitive; his manners coarse and brutish. When Paul and Billie charge him in the last act with undermining decent government he replies: "I don't see what I'm doin' so wrong. This is America, isn't it. Where's all this free enterprise they're always talking about? ... I always did what I want and I'm always gonna." Harry corrupts everyone he touches—his brother, his lawyer and a United States Senator. Harry is the plausible portrait of a crooked tycoon who looks upon corruption as a normal way of life in Washington.

The characterization of Billie Dawn is the best thing in the play. She is the essence of the old-time chorus girl. She is entirely self-satisfied. Having moved out of the chorus into the bed of a rich John she regards herself as a great success. Her pride is fierce; she is quick to object if anyone says anything that seems to disparage her. She screams with rage when Paul assumes that she is in her thirties. She is only twenty-nine, she tells him angrily. Since she had five lines to speak in *Anything Goes* she regards herself not a chorus girl but an actress.

She is also hardheaded. When Paul explains the meaning of his *New Republic* article called "The Yellowing Democratic Manifesto," she retorts: "Well, why didn't you say so?" Billie is authentic and delightful and a legendary character in the postwar American theatre.

Anyone who saw the original production cannot be objective about Billie. She was played by Judy Holliday, a bright, honest, colloquial actress who made every word sound true. It is impossible now to read the text without hearing her flat, artless voice that had undertones of sadness and resignation. Judy Holliday made *Born Yesterday* as memorable as Mr. Kanin did.

And it is gratifying now to realize that not a single act of corruption has taken place in Washington since *Born Yesterday* exposed the technique of buying Senators!

o o o o o o o o o o o o o o o o o o o o o o o o o o o o o o o o o o o o o o

Eugene O'Neill

THE ICEMAN COMETH

o o o o o o o o o o o o o o o o o o o o o o o o o o o o o o o o o o o o o o

Although life is a tragedy and tragedy is austere there were times when Eugene O'Neill felt romantic about it. He loved doom in the theatre. *The Iceman Cometh* is romantic tragedy. Filled with sentimental nostalgia for the vagabond years when he was a waterfront bum, O'Neill wrote *The Iceman Cometh* in 1939 and set it in Harry Hope's West Side waterfront saloon in 1912. That was the period when he had lived in a three-dollar-a-month room above Jimmy-the-Priest's saloon on Fulton Street. But Harry Hope's refuge for the damned also contains O'Neill's memories of another dump he patronized during Prohibition—Tom Wallace's Hell Hole in Greenwich Village. From the eminence of 1939, when O'Neill was America's first dramatist and lived in expensive houses or apartments, the carefree vagrancy of 1912 looked romantic. It was all over and no permanent damage had been done.

Combining these two gin mills and stirring up a lot of raffish memories, O'Neill composed a long, verbose, sluggish drama about a collection of drunken derelicts who sustain their personal pride by cultivating gallant illusions about themselves—"pipe dreams" in O'Neill's phrase—and by convincing themselves that they can return to respectability any time they want to. A garrulous and braggart salesman tries to convince them that they will be happier if they abandon their pipe dreams and face the truth about themselves. He wants to "really save the guy and make him contented with what he is and quit battling himself and find peace for the rest of his life." Nothing could be more disastrous. Dispensing with their illusions threatens to destroy them. In the last act they gratefully return to their habitual drunkenness and their illusions and pipe dreams. Their picturesque lies about themselves make their lives bearable.

The Iceman Cometh (that is, Death cometh) took four and one-half hours to play when it opened at the Martin Beck Theatre on October 9, 1946. As in the case of *Mourning Becomes Electra* in 1931, the audience had to take its dinner in some nearby restaurant during the intermission. But the theme was not so profound, original and intricate that it could not have been dramatized in half that time. O'Neill had seized on it with the enthusiasm of a sophomore. The writing is ponderous. The various characters, who constitute a Who's Who of bums, make long, self-conscious speeches to one another. The dialogue is full of elementary clichés—*booze, bull, open your yap, wise up, bonehead, hick burg,* "I didn't fall for that religious *bunk.*" In 1939 O'Neill was writing the vernacular of 1912 with indiscriminate pedantry.

But it is always dangerous to dismiss O'Neill's prose as flat. It did lack color and lyricism; for instance, it could never state the overtones of *Mourning Becomes Electra.* O'Neill's prose is limited to a kind of slangy inarticulation in which elementary characters cannot really express their feelings. *The Iceman Cometh* is heavy reading.

Nicholas Joy, James Barton, Carl Benton Reid,
Jeanne Cagney, Marcella Markham, Ruth Gilbert
and Dudley Digges in THE ICEMAN COMETH

But put this dialogue in a theatre and let some good actors speak it and it acquires a dark vitality; the power accumulates as one prosy speech is piled on another. Nobody says anything memorable in *The Iceman Cometh,* but Dudley Digges, the saloonkeeper in the original production, left a profound impression of futility and doom on the audience; his monotonous lines expressed some inner premonition of death; and Jason Robards, Jr., the bombastic bunco man in the 1956 production at Circle-in-the-Square, gave the character a feeling of evil mischief and gave the play considerable philosophical significance.

The actors could not have made these dark impressions if the play did not contain the material. Never cross-examine O'Neill off the stage.

o o o o o o o o o o o o o o o o o o o o o o o o o o o o o o o o o o o o o o o o o o o o

Jean-Paul Sartre

NO EXIT

o o o o o o o o o o o o o o o o o o o o o o o o o o o o o o o o o o o o o o o o o o o o

Jean-Paul Sartre wrote *No Exit* when the German Army was occupying France. The play expresses total contempt for authority. It was written by a radical philosopher who at the time was a member of the French underground and who had every reason to feel that the government of his nation had barbarically betrayed its people.

When *No Exit* was produced in an English adaptation at the Biltmore Theatre on November 26, 1946, American audiences had no reason to feel that their government had betrayed them. *No Exit* was alien to all American values at the time. But this terse drama by a pitiless thinker made a lasting impression on the people who saw it because it is a brilliant piece of writing. M. Sartre is an existentialist —a form of nihilistic thought that derives from Kierkegaard and Nietzsche. It views every individual as a separate entity who controls his life by acts of his own will; he cannot look to his government or to religion or to any form of human organization for protection or help. There are not many conscious existentialists in America today, but millions of contemporary Americans lead existentialist lives by flouting law, belief and customs. They are existentialists without knowing it.

Since he is an intellectual M. Sartre is a playwright *manqué*. He either lacks emotion or does not trust it, although emotion is an essential element in art. But M. Sartre's arrangement of characters and the logic of his story give *No Exit* enormous emotional impact—bleak, negative, merciless but horrifying, which is emotion. The play dramatizes the loneliness of man in a disinterested universe.

The setting is the genius of the play. It consists of a close prison-like drawing room with grubby furniture and no décor except an ugly bronze ornament on the mantelpiece. A contemptuous bellboy ushers in the first character—Garcin, a former journalist. "Do you know who I was?" Garcin petulantly inquires of the bellboy who is not giving him much respect. Garcin soons learns the nature of the situation in which he finds himself. He is occupying one room in hell. The tortures he expected are not physical. They are mental and social. No windows, no mirrors, no beds, no toothbrush—nothing that contributes to the self-respect of the individual. The light cannot be turned off. The doorbell does not ring. The door is locked.

In the course of the play two women enter—a lesbian and a harridan who has been consigned to hell because she has killed an unwanted baby. In their own minds all the characters are heroes who are being badly used. But eventually the truth comes out. They are all vicious people. They are condemned to live together in a closed society; each of them is both a rival to the others and a victim of the

Ruth Ford, Annabella and
Claude Dauphin in NO EXIT

others. They cannot establish any relationship that will give comfort to any of them. "We'll stay in this room together, the three of us, for ever and ever. . . . Each of us will act as torturer of the others," says the lesbian. Towards the end of the play Garcin speaks the devastating conclusion: "Hell is other people."

There is something pleasantly ludicrous in the fact that M. Sartre uses a part of mythology (in which he does not believe) to dramatize the sham of mythology. He does not believe in either heaven or hell, but hell is his setting and is his essential dramatic effect. His hell is also unique: it is not underground but overhead (where heaven is); the characters have to look down when they want to see what people on the earth are doing. Using a myth to negate all myths is M. Sartre's cosmic jest.

No Exit is a perfect dramatization of the devastating philosophy of existentialism. The original New York production, directed by John Huston, was brilliantly performed inside a setting that exuded instant claustrophobia, designed by Frederick Kiesler. The actors, all very expert, were Ruth Ford, Annabella, and Claude Dauphin. During the next year or two M. Sartre was a coterie playwright. His *The Respectful Prostitute, The Victors* and *Red Gloves* were produced. But like *No Exit,* none of them was a commercial success. Although New York respected the power of M. Sartre's thought, it unhappily concluded that the theatre is not his natural medium. *No Exit* was the prelude to equally forbidding plays by Samuel Beckett, Eugene Ionesco, Edward Albee and Harold Pinter—all of whom believe that life is not as good as you think it is.

○ ○

Arthur Miller

ALL MY SONS

○ ○

When *All My Sons* opened in the Coronet Theatre on January 29, 1947 everyone knew that a forthright citizen had come into the theatre with some pertinent convictions. Arthur Miller came not as a member of the theatre, but as a delegate from the outside world. His first produced play, *The Man Who Had All the Luck,* had had only four performances when it was produced in 1944, but even then everyone knew that the author was a man to be watched. *All My Sons* brought all his talents into focus—the mind, the passion, the convictions, and the talent for writing.

The theme of *All My Sons,* based on an actual incident, is the responsibility everyone owes to society as a whole. (That is the fundamental theme of most of Mr. Miller's plays.) In the climactic scene of *All My Sons,* Chris tells his aggressive, acquisitive and complacent father: "There's a universe of people outside and you're responsible to it." During the war, which was still a vivid memory in 1947, the father, Joe Keller, had manufactured cylinder heads for combat planes. At one time he had knowingly shipped some cracked cylinder heads out of his factory and they had caused the death of a number of pilots. When the Government charged him with delivering and getting paid for defective merchandise, he had managed to shift the blame to one of his associates. Joe Keller's motive is the opposite of the theme of the play. He is looking after financial security for himself, his son, and his family: "Nothing's bigger than that," he says. "I'm his father and he's my son, and if there's something bigger than that I'll put a bullet in my head."

Everything that Mr. Miller contributed to the play and the rushing vitality of the original performance made the opening of *All My Sons* an exciting occasion. Something of contemporary importance had been said. But Mr. Miller's derivative craftsmanship makes his play look like hackwork today. It is pure Ibsen. It begins with a dramatic symbol—an apple tree that has just blown down—which symbolizes the destruction overseas of the son for whom it was planted. The broken apple tree is very much in the portentous Ibsen tradition. And so is the whole play—the casual opening scenes that create the homely mood and define the intricate relationships of the characters, the cunning intrusion of the plot, the highly-wrought confrontation of the characters after the plot has begun to move, the polemics in the last scene, the reading of a crucial letter at a definitive moment, and the concluding sound of a bullet being fired offstage, like Hedda's suicide in the last scene of *Hedda Gabler*. Mr. Miller's craftsmanship is too contrived for the modern theatre. It eliminates any feeling of spontaneity in the action of the play. It dramatizes what the characters do, and not what they think. It proves a point; it creates nothing.

But it was effective enough in 1947 to alarm insecure Americans who saw Communist plots in everything that was not comfortably banal. Mr. Miller was accused of trying to undermine capitalism by smearing big business. The Civil Affairs Division of the American Military Government refused to let *All My Sons* be presented overseas. The *New Leader*, a dedicated anti-Communist journal, said: "*All My Sons* is fuel for those in Europe that would enflame feeling against the United States. They would say this prize play is typical of capitalistic attitudes in decaying bourgeois America." *All My Sons* provided a prelude to the neurotic fear of communism that turned the United States into a witches' Sabbath a few years later.

Ed Begley in ALL MY SONS

Since playgoers never are intimidated by fanatics, *All My Sons* had a long run. Its audiences were indifferent to the bigotry of the Establishment and respected Mr. Miller's independence and responsibility. Because the play was very much in the social tradition of the Group Theatre (which was also suspected of being subversive by some people), it looked and sounded very much like a Group Theatre play; Elia Kazan, one of the Group Theatre leaders, gave it speed and power in his dynamic style of direction. It was a sensation, not because it was politically daring but because it challenged fundamental parts of the American mythology. In April it received the prize of the New York Drama Critics Circle with the following citation: "To *All My Sons* because of the frank and uncompromising presentation of a timely and important theme, because of the honesty of the writing and the cumulative power of the scenes and because it reveals a genuine instinct for the theatre in an intelligent and thoughtful new playwright."

o o o o o o o o o o o o o o o o o o o o o o o o o o o o o o o o o o o o o o

Tennessee Williams

A STREETCAR NAMED DESIRE

o o o o o o o o o o o o o o o o o o o o o o o o o o o o o o o o o o o o o o

In *A Streetcar Named Desire* Tennessee Williams makes no judgments. He does not say that Blanche Dubois, his neurotic heroine, is wrong or that her sister Stella, and Stella's husband, Stanley Kowalski, are right. All he says is that the division between gentility and grossness exists, and that confrontations between the two are painful.

The play expresses Mr. Williams' mind lucidly. His knowledge of people—especially Southern people—his sensitivity, his extraordinary literary skill, and his personal detachment make *A Streetcar Named Desire* a masterpiece that has lost none of its dark beauty in the last quarter of a century. Although the play represents the antiromantic attitude towards life it is never hostile or censorious. It is full of compassion: it left a permanent mark on the souls of the playgoers who saw it at the Barrymore Theatre, where it opened on December 3, 1947. The anguish of Blanche Dubois is unforgettable.

Two of Mr. Williams' plays had been produced in the previous seven years—*Battle of Angels,* which offended the Boston City Council and obediently closed, and *The Glass Menagerie,* a delicate, rueful play about a withdrawn daughter and her overwhelming mother. It was an instant success when it opened in Chicago and New York in 1945 and permanently relieved Mr. Williams of obscurity and poverty.

There is no plot in *A Streetcar Named Desire*. But the story is illuminating and engrossing and builds up to a shattering climax. Formal plots are seldom as crushing as Mr. Williams' informal story. Set in a noisy, battered corner of New Orleans where Mr. Williams had lived, it records the experience of Blanche Dubois, the last person in a line of Mississippi landowners. She has lost the family home—called Belle Reve—to the banks, and also has lost her job as a school-teacher. Dispossessed and rejected she tries to take refuge in a squalid New Orleans apartment where her sister Stella lives contentedly with her husband Stanley, a Polish factory worker.

The play is the chronological record of the exposure of a genteel Mississippi woman with delusions of social grandeur to her sister's style of living amid commonplace people. Blanche, in a desperate frame of mind, is shocked by the grubbiness of her sister's existence in the tiny, makeshift apartment. The animalism of Stanley and his cronies offends her. She finds herself trapped by a crude style of life that she has always despised. This destroys what little emotional security she has left from her years in Mississippi. Sensitive, fastidious and frightened, she preserves as much dignity as she can by telling little lies about herself. She tries to live behind a mask of wealth and glamour. "I don't want realism," she tells a prospective suitor. "I want magic! Yes, yes, magic! I try to give that to people. I misrepresent things to them. I don't tell truth, I tell what ought to be truth."

As a story this does not seem commensurate with the power the play has to absorb an audience and arouse their sympathy. But Mr. Williams is a literary genius. Although Blanche cannot face reality, he can. His characterization of Blanche is pitiless and sympathetic and thorough. He does not reject the foolish necessities of her character—her psychopathic dependence on dress to keep up appearances, her secret drinking to find relief from the horrors of reality, her fear of the past and her dread of the future—surface pride, interior shame.

Although Blanche is the pivotal character, the characterizations of the other people are equally perceptive. Stella's concern for her sister on the one hand and her content with her life with her loutish husband are objective and understanding. Although Stanley and his cronies are the villains, Mr. Williams knows them as intimately as he understands Blanche's many dilemmas, and he portrays them without prejudice. Stanley is close to a monster, he is so callous and sure of himself, but Mr. Williams respects him as a human being. There is a certain tolerance in Stanley for genuine people; and although his understanding of right and wrong is primitive he has his standards too.

The original performance under the direction of Elia Kazan was another of the theatre's masterpieces. The cast was superb. Marlon Brando's belligerent acting of Stanley was the foundation of his cinema career. Karl Malden's acting of one of Stanley's cronies, Mitch, was not his first, but it made him famous. Jessica Tandy's Blanche, with its procession of moods and fantasies was the essential part of the total masterpiece. And Kim Hunter's spontaneous concern for, and loyalty to, her sister and her tolerant enjoyment of her husband and his pals gave the part of Stella magnetism and stature.

Everything is prosy in *A Streetcar Named Desire*. Everything discussed is elementary and homely. But the play is not a record. It is an act of creation. It received the Pulitzer Prize in 1948.

o o o o o o o o o o o o o o o o o o o o o o o o o o o o o o o o o o o

Thomas Heggen and Joshua Logan

MISTER ROBERTS

u u u u u u u u u u u u u u u u u u u u u u u u u u u u u u u u u u u

In 1948, two and one-half years after the Japanese surrender, it was possible to be hilarious about World War II. It had taken six years before Laurence Stallings and Maxwell Anderson were sufficiently disillusioned about World War I to write *What Price Glory?* After World War II no one was under any illusions about anything. Everyone knew that war was beneath the contempt of civilized nations. What Fanny Kemble had called "the pomp and circumstance of glorious war" in 1850 was recognized in 1948 as a degenerative disease.

Thomas Heggen and Joshua Logan knew that—among a great many more barbaric things—war is boring. Mr. Heggen had served in the Navy for three years. Mr. Logan had served for four years in Air Force Combat Intelligence. *Mister Roberts* had originally been a novel written by Mr. Heggen. He and Mr. Logan then turned it into a popular comedy about the seething boredom of the crew of a Navy cargo ship—the AK-601 which never got into a combat zone while the shooting was going on. Doc, the ship's medical officer, had never seen a battleship.

The ship's only distinction had been winning the Admiral John F. Finchley award for, as Mr. Roberts stated it, "delivering more toothpaste and toilet paper than any other cargo ship in a safe area of the Pacific." The story of *Mister Roberts* explores a feud between a tyrannical old-style skipper with a sadistic contempt for his crew and a young first officer, Mister Roberts, who longs for reassignment to a combat vessel. Roberts bombs the skipper with a series of letters to the Navy Department requesting reassignment. The skipper marks all of them "disapproved." Halfway through the comedy the skipper agrees to give the crew shore liberty if Roberts will agree not to write any more reassignment letters. When the crew discover inadvertently that Roberts has sacrificed his hopes for reassignment in exchange for shore liberty for his shipmates, they forge the captain's signature to another petition for reassignment and Roberts gets his wish.

The story is only a device for holding the comedy together. The real theme is the ludicrous disparity between the glamour of war and the unbearable banality of service in a cargo ship. In the words of Roberts, they are continually sailing between Tedium and Apathy with occasional sidetrips to Monotony. They have a distorted view of life. Their life is ingrown. Everything is out of proportion. Their emotions are overwrought. The fury with which they try to make Johnny Walker Scotch out of hospital alcohol, Coca-Cola, and a drop of iodine is comic because it is desperate. The sight of a female nurse provokes panic. The animal spirits aroused by shore liberty are ludicrous because they are compensation for the unnatural discipline of life at sea.

Although the dialogue seems funny, it is not spiked with jokes or gags. Nothing memorable is said. The lines are funny because they consist of the small talk of some high-strung young men who have lost contact with reality.

There is a fundamental flaw in *Mister Roberts*. As the story goes skittering along, the authors cannot resist the temptation to be heroic in a stiff upperlip vein. Roberts becomes a man of insufferable honor when he silently sacrifices his personal ambition in exchange for shore liberty for the crew. The crew are insufferably magnanimous when they discover that they have misjudged him. In the last scene Roberts' heroic death in a combat destroyer, reported in a letter sent

Henry Fonda in MISTER ROBERTS

to AK-601 by a friend, is part of the ancient hokum of popular comedy and it triumphs over the derision of war.

It was difficult to be objective about the play when it opened because the performance was uproarious. Henry Fonda, returning to the stage after twelve years of incarceration in Hollywood, underplayed the part of Mister Roberts in a winning style that could not be defined or analyzed; while David Wayne as a scatterbrained ensign and Robert Keith as the sardonic medical officer and William Harrigan as the crude skipper brought color, individuality and vitality to the performance.

War looked ridiculous in *Mister Roberts*—a step in the right direction.

○ ○

Jean Giraudoux

THE MADWOMAN OF CHAILLOT

○ ○

Although *The Madwoman of Chaillot* virtually exterminates modern society, it hardly speaks an angry word. Jean Giraudoux had the lightest and most urbane sense of humor and the daintiest sense of irony. In one important respect his imagination resembled Lewis Carroll's: it was mad in the most logical way. Like *Alice in Wonderland, The Madwoman of Chaillot* is inspired lunacy. No denunciation of the rapacity, perfidy and malevolence of big business has ever been more ruthless and at the same time more entertaining. Giraudoux liked people and had a lethal sense of humor about their follies.

The version put on at the Belasco Theatre on December 27, 1948 was Maurice Valency's English adaptation of the original French script. Mr. Valency simplified the original, which was capricious in form and intricate in style. It is likely that Mr. Valency's pithy adaptation is largely responsible for the enthusiasm American theatregoers have for the play.

Everything about *The Madwoman of Chaillot* is elegant and smart in the beginning. It opens on the terrace of a fashionable café "in the stately quarter of Paris known as Chaillot," and "the time is a little before noon in the spring of next year." A rich, self-assured businessman and a proper baron are conversing at a table—incidentally treating other people with the greatest condescension. The businessman has just organized an extravagantly capitalized corporation —International Substrate of Paris, Inc., and he wants the baron to lend his name to the board of directors. There is only one weak point in the corporation: it has no function. "The trouble is we have a tremendous capital and not the slightest idea what to do with it," says the president. He does not regard this as a serious weakness: "A stock certificate is not a tool, like a shovel, or a commodity like a pound of cheese," he tells the baron. "What we sell a customer is not a share in a business but a view of the Elysian Fields. A financier is a creative artist. Our function is to stimulate the imagination. We are poets!"

The Prospector, who represents one of M. Giraudoux's plunderers of the world, strolls in with the solution. He has found oil directly beneath the plaza of Chaillot. He proposes to wipe the buildings out of the way, sink a well and make a fortune. "Civilization gets in our way all the time," he concedes. But as a man of affairs he knows how to bribe anyone who stands in his way and he is already corrupting the government. Through all this amusing exposition M. Giraudoux writes with sobriety and reason.

But as the play moves on it is plain that M. Giraudoux's bland style is part of his weapon. He is undermining his most reasonable characters. His businessmen are the mad characters. They are the ones that do not understand reality. They are opposed by four raffish old crones who talk nonsense and behave sensibly. Since these crones believe in nothing but love and beauty, they look mad to sophisticated people. But they are the ones who know that something catastrophic is about to happen and they know how to deal with it— ruthlessly. According to their chief adviser, The Ragpicker: "The pimps have taken over the world. They don't do anything, they don't make anything—they just stand there and take their cut.... Look at the shopkeepers. Do you ever see one smiling at a customer any more? Certainly not. Their smiles are strictly for the pimps." The madwomen's executive foreman is The Sewerman. After consulting with the madwomen he opens an endless stairway that goes down through

Marita Hunt and Estelle Winwood
in THE MADWOMAN OF CHAILLOT

the sewer to Hell and from which no one ever returns. The business-men go down there under the impression that they are duping the madwomen—who, in fact, are duping them.

Everything is immediately lovely once the businessmen are gone. "Now you can breathe again. Now you can see," says the waiter. "The air is pure! The sky is clear!" says another. "On the street utter strangers are shaking hands, they don't know why, and offering each other almond bars!" says the police sergeant. The conclusion is tri-umphant and nutty.

There are no clever remarks in *The Madwoman of Chaillot,* no witty phrases, nor are there any moral conclusions that would give M. Giraudoux the stature of a prophet. The humor consists in a gen-teel reversal of standards by which the sane people emerge as mad and the madwomen are the saviours of society. In addition to being a man of the world M. Giraudoux was a poet. He had an affectionate feeling for the human race. In this quizzical play madness becomes kindness and generosity.

In the 1948 production, *The Madwoman of Chaillot* was per-formed with the most comical sobriety and dignity. Everything looked very serious indeed. None of the actors indicated that he was playing in a comic fantasy. They all accepted madness as common sense. Liv-ing in an occupied country in the early 1940's during a barbaric war Jean Giraudoux wrote a civilized play that envisioned a decent world. Perhaps he was an inspired madman.

The Madwoman of Chaillot won the New York Drama Critics Circle award in 1949.

o o o o o o o o o o o o o o o o o o o o o o o o o o o o o o o o o o o o o o o o o

Arthur Miller

DEATH OF A SALESMAN

o o o o o o o o o o o o o o o o o o o o o o o o o o o o o o o o o o o o o o o o

After dramatizing a pertinent American topic in *All My Sons* in 1947 Arthur Miller plunged wide and deep into the mythology of America. *Death of a Salesman*, which opened at the Morosco Theatre on February 10, 1949, is his masterpiece, full of understanding, full of sympathy, written with loyalty and respect. In its technical versatility as well as its knowledge of character, *Death of a Salesman* is more like a spontaneous creation than a composition.

In *All My Sons* Mr. Miller wrote workmanlike prose in the manner of Ibsen; it told a story but did not express a point of view. Mr. Miller's affection for Willy Loman, the salesman of the title, endows the homely opening scene of *Death of a Salesman* with great warmth and intimacy, and Mr. Miller's personal commitment carries an indomitable story to a tragic conclusion.

Nothing of great importance is at stake in *Death of a Salesman*. An ordinary traveling salesman—who used to be called a "drummer"—is getting old and losing vitality and drifting into poverty and obscurity. Mr. Miller does not take this for granted; he knows that the slow, heartless, mechanical dissolution of a flashy salesman is an agonizing experience. He makes a notable event out of it. He regards it as a painful flaw in the American dream.

Willy's patient wife, Linda, describes it to her two four-flushing

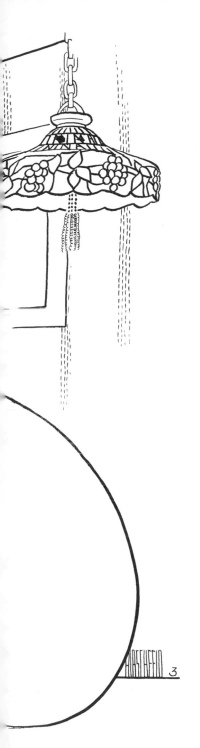

Mildred Dunnock and Lee J. Cobb
in DEATH OF A SALESMAN

3

sons in homely words that would apply to millions of other Americans: "I don't say he's a great man. Willy Loman never made a lot of money. His name was never in the paper. He's not the finest character that ever lived. But he's a human being, and a terrible thing is happening to him. So attention must be paid. He's not to be allowed to fall into his grave like an old dog. Attention, attention must be finally paid to such a person." In the opening performance those words were spoken in the tired, plaintive voice of Mildred Dunnock and made an indelible impression on everyone who heard them. They have the universality and devotion of great literature.

Willy has done nothing really wrong—a little petty stealing or cheating, perhaps, but nothing really evil or unlawful. His tragedy consists in his belief in an empty dream. The gaudy, flamboyant dream of commercial success is his credo. He is not concerned with the integrity of the product he sells. He uses it as a hand prop in his swagger, convivial, cunning performance on the traveling salesman's road. To him success is a form of prostitution. He has come to believe his own performance. To sustain his pride he also believes the extravagant lies his two sons tell him about themselves. Like him they are egotists and braggarts. They have all lost contact with truth and reality.

In the last scene when family and friends have collected for Willy's funeral, one of the neighbors describes the evanescent nature of the traveling salesman's career; and this speech constitutes a requiem at the grave of an obscure, average, loyal American: "Willy was a salesman. And for a salesman, there is no rock bottom to the life. He doesn't put a bolt to a nut, he don't tell you the law or give you medicine. He's a man out there in the blue, riding on a smile and a shoeshine. And when they start not smiling back—that's an earthquake. And then when you get yourself a couple of spots on your hat, and you're finished. Nobody dast blame this man. A salesman is got to dream, boy. It comes with the territory."

Nobody had written about the dark side of the American fantasy with the sympathy and knowledge Mr. Miller brought to it, and audiences were overwhelmed. The battle of the books began immediately. Theatregoers who remembered the magisterial words of Aristotle, who lived more than twenty-one centuries before, said that what happened to Willy made him a pathetic figure; but, since he was not a king, a prince, a rich man or at the least a college graduate, he was not qualified to be a tragic victim. "There is no tragic flaw in *Death of a Salesman,*" said one of the most pious of the academics. "I am never impressed that Willy Loman, as Mr. Miller has described him, ever shows that he has the stuff or the possibilities to be anything better than he is."

Willy is no hero; he is only an ordinary opportunist. But Mr. Miller is greater than Aristotle in one respect: he knows that Willy Loman's anguish is just as painful as if he were a big shot, and that Willy is entitled to the same degree of compassion. And there is another point of view: Willy Loman's tragedy is also the tragedy of a tarnished civilization that equates salesmanship with buncombe. Willy does in a small way what vast corporations do in a big way through the techniques of showmanship, advertising and fraud.

Willy Loman is part of America. It was Mr. Miller's genius to put the tragedy of a small man on the level of a big executive.

o o o o o o o o o o o o o o o o o o o o o o o o o o o o o o o o o o o o o o

Richard Rodgers, Oscar Hammerstein II
and Joshua Logan

SOUTH PACIFIC

o o o o o o o o o o o o o o o o o o o o o o o o o o o o o o o o o o o o o o

Since *South Pacific* was designed to entertain the audience and succeeded in doing so for 1,925 performances, discussion of its human

content may seem to be beside the point. But in view of the banality
and stereotypes of most musical shows, like *No, No Nanette, Irene,*
and *The Student Prince,* the fundamental humanity of *South Pacific*
cannot be ignored. It is interested in the character of its chief men
and women. It discusses race prejudice in ethical terms. It belongs to
the literature of the human race in music as well as in words.

Using James Michener's *Tales of the South Pacific* as their source
book, Oscar Hammerstein II and Joshua Logan wrote the book. Mr.
Hammerstein wrote the lyrics. Richard Rodgers wrote the music.
South Pacific opened at the Majestic Theatre on April 7, 1949, to an
audience that was moved as well as delighted.

The character delineation begins almost at once. When Ensign
Nellie Forbush (played by Mary Martin) enters to visit Emile de
Becque's house on an island in the South Pacific, she sings a meditative song that states the fundamental quality of her character: She
defines herself as a "cock-eyed optimist"—

> *I hear the human race*
> *Is falling on its face*
> *And hasn't far to go,*
> *But ev'ry whippoorwill*
> *Is selling me a bill,*
> *And telling me it just ain't so.*

A native of Little Rock, Arkansas, Nellie is provincial and inex-
perienced and goodhearted. Her character faces the crucial test when
she finds that Emile de Becque's two children are half Polynesian—
children of a native wife now dead. She does not know why she finds
this circumstance so revolting. At first it seems to her immoral and
degenerate. But she changes. "What piffle! What a pinhead!" she
exclaims much later when she realizes that she loves de Becque.

Since Emile de Becque (played by Ezio Pinza) is already a man
of the world, his character does not undergo any serious changes. But
all the other people in *South Pacific* undergo deeper character devel-
opment than is the case in the standard musical show. Bloody Mary

Mary Martin and Ezio Pinza in SOUTH PACIFIC

(played by Juanita Hall), the coarse Tonkinese peddler, is extremely well characterized; she is noisy, cunning, primitive. Temperamentally unstable, she switches from friendly to hostile in a flash. She is anything but romantic, which is the staple of the average musical show. But the author and the composer have enough respect for her to portray her as a human being.

Luther Billis, the sergeant (played by Myron McCormick), is a fully-delineated character—a bluffer, an operator, ignorant, pompous. He never learns anything from anyone, but maneuvers through life by the skin of his teeth. And Lieutenant Joseph Cable (played by William Tabbert) is an individual also. He learns how inadequate his university education is when he falls in love with a charming native girl. "You've Got to Be Taught to Hate and Fear" is the learning song the lyricist and the composer have written for him. It expresses their liberal philosophy. There are ethical principles about civilized people at stake amid the theatrical exuberances of *South Pacific*. Is this the reason why the authors and the composer give an impression of working from strength? Does belief in the human race stimulate their creative capacities? Their show is full of events and vitality.

Apart from its social principles "South Pacific" is abundant and festive. There is an endless sense of antic running through it. Mr. Rodgers has a recognizable style as a composer; the style is rich in melody. But his manner is so varied that the songs sound as though he had never composed any others. "Some Enchanted Evening" is formal romance, and excellent in kind. But it is impossible to find any common element in this virtuoso score—the rhapsody of Nellie's "cock-eyed optimist" song; the jazzy "I'm Gonna to Wash That Man Right Out-a My Hair"; the tender lyric, "Younger Than Springtime"; Bloody Mary's wistful serenade to Bali Ha'i. And there has never been a more spontaneous male ballad than "There's Nothing Like a Dame," which is a roaring salute to females.

In every respect *South Pacific* is a professional musical comedy. But it has one great distinction. It is compassionate about human beings. And it's "stuck, like a dope/with a thing called hope" and can't get it out of the text or the music.

1950-1960

Julian Mayfield in LOST IN THE STARS

○ ○

Maxwell Anderson and Kurt Weill

LOST IN THE STARS

○ ○

Lost in the Stars opened at the Music Box on October 30, 1949, and ran for 273 performances. It was a musical tragedy about the cruelties of segregation in South Africa, written out of Alan Paton's novel, *Cry the Beloved Country,* by Maxwell Anderson, with a score by Kurt Weill.

Mr. Anderson and Mr. Weill, neighbors in New City, N.Y., had been attracted to a theme that had universal significance. In 1949 relations between the blacks and the whites in the United States were consistently callous and frequently cruel, but this was not the major concern of the nation. In South Africa segregation was—and is—the fundamental principle of the state—a legalized institution administered by the police and the court. Mr. Paton's monumental novel, which was widely read in the United States, expressed the ordeal of daily life in South Africa with the sensitivity of a man of conscience.

In the context of 1949 *Lost in the Stars* gave Broadway audiences a deeply moving experience. Mr. Weill's score was particularly eloquent—some of it was show music with a cabaret setting, but most of it transmuted the fears and the hatreds, the wildness and anguish of elemental characters into a poignant lament. But in book form

213

today, with the rich sound of the music stilled, *Lost in the Stars* seems superficial. The libretto is thin, most of the verse is facile, the sympathy is pious, and the storytelling is routine.

Although the style is mythic in the first scenes it soon subsides into hackwork until the last scene, which is the chief emotional part of the play. A black country preacher and a contemptuous white planter are brought together by a common experience that has shaken them out of their separate solidarities. The preacher's son has unintentionally killed the white man's son. On both sides the situation is ironic. For the white man's son is an enemy of segregation, and the preacher's son is not a common criminal. Both fathers have something very genuine to mourn. "Let us forgive each other," the white planter says to the black preacher in the last scene, and when the curtain comes down the audience has reason to believe that something wholesome and creative has been accomplished. This is the one part of the play that contributes to the theme and does not exploit it.

The basic form of *Lost in the Stars* is epic. On steps leading from the orchestra pit to the stage a chorus of singers comments on the play in haunting music suitable for a classic tragedy. But Mr. Anderson's libretto does not have much spiritual exaltation. The story of a poor preacher seeking his lost son in Johannesburg and of an attempted robbery that leads to murder is mediocre playwriting in the form of a thriller. The play also includes a flamboyant cabaret scene better suited to a flashy Broadway revue.

The freshest item in the play is a song that Mr. Weill and Mr. Anderson wrote long before they became interested in Mr. Paton's novel. It has more substance, imagination and momentum than the play to which it has been appended. The words of the song follow:

> *Before Lord God made the sea and the land*
> *He held all the stars in the palm of his hand,*
> *And they ran through his fingers like grains of sand,*
> *   And one little star fell alone.*
>
> *Then the Lord God hunted through the wide night air*
> *For the little dark star on the wind down there—*

And he stated and promised he'd take special care
    So it wouldn't get lost again.

Now a man don't mind if the stars grow dim
And the clouds blow over and darken him,
So long as the Lord God's watching over them,
    Keeping track how it all goes on.

But I've been walking through the night and the day
Till my eyes get weary and my head turns gray,
And sometimes it seems maybe God's gone away,
Forgetting the promise we heard him say—
And we're lost out here in the stars—
    Little stars, big stars,
    Blowing through the night,
    And we're lost out here in the stars.

Lost in the Stars was staged with vivid color and flaring motion by Rouben Mamoulian, who had created the sweeping performance of *Porgy* twenty-two years previously. The part of the preacher was played and sung by Todd Duncan, who had distinguished himself in the Gershwin *Porgy and Bess,* and the part of the white planter was played by Leslie Banks, an English actor better known for his style of dry comedy. By 1949 some of the best black actors of the Twenties and Thirties were gone. But Georgette Harvey, from the original company of *Porgy,* was on hand, and so was William Marshall, who had once played in *The Green Pastures,* and there were many new black actors who could contribute the vitality of motion and sound that *Lost in the Stars* required. In the years since 1949 most of the vitality has gone out of the script. Only an attempt to make a human statement remains.

o o o o o o o o o o o o o o o o o o o o o o o o o o o o o o o o o o o o o o o o

Abe Burrows, Jo Swerling and Frank Loesser

GUYS AND DOLLS

o o o o o o o o o o o o o o o o o o o o o o o o o o o o o o o o o o o o o o o o

Guys and Dolls is a musical comedy about Broadway, produced on Broadway, and played by Broadway actors. Also, patronized chiefly by Broadway audiences for 1200 performances. But it is no house organ. Although it provides a colorful show with a lively book, witty music and overwhelming scenes, it is also an amusing analysis of character. For the honky-tonk personnel of this carnival—night-club chanteuses, chorus girls, crapshooters, cops, Salvation Army sentinels —have one thing in common. They are completely absorbed in their own world. The Times Square terrain is their microcosm. The tensions, the suspicions and feuds, the petty triumphs and disasters, the gaudy romances, the dingy dives seem to them thoroughly normal.

They cannot imagine the orderly bourgeois world that surrounds them—the world of civilians. It seems to them boring and backward. They are serious people who try to live up to the standards of their own milieu. They are not against the rest of the world. But it seems to them alien and dull and they instinctively shrink away from it. They know the neighborhood cops, but they try to avoid tangling with them. It is a shallow, infantile world without taste or enlightenment. But it is the only world they know or want to know, and Nicely-Nicely Johnson, Benny Southstreet, Rusty Charlie, Nathan Detroit and

Harry the Horse are not interested in anyone who is not a part of it.

Guys and Dolls, which opened at the Forty-sixth Street Theatre on November 24, 1950, is based on a Broadway story, "The Idyll of Miss Sarah Brown," by Damon Runyon, the true recorder of Broadway society. Abe Burrows and Jo Swerling wrote the book. Frank Loesser wrote the score and the lyrics. Everything these people put on paper was superb. And since the performance by a memorable cast and the production were also perfect, George S. Kaufman should be credited with the direction, which was the last of his many triumphs. Part of the wit of *Guys and Dolls* is in Mr. Loesser's use of respectable musical forms to depict ignominious people. The score begins with "A Fugue for Tinhorns," in which Nicely-Nicely Johnson, Benny Southstreet and Rusty Charlie compare their selections from the morning scratch sheet. The fugue, with its repetition of theme and its sidewalk vernacular, introduces the note of amiable derision that characterizes the whole show.

> *I got the horse right here*
> *The name is Paul Revere*

sings Nicely-Nicely. And then Benny sings:

> *I'm pickin' Valentine, 'cause on the morning line*
> *The guy has got him figured as five to nine.*

Rusty Charlie counters:

> *But look at Epitaph. He wins it by a half*
> *According to this here in the* Telegraph.

There are no heroes in *Guys and Dolls.* It is a democracy of hucksters, operators, and heated personalities. Nathan Detroit (played by Sam Levene) is desperate; he is trying to find a place where his floating crap game can be played without benefit of the police. Sarah Brown (played by Isabel Bigley) is desperate and depressed. She

Douglas Deane, Tom Pedi, Stubby Kaye,
John Silver, Robert Alda, Sam Levene, B. S. Pully,
Vivian Blaine, Pat Rooney, Sr. and
Isabel Bigley in GUYS AND DOLLS

does not seem to be able to attract enough sinners into the Salvation Army mission. Sky Masterson (played by Robert Alda) is desperate. A professional gambler and an experienced cynic, he has fallen in love with a lady.

Miss Adelaide (played by Vivian Blaine) is desperate. She has been engaged to Nathan Detroit for fourteen years and does not seem to be getting any closer to the altar. When she is feuding with Nathan she cannot think straight. "Tell him I never want to talk to him again and have him call me here," she snaps at a mutual friend. While the feud is going on he can't do anything right. If he turns up at the place where he said he would be she is just as furious: "Just when he should be lying he's telling the truth," she exclaims with virtuous indignation.

They are all innocents lost in a furtive world. But their world is also fabulous, and it would be wise not to denigrate it. Amid all its follies and obscenities it still can create a musical show like *Guys and Dolls* which is full of insight and wit as well as uproar and melody.

o o o o o o o o o o o o o o o o o o o o o o o o o o o o o o o o o o o o o o

Arthur Miller

THE CRUCIBLE

o o o o o o o o o o o o o o o o o o o o o o o o o o o o o o o o o o o o o o

In 1953, when the scourge of McCarthyism was devastating the land, Arthur Miller wrote *The Crucible*, a drama about the Salem witch trials of 1692. The play opened at the Martin Beck Theatre on January 23. Since Mr. Miller did not approve of corruption in industry (see *All My Sons*, 1947) he was suspected of being a Communist, bent on undermining the American system of predatory enterprise. *The Crucible* was everywhere accepted as an attack on McCarthyism; and since most people were either afraid of McCarthyism or believed in it, Mr. Miller's courage was admired on Broadway. *The Crucible* ran for 197 performances.

There are certain analogies between the hysterical witch-hunting by the Salem Puritans of 1692 and the derisive witch-hunting of McCarthy two and one-half centuries later. Fear, ignorance, delusions, bigotry and malice were common to both; and the label of "witch-hunting" was applied to McCarthyism accordingly. In Salem citizens had been charged with being instruments of the devil for no reason. Suspicion was accepted as evidence of guilt. A citizen who read books was suspected of being untrustworthy. Not going to church was regarded as a sign of subversion. Any variation from the norm was dangerous. John Proctor is the chief victim in *The Crucible*. When some irresponsible girls accuse him of doing the devil's work and are believed by the court he asks bitterly: "Is the accuser always holy now?" In the early 1950's the principal accuser was Senator Joseph McCarthy of Wisconsin, and he became the malign hero of the day. In both instances—1692 and the 1950's—the bigots were triumphant.

But now that McCarthyism has been absorbed into the bloodstream of America and is no longer a deliberate crusade, *The Crucible* is less powerful than it was in 1953. There are disparities that seem more significant now than they did then. A streak of supernaturalism runs through it, and supernaturalism was not a factor in McCarthyism. In the first scene Betty Parris' state of unconsciousness defies rational explanation. She and some other girls have been seen "dancing in the forest" and are therefore suspected of being children of the devil—"trafficking with spirits in the forest." The dancing has been real. But her prolonged state of unconsciousness seems to have some supernaturalistic origin when the play opens. By adhering to the facts of the Salem trials Mr. Miller weakens the comparison to McCarthyism.

The aggressive actions of Government authority are recognizable in terms of McCarthyism. The sanctimoniousness of the deputy governor, the frightened malevolence of the local preacher are consistent with McCarthyism. A witness who saves himself by accusing someone else and the pious insistence on confession by the judges are consistent with the corrupt techniques of the House Committee on Un-American Activities. But as the play goes on, the complications in the story and in the relationships of the characters become so confusing that it is difficult to be sure who is on which side. Since *The Crucible* is melodrama the characterizations are superficial and detached. The literary style is artificial. On the whole, Mr. Miller made his political points more effectively in his revision of Ibsen's *An Enemy of the People* in 1950.

There are some relevant comments by the author in the published text of *The Crucible*. Mr. Miller observes that the Salem witch trial came at the time when the emphasis in the political order was changing. Hard work and strict adherence to order had established the

Arthur Kennedy, Jennie Egan and Walter Hampden in THE CRUCIBLE

community so securely that a relaxation in theocratic authority was possible. The time had come, Mr. Miller says, "when the repressions of order were heavier than seemed warranted. . . . The witch-hunt was a perverse manifestation of the panic which set in among all classes when the balance began to turn towards greater individual freedom."

McCarthyism, however, did not represent any change in the political status of the individual. It was a cynical scheme for grabbing power. McCarthy wanted to advance his political career and he discovered that millions of American citizens were as ignorant and bigoted and as fearful and vicious as the people of Salem in 1692, and that played into his hands. Fourteen years after the Salem trial the jury retracted its accusations—too late to save the lives of those who had been hanged. In 1954 the U.S. Senate censured McCarthy for conduct unbecoming a Senator.

But nobody has retracted.

o o o o o o o o o o o o o o o o o o o o o o o o o o o o o o o o o o o o o o o o o o o o o

William Inge

PICNIC

o o o o o o o o o o o o o o o o o o o o o o o o o o o o o o o o o o o o o o o o o o o

It is a small town in Kansas. It is a hot Labor Day—the day before school reopens. The action occurs in the dooryard of two shabby houses divided by a picket fence and occupied by two widows. In addition to the widows the neighborhood includes the two daughters of Mrs. Owens (one of the widows) and a female schoolteacher who boards with them. No male resides in the neighborhood, although mating is everyone's chief preoccupation. The women are not aware of being starved for male companionship. They are hardly aware of anything except the routine of everyday living. But unconsciously they long to escape from a frowzy neighborhood and from constant insecurity, and men are the only possible agents of change.

This is the preliminary situation in William Inge's *Picnic*, which opened at the Music Box on February 19, 1953. It might have been the prologue to another homely comedy or to a derisive cartoon in the style of Sinclair Lewis' *Main Street*. For it was an American article of faith at the time that people in small Middle Western towns are ridiculous. But *Picnic* was written by a man who grew up in a Middle Western town. To him the characters were not ridiculous, although they were commonplace; and he had something serious to say about them before the final curtain.

The torpor of the neighborhood is dispelled by the appearance of a braggart bum with a marvelous physique and a flimsy college education. He is in search of the big break common to the fantasy of American civilization. At the moment he is down on his luck and has prevailed upon one of the widows to give him a free breakfast in exchange for doing some chores around the house. In the exhausting heat of this Labor Day he goes about his work stripped to the waist. The women are shocked or startled. He is chanticleer in a hen yard. None of the women can keep her mind on her work when Hal (for that is his name) exudes plenty *machismo*.

During the first half of the play this female infatuation with the male display is amusing. The schoolteacher, for example, rebels against the timidity of her suitor and insists on his marrying her at once. "You gotta marry me, Howard," she says. "Please marry me, Howard." Madge, Mrs. Owens' older daughter and an acknowledged beauty, is suddenly dissatisfied with the wealthy young man to whom she is engaged. An uneventful future has always depressed her despite the prospect of being the wife of the son of the most important family in town. Hal's blatant masculinity paralyzes her.

If Mr. Inge were content with the stale craftsmanship of the old theatre he would have resolved all these problems happily and provided everyone with the best situation in this best of all possible worlds. But he understands why his people behave as they do. He is concerned with their shapeless aspirations—Madge's vague dreams of some sort of emotional fulfillment; her mother's resolve to see both of her daughters settled; Madge's sister's childish hope of becoming a librarian with access to thousands of books. Even Hal: Hal would like to have "something in a nice office where I can wear a tie and have a sweet little secretary and talk over the telephone about enterprises and things." All their dreams are hackneyed.

And none of them is fulfilled. In the last scene Hal skips town after having knocked out a policeman. He hopes to get a job as a bellhop in a Houston hotel. Although Madge knows all about him she

Ralph Meeker and Janice Rule in PICNIC

throws away her security and goes after him. "He's no good," her mother tells her. "He'll never be able to support you. When he does have a job he'll spend all his money on booze. After a while there'll be other women."

All true. Mr. Inge is under no illusions. He knows that commonplace characters have commonplace lives. The distinction of *Picnic* is the depth of the characterizations and the integrity of the story. Mr. Inge, the chronicler, does not take sides.

Picnic was extremely well staged; it was acted by a cast of winning, talented players, including some who were then or have since become notable—Kim Stanley, Janice Rule, Ralph Meeker, Eileen Heckart, Peggy Conklin, Ruth McDevitt; and it was probably the last time Paul Newman acted a secondary part without distinction.

Picnic won the Pulitzer Prize and the Critics Circle award.

o o o o o o o o o o o o o o o o o o o o o o o o o o o o o o o o o o o o o o o o o o o o o o o

Tennessee Williams

CAMINO REAL

o o o o o o o o o o o o o o o o o o o o o o o o o o o o o o o o o o o o o o o o o o o o o o

In 1953 Tennessee Williams wrote a beautiful play about a hideous subject. *Camino Real,* which opened at the National Theatre on March 19 of that year, reveals the horrors and cruelties of life. Although it was beautiful acted as well as beautifully written, it had only sixty performances because audiences found it repellent. Mr. Williams' dark view of life appalled them.

Hurd Hatfield, Joseph Anthony, Eli Wallach,
Jenny Goldstein, Jo Van Fleet and
Frank Silvera in CAMINO REAL

Many theatregoers also complained that they did not understand it. Probably they did not want to understand it. For the play is clear enough. Mr. Williams' literary gifts have never been better used than in this sad fantasy on the bitterness of human beings. *Camino Real* is a desolate play. On one side of the stage is a luxury hotel and on the other, Skid Row. A barrier in the rear leads into "Terra Incognito." The forestage is a crumbling plaza where the thirty-nine characters and groups of nameless people loiter without purpose.

In the published version of the play, which differs from the acted version, Mr. Williams quotes an illuminating line from Dante's "Inferno": "In the middle of the journey of our life I came to myself in a dark wood where the straight way was lost." That defines the spiritual locale. It could be taken literally, except for one factor. Any man who can compose an organic drama out of such diffuse materials has not lost the straight way to literature. Anything as artistically energetic as *Camino Real* refutes the apathy of the theme.

The cast of characters represents the whole compass of life: street cleaners, who are really jeering and aggressive undertakers, a merciless loan shark, heartless policemen, an evil gypsy and other people representative of our civilization; there are also some characters with specific significance—Kilroy, the naïve, improvident American; Casanova, the battered, desperate old man who was once a promiscuous lover; Camille, now dying of TB; Lord Byron, setting out for Athens again; Don Quixote, whose radiant dreams are not defiled by the obscene realities in which he lives.

They move around among the other people, but they are alone. They fear association with other people. "The most dangerous word in any human tongue is the word for brother," says the hotel padrone. "It is inflammatory. . . . For what is a brother but someone to get ahead of, to cheat, to lie to, to undersell in the market." Camino Real is a desolate place and the drama about it is a prologue to death.

It would be intolerable if Mr. Williams were not such an eloquent writer. He gives the play a plausible dimension. "We're all of us guinea pigs in the laboratory of God," says the disillusioned gypsy. "Humanity is just a work in progress." Gazing down the Camino Real as evening dims the light, the hotel manager says: "Can this be all? Is there nothing more? Is this what the glittering wheels of the heavens turn for?" Is creation no match for death?

Technically, the ending of *Camino Real* is happy. When Don Quixote comes on in the last scene the fountains in the plaza miraculously start flowing sweetly and loudly. And Don Quixote, the foolish knight, has the words that save Kilroy from total degradation: "Don't! Pity! Your! Self!," he exclaims. "Wounds of vanity . . . are better accepted with a tolerant smile." And as he climbs the steps to "Terra Incognito" he gives an exultant shout: "The violets in the mountains have broken the rocks!" The softness of faith has triumphed over the hardness of civilization. For a moment or two the conclusion pushes the ordeal of life away.

But it is doubtful that Mr. Williams believes it. His evidence for the savagery of life is too convincing. And probably that is why audiences did not like *Camino Real*. They could not imagine that Mr. Williams' dark view of life would seem less mythical twenty years later. It is more like reality today.

o o o o o o o o o o o o o o o o o o o o o o o o o o o o o o o o o o o o

Jean Giraudoux

TIGER AT THE GATES

o o o o o o o o o o o o o o o o o o o o o o o o o o o o o o o o o o o o

The opening lines of Jean Giraudoux' *Tiger at the Gates* summarize the argument of the play. Andromache, wife of Hector, tells Cassandra, her sister-in-law: "There's not going to be a Trojan War, Cassandra." Cassandra, the prophet without a constituency, replies: "I shall take that bet, Andromache."

When the play appeared in France in 1935 Giraudoux called it: *La Guerre de Troie n'aura pas lieu*. When Christopher Fry's English adaptation was produced at the Plymouth Theatre on October 3, 1955, the title was changed to *Tiger at the Gates*—"tiger" being Giraudoux's metaphor for destiny. The tiger of war has been sleeping, but Cassandra believes he is being prodded awake by cocksure, belligerent statements by politicians, army commanders, poets and intellectuals. Cassandra believes that there will be a war because human beings take war for granted as a normal part of civilized life.

Giraudoux had a right to this pessimistic opinion. He fought in the French Army in World War I. After being wounded he was withdrawn from the front and reassigned to Harvard University to train the students for service in the U.S. Army. By the time of World War II he had had extensive service as a French diplomat and he knew a good deal about the fatuous arguments and the sanctimonious bombast that precipitate wars.

Tiger at the Gates is full of wisdom and wit. Setting his play in the legendary period of Helen of Troy Giraudoux can discuss war in terms of mythology without awakening the jingoistic prejudices of his contemporaries. There is no reason for the war, as Andromache declares. Helen and Paris do not really love each other. They are incapable of honest emotions. Paris is a poseur and philanderer. Helen is a self-centered trollop who does not love anyone except herself and does not know anything outside herself. There could hardly be a less romantic pair than these petty egotists.

But *Tiger at the Gates,* in its many moods of ridicule and shrewdness, shows how the instinct for war overcomes common sense. The Trojan citizens want war to shore up their illusory national honor. Returning Helen to her Greek husband, which would be one way of avoiding war, would be an unacceptable sign of national cowardice. The scientists want war. So do the poets: "As soon as war is declared, it would be impossible to hold the poets back," says Hecuba.

Michael Redgrave and Diane Cilento
in TIGER AT THE GATES

Giraudoux reserves his most lethal wit for the international jurist. Busiris cites three breaches of the international law which, he says, Troy cannot ignore. During the conversation it develops that every nation that has followed Busiris' advice in the past has been destroyed by the enemy. But that does not disturb his confidence in his own superiority. He can argue any side. When Hector threatens to imprison him, Busiris can also cite legal reasons for not going to war. He can be on any side that is to his advantage.

When the Greeks invade the Trojan harbor and start coming ashore the argument descends from law to insult and national honor and national wealth—very witty but also sad and woeful. A believer in reality, Giraudoux is conceding the impossibility of banishing war. When Hector and Ulysses, leaders of the opposite sides, argue whether to go to war or not, Ulysses remarks: "The universe knows that destiny wasn't preparing alternative ways for civilization to flower. It was contriving the dance of death, letting loose the brutality and human folly which is all that the gods are really contented by. . . . It is Destiny's way of contriving things, inevitably."

When Giraudoux wrote *Tiger at the Gates* in 1935 for French audiences, war with Germany was a matter of grave concern. Excepting Germany and Japan, the whole world was trying to find ways of avoiding it. But four years after Giraudoux's play appeared it turned out that he was right in recognizing war as an integral part of civilization. His tandem experiences as writer and diplomat had coincided. In the middle of the play Andromache says: "Everyone, when there's war in the air, learns to live with a new element: falsehood. Everyone lies."

Giraudoux wrote the play before the lying was again necessary.

o o o o o o o o o o o o o o o o o o o o o o o o o o o o o o o o o o o o o o o o o o o

William Inge

BUS STOP

o o o o o o o o o o o o o o o o o o o o o o o o o o o o o o o o o o o o o o o o o o o

If it were not for William Inge's insight *Bus Stop*, which opened at the Music Box on March 2, 1955, would be routine popular comedy. The situation is standard: Five passengers on a bus are marooned overnight in a slatternly street-corner restaurant because of a March blizzard. During the course of their isolation they reveal a good deal about themselves and learn a lot about one another. Standard procedure in a comedy based on a platitudinous situation.

But there are extenuating circumstances that remove *Bus Stop* from commonplace theatre. The slatternly restaurant has a personality. It is "set in a small Kansas town about thirty miles west of Kansas City"—familiar territory to Mr. Inge. He was born in Independence, Kansas, graduated from the University of Kansas, wrote criticism for a St. Louis, Missouri, newspaper, and he knows all about the characters in this play. All except one of them—an educated dipsomaniac on the lam—are simple people with good hearts and normal expectations of life. They have no problems that are not personal— no causes, no ideology, no politics. They are completely engulfed in their own milieu.

When the curtain goes up Grace, a grass widow and Elma, a high-school student and part-time waitress, are preparing for the

arrival of the regular bus. They are preparing fresh coffee, home-
made pies and cakes and sandwiches. The local sheriff has drifted in
to keep warm. When the bus arrives, Cherie, a night-club singer wearing garish, rumpled clothes, bursts in and says she is being pursued
by a cowboy. She is afraid of him; she asks the sheriff to protect her.
The other characters consist of the bus driver, who feels at home in
Grace's restaurant, the drunken professor hurrying across the state
line to escape the police, and the cowboy and his pal. Before long the
restaurant, isolated in the snow storm, is boiling with temperament
and confusion.

What is the characters' one obsession? Sex. Everything else
seems to them superficial. How the girl can catch the boy or the boy
the girl is all that concerns them. The bus driver and Grace arrange
a surreptitious rendezvous in her empty apartment upstairs. Nobody
notices their separate departures. But Elma, the high-school girl, is
completely unworldly. Without realizing it she almost becomes involved in an assignation with the pickled professor who has a yen
for virgins.

The two essential characters in the comedy, however, are Cherie,
the night-club singer, and Bo, the amorous cowboy. They both have
gaudy illusions about themselves. Cherie thinks of herself as an artist.
She does not call herself a singer but—in her illiterate French—a
"chanteusy." Actually she is a cheap tart from the Ozarks. Bo is a
braggart male. He pictures himself as the conqueror of whatever he
wants. At the moment all he wants is to marry Cherie and install her
in his Montana ranch house as head of a family. He cannot imagine
why she resists him: "Well, I . . . I just never realized . . . a girl might
not love me," he says mournfully at the end of Act One.

Cherie's resistance is largely ignorance. A natural tart, she is
afraid of marriage. Her career dreams are elementary: "There's a
hillbilly program on one of the radio stations. I might git a job on it.
If I don't I'll prob'ly git me a job in Liggett's or Walgreen's. Then
after a while I'll prob'ly marry some guy, whether I think I love him
or not. Who'm I to keep insistin' I should fall in love or not? You
hear all about love when yo'r a kid and jest take it for granted that

such a thing really exists. Maybe ya have to find out for yourself it don't. Maybe everyone's afraid to tell ya." Elma, a small-town girl, has a completely different view: "I'm sort of idealistic about things," she remarks. "I like to think that people fall in love and stay that way, forever and ever."

After Bo has been humiliated, not only by Cherie but also by the sheriff, who beats him up, he is less overbearing and more appealing, and Cherie accepts him: "Ain't it wonderful when someone so awful turns out t'be so nice?" she observes to Elma. "We're gitting married. I'm going to Montana." What has seemed impossibly complicated has turned out to be simple.

And that is the theme of *Bus Stop*. The grass widow and the bus driver are the only characters who know what to do when they suddenly have a mutually fond feeling. They sneak upstairs and go to bed while the others are playing pingpong with words. Faced with realities, the others can't cope, and that is why Mr. Inge's *Bus Stop* is a lumpish, Kansas variation on Chekhov's *The Cherry Orchard*.

Kim Stanley and Albert Salmi appeared in the two chief parts in the original production of *Bus Stop,* under the direction of Harold Clurman. It was a resounding delight.

o o o o o o o o o o o o o o o o o o o o o o o o o o o o o o o o o o o o o o o o o o o o

Frances Goodrich and Albert Hackett

THE DIARY OF ANNE FRANK

o o o o o o o o o o o o o o o o o o o o o o o o o o o o o o o o o o o o o o o o o o o o

There is a poignant contrast in the structure of *The Diary of Anne Frank*. On the one side—and never seen—the massive, primitive brutality of the Nazis in Amsterdam in July of 1942. On the other side, the innocent brightness of a thirteen-year-old girl who believes, "in spite of everything, that people are good at heart." In real life the Nazis were crushed in May of 1945. Two months before that date Anne Frank died in the Belsen concentration camp where the Nazis incarcerated and exterminated Jews. But the excitement and hope of Anne were never crushed. She faced a crisis without surrendering belief. Despite their power, the belief of the Nazis is dead.

Although *The Diary of Anne Frank* made a profound impression on audiences—including German audiences who received it in silence and sorrow—it has no thesis. It points no moral; it makes no polemical statements. The rhetoric is colloquial. Frances Goodrich and Albert Hackett (Mr. and Mrs. Hackett), who wrote it, do not intrude on Anne's thoughts or experience. Through sympathy and understanding they composed a deeply moving portrait of a small group of isolated human beings who oppose the Nazi mass ferocity with civilized behavior. In the last scene, when the Nazis are banging on the door of the garret where the Amsterdam Jews have been hiding, Anne's voice is heard reading from her diary: "Goodbye for a while. P.S. please, Miep or Mr. Kraler, or anyone else. If you should find this diary, will you please keep it safe for me, because some day I hope. . . ." Some day is now and the diary is safe.

In real life Anne was the youngest of eight Jews who hid for two years and one month in a cramped attic over a warehouse in Amsterdam. Anne kept a diary all through their terrible ordeal. It was found after her death. Some of it is transcribed in the play. But Mr. and Mrs. Hackett found it necessary through most of the play to use their own words and construct a form that seemed to them most illuminating.

The play chronicles the group life of the eight Jews crowded in a small, isolated space. The discipline they have to observe is formidable. While people are working in the warehouse downstairs they have to keep completely quiet. They move around cautiously in their stocking feet. They cannot draw water because it would rumble in the pipes downstairs. They have to remain invisible to people in the street or in neighborhood buildings. Living close together day after day they get on one another's nerves. All of them dream of a day when they can be free of one another. Most of the things said are harsh or wounding; very little is sociable or joyous.

But Anne is a completely disarming girl. She talks constantly; in school she was known as Mrs. Quack Quack. She is brash, self-centered and vain. "I'm going to be remarkable," she confides to one of the other refugees. "I'm going to be a famous dancer or singer— or something wonderful." She is also aware of her abrasive personality: "I do it all wrong," she confesses. "I say too much. I go too far. I hurt people's feelings." In the play Anne is not an idealized character.

But her adolescent temperament includes a purity of spirit that

Dennie Moore, Lou Jacobi, Gusti Huber,
Joseph Schildkraut, Eva Rubinstein, Jack Gilford
and Susan Strasberg in THE DIARY OF ANNE FRANK

gives the play a touching and exalting ambiance. The audience already knows that Anne's radiant hopes will never be fulfilled, and it knows that the dingy garret is surrounded by the Nazis, who, after the play is over, will destroy her. The authors do not have to explain the nature of the unseen enemy. But without intruding on Anne's imaginative world they still keep her dreams and her restlessness and wonder in perspective; and through her instinctive good will they conclude the play on an unspoken note of forgiveness. The original production at the Cort Theatre on October 5, 1955, was inspired.

Garson Kanin accepted the responsibility of directing it as a public trust. All the actors, especially Susan Strasberg as Anne and Joseph Schildkraut as her father, played with great tenderness and personal reticence. It was a memorable occasion, like a requiem for World War II.

The Diary of Anne Frank received the Pulitzer Prize in 1956.

o o o o o o o o o o o o o o o o o o o o o o o o o o o o o o o o o o o o o o o o

Samuel Beckett

WAITING FOR GODOT

o o o o o o o o o o o o o o o o o o o o o o o o o o o o o o o o o o o o o o o o

In the first act of *Waiting for Godot* Pozzo inquires of Estragon: "What is your name?" "Adam" is Estragon's reply.

That's one clue to the meaning of Samuel Beckett's ironically ambiguous tragicomedy which opened at the John Golden Theatre on April 19, 1956. There are a few other tangential clues. But *Waiting for Godot* is not to be explained. It is a metaphor of life by a gifted dramatist who can make his enigma seem full of ludicrous portents. And if the theatregoer complains that it is futile, Mr. Beckett can make a similar complaint: that the life of human beings on earth is monumentally futile. A civilization that shines with human ideals cannot be imposed on a natural order that imposes death on everything.

Pozzo, the braggart big shot, remarks about human beings in a ghoulishly humorous vein: "They give birth astride of a grave, the light gleams an instant, then it's night once more." Vladimir carries

*Kurt Kasznar, Alvin Epstein, Bert Lahr and
E. G. Marshall in* WAITING FOR GODOT

the same figure one step further: "Down in the hole, lingeringly, the gravedigger puts on the forceps." It is the cosmic jest—ruthless and immutable.

In *Waiting for Godot* four strange people are waiting for something that will never happen. They are two vagabonds, Estragon and Vladimir, who are loitering beside a gaunt tree on a lonely country road; a big shot named Pozzo who is driving an overburdened slave at the end of a rope, and a rather shy messenger boy. When the play begins, Estragon is trying to pull off a boot that is too small for him. The first line of the play is his dogma throughout the play: "Nothing to be done." Estragon and Vladimir keep on talking in simple declarative sentences that mark time. They don't know what they are doing. They don't know who Godot is.

In the midst of their torpid conversation a frail slave, overburdened with baggage, comes on stage with a rope around his neck. He is followed by Pozzo, who carries a whip. Unlike the vagabonds Pozzo is full of energy and decision. He is the master exploiting the masses. When he returns in the second act he is blind and helpless, but he is still driving the slave. Otherwise nothing happens in the play. "We'll hang ourselves tomorrow," Vladimir says in the last scene, "unless Godot comes." The point of the play is that Godot never comes.

Who is Godot? When the play was new, many people assumed that Godot was God. But Mr. Beckett denies that. He says Godot is a common French name that attracted him when he was writing the play. No matter who Godot may be, the play cannot be explained in objective terms. It is part of the empty eternity Mr. Beckett is describing—an interruption of eternal silence.

If it were taken literally, the play would be depressing. For it says that the civilized life we are trying to create with so much energy and idealism is futile. It will be devoured by the death that consumes everything. But Mr. Beckett is not an angry writer. His image of nothing is comic. We laugh, perhaps in self-defense. The dialogue is pithy, the lazy images are droll, and the whole concept is too grotesque to be accepted without a grin of conspiracy. And we may take note of the fact that the play does not include any women. If it did, life might not seem so empty to Estragon and Vladimir, and there might be some continuity to life—a continuity of banality perhaps, but at least something less dismal than the text of this play describes.

When *Waiting for Godot* opened in New York (after the original productions in Paris and London) the producer had the good taste to cast it with personable actors—Bert Lahr and E. G. Marshall as Estragon and Vladimir and Kurt Kasznar and Alvin Epstein as Pozzo and the slave. The production staged by Herbert Berghof had a surface of straight-faced seriousness like Mr. Beckett's writing. The production had only fifty-nine performances, for the public had a perverse unwillingness to see itself demolished on the stage. It may prove Mr. Beckett's theory that the public behaved in accordance with the last lines of the play:

VLADIMIR. Well? Shall we go?
ESTRAGON. Yes, let's go.

But they do not go. They continue waiting for Godot.

o o o o o o o o o o o o o o o o o o o o o o o o o o o o o o o o o o o o o o o o o o o o

*Leonard Bernstein, Arthur Laurents and
Stephen Sondheim*

WEST SIDE STORY

o o o o o o o o o o o o o o o o o o o o o o o o o o o o o o o o o o o o o o o o o o o o

The romantic plazas of Verona in the Middle Ages have nothing in common with the eroded alleys and filthy streets of Harlem in the twentieth century. But that did not deter some imaginative theatre

*Ken LeRoy, Mickey Calin, Larry Kert and
Carol Lawrence in* WEST SIDE STORY

people from putting Shakespeare's *Romeo and Juliet* into that blighted region in a superb music drama, *West Side Story,* which opened at the Winter Garden on September 26, 1957. It revealed social insights that no one expects from the musical stage.

The translation of the romantic tragedy of *Romeo and Juliet* into the strident vernacular of a New York ghetto was made by Arthur Laurents, who wrote the libretto, and Stephen Sondheim, who wrote the lyrics. Leonard Bernstein, who had previously caught the sharp beat of Manhattan in *On the Town* and *Wonderful Town,* composed a swift, astringent score that communicated the neurotic violence of the story. And Jerome Robbins, the choreographer, staged a performance that was like an explosion. In his *Romeo and Juliet* Shakespeare was writing about a mythical place in a mythical time. *West Side Story* screams with the fears and bitterness of today.

The proportions of the two dramas differ radically. In Shakespeare's play the thwarted love between Romeo and Juliet dominates the stage. In *West Side Story* Tony (Romeo) is a lieutenant in a street gang called the Jets, and Maria (Juliet) is the sister of the leader of the rival gang, the Sharks. Maria is looking forward to a neighborhood dance—not a ball—because she thinks it will be the "real beginning of my life as a young lady in America." Tony and Maria fall in love instantly at the dance. Their balcony scene consists of a furtive meeting on a tenement fire escape. In the original production it was an affecting scene because of the charm and lyric voice of Carol Lawrence as Maria and Larry Kert's openness and force in the part of Tony. The song the lovers sing illustrates the sad difference between Shakespeare's golden lyricism and the tight colloquialism of two tenement young people:

> *Tonight, tonight,*
> *The world is full of light,*
> *With suns and moons all over the place.*
> *Tonight, tonight,*
> *The world is wild and bright,*
> *Going mad, shooting sparks into space.*

Today the world is just an address,
A place for me to live in,
No better than all right,
But there you are
And what was just a world is a star
Tonight!

But the reckless and racial hostilities of the two gangs dominate *West Side Story*. The leader of one gang addresses the leader of the other: "Everyone of you hates everyone of us, and we hate you right back. I don't drink with nobody I hate. I don't shake hands with nobody I hate. Let's get at it;" and the two gangs start fighting with clubs and knives in an open space behind a mesh fence and under a highway. The Jets pride themselves on being American—that is, all of them were born in America, although of different races. All the Sharks are Puerto Ricans.

The enmity is visceral. It is impervious to reason. A social worker tries to break down the hostility by getting both gangs to attend the dance, but he does not succeed. The enmity is also impervious to the law. A police lieutenant and a patrolman try to intervene, but they are outwitted. The young men are not vicious. They are lively boys caught up in the mass evil of a wild city. Nothing can remove the intangible barriers between two sets of young bigots whose mutual hostility is as elusive as air and fire.

Since the characters speak a vernacular that has no eloquence, Mr. Bernstein's score creates the mood with nervous virtuosity—vibrant, reckless, the joy constricted, the romance haunted. Even in the dance scene the excitement is darkened by some unspoken fatality. The dancing is wild and frantic and the hall is like the threshold to a tomb.

West Side Story lacks the literary glory of *Romeo and Juliet*. It also shifts the emphasis away from the lovers to the street gangs. But it makes a valid and harrowing comment on the life of an American city. Out of myth and into reality—"where civil blood makes civil hands unclean."

o o o o o o o o o o o o o o o o o o o o o o o o o o o o o o o o o o o o o o o o o o

Friedrich Duerrenmatt

THE VISIT

o o o o o o o o o o o o o o o o o o o o o o o o o o o o o o o o o o o o o o o o o o

In *The Visit* Friedrich Duerrenmatt's contempt for the moral codes of human beings is so devastating that at first it looks like a grisly joke. It shows the townspeople of Güllen, "somewhere in Europe," agreeing to murder one of their leading citizens in exchange for a gift of one billion marks.

In Maurice Valency's urbane adaptation the play is so well written, the dialogue is so temperate and logical that ultimately the theme has to be taken seriously as a criticism—a shocking criticism—of life. Güllen is a variant on a word that means "sewage" in the German of Switzerland, where Herr Duerrenmatt lives.

The story is simple, like the plot for a bitter ballet. When Claire Zachanassian lived in Güllen as a girl she was in love with Anton Schill, who adored her, and they had a child. At a trial for bastardy he denied his responsibility and bribed two of his fellow citizens to testify in his behalf. Claire left town in disgrace. By practising the life of a whore and by financial shrewdness she became a fabulously wealthy woman. Coming back to Güllen as a distinguished visitor after an absence of many years she makes her monstrous offer. "The world made me a whore," she says, "and now I make the world a brothel." She knows the world very well indeed. Initially the citizens do not want to kill Anton Schill, who is one of their most respected citzens; they are aghast; they cannot believe that the proposal is serious. But eventually they accept her terms. When she leaves town triumphantly her imposing entourage carries the dead body of Anton Schill in the coffin she had brought when she arrived.

Although *The Visit* is written in sedate prose, the first act emerges on the stage as a humorous fantasy. Claire's entrance at the railroad station is comically regal. She has stopped the train by pulling the emergency cord. When the conductor argues with her she casually hands him a bribe of four thousand marks, leaving him impressed and pleased. The local people, who hope she will rescue Güllen from terrible poverty, overwhelm her with insincere compliments and servility. This also is comic.

But in the second act it is plain that *The Visit* is not comic. It is a ghastly criticism of life. Claire means what she says; and *The Visit* brilliantly portrays the slow, mass corruption of the common people. At first they rally to the defense of their citizen, whom they have already nominated to be the next burgomaster. But gradually and stealthily they turn against him. They begin spending the money before they have received it. They hypocritically convince themselves that since Claire was unjustly treated years ago she is entitled to restitution now. As time goes on, they become so corrupted that they make a joint declaration in town meeting that they will murder Anton Schill "not out of love for worldly gain but out of love for the right, to purify the town guilt, to reaffirm our faith in the eternal power of justice." They murder Anton Schill sanctimoniously. The cold logic of the story makes *The Visit* believable and horrifying.

Give Herr Duerrenmatt full credit for the skill with which he has made a fantastic theme look and sound reasonable. But when *The Visit* opened at the Lunt-Fontanne Theatre on May 6, 1958, the gruesome impact it made derived also from the cold virtuosity of Peter Brook's staging and the magnificent acting of Lynn Fontanne and Alfred Lunt. For years they had been squandering talent on trivial comedies cut to their measure. But their acting in *The Visit,* which marked the conclusion of their long stage career, reminded theatre-

John Wyse, Lynn Fontanne and
Alfred Lunt in THE VISIT

goers that they were great actors in any genre—perfectionists in details, magnetic in style. After the ironic grandeur of Miss Fontanne's entrance she deepened the characterization by describing Claire's surface coolness as a form of interior ferocity and the elegance as the worldly mask of a vicious woman. As Anton Schill, Alfred Lunt gave an equally stunning and meticulous performance. The scene in which Anton Schill tries to leave town became a memorable piece of pantomime—terror and loneliness and wordless despair.

If there had been an overwrought word in the dialogue or a spurious gesture in the acting, or a soft interlude in the direction, *The Visit* would have fallen apart and its hard theme would have degenerated into pathos. But everything about the production rang true and this fastidiously written play rudely destroyed some familiar myths about the moral integrity of civilized people. The most intelligible of the plays of disillusion and disdain, *The Visit* is also the most genuine and appalling.

○ ○

Archibald MacLeish

J. B.

○ ○

In *J.B.* Archibald MacLeish asks the unanswerable question: Is God just? *J.B.* is a modern version of the ambiguous myth of Job—the verse sharp, the story merciless, the characters out of the inferno of today. The play had an imaginative production at the ANTA Theatre where it opened on December 11, 1958, and it received the Pulitzer Prize the next spring.

Since Mr. MacLeish is neither God nor Satan he cannot explain the mystery of Job's tribulations more creatively than the authors (apparently there were three) did in the original Bible story. Mr. MacLeish is cursed with the skepticism of modern thinking. The questions he asks are modern conundrums:

> *If God is God He is not good,*
> *If God is good He is not God,*
> *Take the even, take the odd ...*

or,

> *If God is Will*
> *And Will is well*
> *Then what is ill?*
> *God still?*

The cosmic questions—does God treat man justly, is God merciful? —deserve something more responsible than rhymes like these.

But the spectacle of J.B.'s (Job's) afflictions becomes increasingly overpowering in this drama because it comes out of the history of modern times. J.B. is a wealthy family man who believes implacably in the goodness of God. When the play begins on a spiral setting that encompasses Heaven as well as Earth, J.B., his wife Sarah, and their five children are sitting down to a bountiful Thanksgiving dinner, meekly served by two family servants. The family recites the Lord's Prayer, obediently but not humbly. Sarah believes that they should not take God's bounty for granted: "God doesn't give all this for nothing," she observes. But J.B. has no misgivings about God; he has never doubted that God has always been on his side, and he is grateful for God's many gifts and for his protection. J.B.'s happy, comfortable home symbolizes the mass ideal of America.

But the gratuitous afflictions God lays on J.B. are overwhelming, not only because they illustrate the calamities of today but also

*Christopher Plummer, Raymond Massey
and Pat Hingle in* J.B.

because Mr. MacLeish's verse expresses J.B.'s anguish ruthlessly. A son is killed in the army, not in combat, but through the carelessness of an officer. Two daughters are killed in an automobile accident; another daughter is raped and murdered, Sarah is nearly killed by a bomb that wrecks everything the family owns, J.B. nearly dies in a flood.

Sarah is bitter: "What had they done—those children? What had *we* done?" J.B. is shocked and grieved. But he never repudiates his belief in God. "God is just," he exclaims in the midst of his calamities. J.B. thinks he is being punished for some sin of which he is not aware. But one of the comforters puts it very bluntly: "Your sin is simple," he says. "You were born a man!"

In the last scene Mr. MacLeish accepts reality. When Sarah says that there is no justice, but only love, J.B. agrees. "God does not love. He Is," says J.B. God's existence is the only reality. When the final curtain comes down, he and Sarah reduce their area of faith to the comfort and beneficence of love:

> *The candles in churches are out.*
> *The lights have gone out of the sky.*
> *Blow on the coal of the heart*
> *And we'll see by and by.*

J.B. does not conclude with the bountifulness of the Bible story, which must have been rewritten by some hired Pollyanna. Amid the desolation of the modern world God does not reward J.B. for the tenacity of his faith. But in comparison with the devastation of their experience Sarah's belief in love is merciful: "That's the wonder," she says and it is. Can it bind the sweet influences of the Pleiades? No doubt it can. For *J.B.* demonstrates the helplessness of dogma to create a tolerable world.

o o o o o o o o o o o o o o o o o o o o o o o o o o o o o o o o o o o o o o o

Lorraine Hansberry

A RAISIN IN THE SUN

o o o o o o o o o o o o o o o o o o o o o o o o o o o o o o o o o o o o o o o

The title of Lorraine Hansberry's play, *A Raisin in the Sun,* which opened at the Longacre Theatre on March 11, 1959, comes from a gentle poem by Langston Hughes—

> *What happens to a dream deferred?*
> *Does it dry up*
> *Like a raisin in the sun?*

In the case of Miss Hansberry's play it makes a gallant break with the poverty and docility of a Negro family in Chicago.

Having emigrated from Chicago to Greenwich Village, and having dedicated her play "To Mama: in gratitude for the dream," Miss Hansberry is obviously writing out of personal experience and observation, and that may be why *A Raisin In the Sun* is not a revolutionary play on a revolutionary subject but a passionate statement of home truths about representative people. Throughout most of the play Miss Hansberry calls her characters "colored people;" she uses "Negroes" in the last scenes. Although she is writing about minority people who are handicapped by race prejudice she writes as part of the American civilization.

In the play Mama is the matriarch of a poor Negro family on the South Side of Chicago in the late 1950's. When she and her late husband had moved into this "rat trap," as she calls it, just after they had been married, they expected to stay no more than a year. But she has been here all her mature life. Her children were born here and still live here: her son, who is a white man's chauffeur; her son's wife, who keeps house at home and works as a domestic for white people; their son, who is in school, and Mama's daughter, who is in school and wants to become a doctor of medicine. The cramped, slatternly inconvenient apartment is the dismal prologue to Mama's "dream deferred."

She is about to receive her husband's life insurance of $10,000. That is the basis of the plot. The availability of that substantial sum of money divides the family. The son wants to invest it in a neighborhood liquor store. The daughter is going to need money for tuition in medical school. Mama is responsive to everyone's needs. She pays $3,000 down on a house in a white neighborhood, and splits the rest of the money between her son and daughter. Money causes the pain and the anxiety in Miss Hansberry's play. Replying to her son's statement that money is life, Mama says: "So now it's life. Money is life. Once upon a time freedom used to be life—now it's money."

The plot gives the play tension and a theatrical climax. But its great virtue is the illumination Miss Hansberry brings to her characters—the bitterness and greed of the married son ("We are a group of men tied to a race of women with small minds"), the patient, industrious wife, the daughter, Beneatha, who represents the liberated student who has strong opinions about cultural questions and is full of ambition, and Mama, a woman of little education and great moral scruples. There is also a rich young suitor, who is bored with Negro problems, and a joyous young African man full of hope. Most of the members of the family are short tempered. But a white man representing a white community brings them together. He is a sanctimonious segregationist: "It is a matter of the people of Clybourne Park believing, rightly or wrongly," he says, "that for the happiness of all concerned that our Negro families are happier when they live in their

own communities." In the end the opposition of the white people is
the element that unites the Negro family.

    A Raisin in the Sun is not an organic expression of an idea; it is
artistically undistinguished. But Miss Hansberry's intimate knowledge of the people, her respect and affection for Mama, who dominates the play by simplicity and moral standards and whose country
manners are invariably above reproach; her sympathy and skepticism
about the racial programs; her criticisms of some of her colored people; her independent mind and her kindness make *A Raisin in the Sun*
an admirable and instructive drama.

    It was played by a cast of dedicated actors who believed what

Sidney Poitier and Claudia McNeil
in A RAISIN IN THE SUN

the author had given them to say— Claudia McNeil as Mama, and Ruby Dee, Sidney Poitier, Diana Sands, Louis Gossett and Lonne Elder III in other parts. *A Raisin in the Sun* had 530 performances and won the Critics Circle award. As Mama's son, Walter, tells the white man who wants to keep the Negroes out of Clybourne Park: "We are very proud. . . . My son makes the sixth generation of our family in this country. . . . We don't want to make no trouble for nobody or fight no causes—but we will try to be good neighbors. That's all we got to say. We don't want your money." "That's what the man said," Walter's aggressive sister remarks defiantly.

Paddy Chayefsky

THE TENTH MAN

To Paddy Chayefsky, author of *The Tenth Man* which opened at the Booth Theatre on November 5, 1959, Judaism and neighborhood life are the same thing. The setting of his shrewd play is a Mineola, Long Island, synagogue that looks untidy and abandoned; in the words of the most articulate character: "Really, if it wasn't for the Holy Ark this place would look like the local headquarters of the American Labor Party."

At six-thirty on a freezing morning it is the meeting place of some caustic idlers who are united only by the fact that all of them are Jews. One, who is wearing a white linen prayer shawl and a small black skullcap, is completely absorbed in praying at the altar. He is not aware that any other mortals exist. The others ignore him. They consist of the sexton, who manages the synagogue in an off-hand manner, an intellectually alert atheist who regards praying as "pietistic humbug," and a few other elderly men who are at loose ends and use the synagogue as a convenient meeting place.

They like to talk. Talk gives them individual importance and keeps boredom away. They have strong and contrary opinions. Their sentences have a Yiddish inflection, and end in a kind of ritualistic melancholy. They give homely images to abstract ideas: "My daughter-in-law, may she grow rich and buy a hotel with a thousand rooms and be found dead in every one of them."

One of the men who comes in later has a problem. His granddaughter is mentally unbalanced—a catatonic schizophrenic, in the jargon of modern science. But he believes that she is possessed of a dybbuk. The others are skeptical of anything so primitive as a dybbuk. But it is the genius of these neighborhood Jews to take an interest in any idea. They agree to collaborate on a traditional exorcism, conducted by the man at the altar in his prayer shawl. "A dybbuk is a migratory soul that possesses the body of another human being in order to return to heaven," says one of the members. "I wrote several articles on the matter for Yiddish publications."

In order to complete the quorum of ten men needed for a prayer service, the sexton solicits a young man on the street—Arthur, by name, who believes in nothing but is willing to oblige. He thinks men have invented religion to give themselves importance: "You have invented it all—the guilt, God, forgiveness, the whole world, dybbuks, love, passion, fulfillment—the whole fantastic mess of pottage—because it is unbearable for you to bear the pain of insignificance." He is a compulsive drinker and is going to a psychiatrist to get straightened out.

The girl with the dybbuk believes that Arthur, too, has a dybbuk—"some sad little turnkey, who drifts about inside you, locking up all the little doors, and saying: 'You are dead. You are dead'." She is right. When the ritual of exorcism is finished, it is not the girl but

George Voskovec, Lou Jacobi,
Arnold Marle, Jacob Ben-Ami and Risa Schwartz
in THE TENTH MAN

Arthur who is freed of a dybbuk—freed of disbelief and hatred. **Mr. Chayefsky** has concluded his play with a little joke that translates modern psychiatry into ancient dybbukry and transmutes *The Tenth Man* into a comic Bible story.

But his portrait of a ramshackle neighborhood synagogue and a group of crotchety yet fraternal old men is his triumph. Neighborhood gossip and religious ritual occur simultaneously. The men argue with great relish about religion and their relatives, and everything has a practical ring. There is no mysticism about their beliefs. Talking to a new rabbi on the telephone, the rabbi of Mr. Chayefsky's synagogue says that preaching about God to a congregation is not enough: "You've got to be a go-getter, unfortunately."

Religion is the foundation of the lives of the characters in the Mineola synagogue. They put on their phylacteries. They say ritualistic prayers. They join hands in a tribal dance. But Mr. Chayefsky is always making something local out of something occult and mythical. He never loses the common touch. The concluding sentence states the theme without rhetorical flourishes: Speaking of Arthur, the non-believer, one of the old men says: "He still doesn't believe in God. He simply wants to love. And when you stop and think about it, gentlemen, is there any difference?" Note the conclusion of *J.B.*

1960-1973

Angela Lansbury and Joan Plowright
in A TASTE OF HONEY

Shelagh Delaney

A TASTE OF HONEY

When Shelagh Delaney, at the age of nineteen, was ushering in a Manchester, England, theatre she saw a play by Terence Rattigan that seemed to her too trivial. She thought that she could write a better one. After she had finished it and labeled it *A Taste of Honey*, she sent the manuscript to Joan Littlewood, the enterprising director of the Theatre Royale in London, and asked Miss Littlewood's opinion. She asked to have the manuscript returned because "whatever kind of theatrical atrocity it may be it means a lot to me." It also meant a lot to Miss Littlewood, who produced it in London. The play later opened at the Lyceum Theatre in New York on October 4, 1960.

Since Miss Delaney was not then an experienced playwright *A Taste of Honey* has limitations. It is tight and narrow; the dialogue is all in one key. But the originality of her portrait of poor people in Manchester and her obsession with honesty outweigh the advantages that more versatile craftsmanship might have provided. Her characters are imprisoned in poverty. They are hard and bitter. But they are also self-contained. They do not blame their misfortune on outside forces—the state or the economy. Although they accept their fate with rancor and virulence they do not expect to evade it. Being self-centered they cannot really imagine a better life.

Helen, the mother of Jo, and, in Miss Delaney's words a "semi-whore," tells her daughter: "Listen, Jo . . . there's two *w's* in your future—work or want. . . . We're all at the steering wheel of our own destiny, careening along like drunken drivers." That's about the only rhetoric in the play. Everything else is in a shrill and gross vernacular.

A Taste of Honey is set in a cold, dreary, dirty flat in Manchester in a building surrounded by a gas works, a slaughter house and a cemetery. Helen and Jo hate each other. Helen, a widow, resents the fact that her daughter is constantly underfoot and impedes her natural promiscuity. Jo blames her mother for everything—for having given birth to her, for the harshness of their lives. Jo has a few rather pathetic visions of something better than ugliness—flowers that can be grown in a pot, and drawing pictures. "I'm not just talented," she tells her mother. "I'm geniused."

The first act consists of a pitiless statement of the starved, sordid lives of two defenseless women. But the second act introduces a note of humanity that puts the play on another level. Jo is pregnant by a Negro sailor who has abandoned her. She is working all day in a shoe store and much of the night in a bar to pay her bills. A homosexual art student named Geoffrey moves in with her, realizes that she is incapable of planning and of solving her problems, and for no reason except common sympathy takes charge. Jo talks continuously in her characteristic vein of insulting, belligerent, jeering conversation. She is incapable of gentleness. But Geoffrey shops for food, cleans the room, makes plans for the delivery of her baby, scrounges a basket that can be used for a cradle and even sews baby clothes. Under the hard surface of this relentless play there is a merciful interior—nothing more than kindness really, but kindness is almost as creative as love in this environment.

If Miss Delaney were a more experienced playwright she could remove some of the ambiguities of *A Taste of Honey*. She is so determined not to be sentimental or militant that she does not account for all the circumstances that affect her characters. She tries to be objective. But the natural warmth of a compassionate young woman tempers her objectivity in the last act and makes art out of reporting. What trained sociologists would define as "disadvantaged people" are poor people in Miss Delaney's play and they have vivid lives of their own—undisciplined, spiteful, illogical, vicious, filthy but independent. Miss Delaney does not condescend to them; she does not pity them. She respects their vitality.

o o o o o o o o o o o o o o o o o o o o o o o o o o o o o o o o o o o o o o o

Eugène Ionesco

RHINOCEROS

o o o o o o o o o o o o o o o o o o o o o o o o o o o o o o o o o o o o o o o

Although Eugène Ionesco despises contemporary civilization he has not lost his sense of humor. His *Rhinoceros*, which was acted at the Longacre Theatre on January 9, 1961, in Derek Prouse's translation, is a funny and lively play. The basic idea is ludicrously grotesque: Ionesco portrays human beings who cannot resist the exotic opportunity of turning themselves into rhinoceroses. The playgoer knows that this is physically impossible. But after seeing *Rhinoceros*, and rereading the text, one cannot be sure of anything. For the intellectuals in M. Ionesco's lampoon are so sure of themselves that they behave like fools.

The logician, for example: his pedantic logic leads him straight into absurdities. Since cats have four paws he declares that all four-

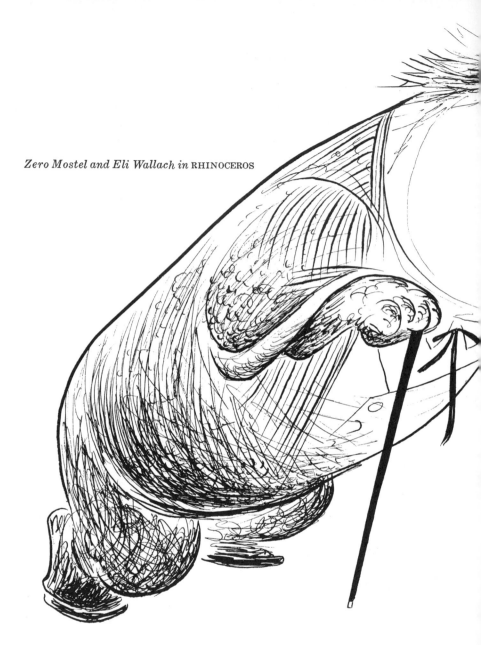

legged animals are cats. "My dog has four paws," the Old Gentleman politely protests. "Then it's a cat," the Logician declares. The Old Gentleman can only agree that "Logic is a very beautiful thing." "Another syllogism," the Logician points out: "All cats die. Socrates is dead. Therefore, Socrates is a cat."

All this upside-down chatter is droll, written with sharpness and agility. But it is of secondary importance in the play. *Rhinoceros* concerns human beings who meekly turn themselves into rhinoceroses in conformance to a vogue. They are sheep before they become rhinoceroses. When the rhinoceroses first appear in the community, people protest. The noise of their trumpeting, the damage they do to established customs and institutions repel the public. But as more and more people become rhinoceroses the remaining people happily conform. "We must move with the times," one smug intellectual observes when he makes the absurd decision. Eventually public opinion begins to agree that rhinoceroses are the desirable species. "They are the ones that are right," says one servile secretary. "They're like gods." Confronted with a crisis, most of the human beings enthusiastically debase themselves by running with the mob.

M. Ionesco's preposterous image of making rhinoceroses out of human beings becomes static after it has been initially stated. One of the most colorless of his characters, Mrs. Boeuf, startles the others by announcing that her absent husband has become a rhinoceros. "Oh, Boeuf, my poor Boeuf, what's happened to you!" she says in a tone of lament. There is nothing in the rest of the play as fantastic as that. The rest of the play consists of different aspects of the same image.

But M. Ionesco's wittily contemptuous view of the inadequacies of civilized people remains unimpaired. They are egotists; they cannot listen to the other characters; they cannot cope with the seriousness of their situation. They are compulsive talkers of pretentious nonsense.

When the first rhinoceros upsets the decorum of the community their comments are entertainingly inadequate. "Oh, a rhinoceros," an intellectual casually remarks when he sees the first one. "Well, of all things," says another. "You don't often see that," exclaims the proprietor of a street café. A café guest whose conversation has been interrupted by the rhinoceros protests against the intrusion of "a stupid quadruped not worth talking about. . . . Why go on at me," he growls, "just because some wretched perissodactyle happens to pass by?"

Unable to grasp the significance of the new invasion the characters run off into irrelevancies that flatter their egoes. A cat has been killed by a rhinoceros. One of the bystanders asks what color the cat was, but he promptly forgets the cat and initiates a pious discussion of the "color bar." "The color bar is something I feel strongly about.

I hate it," he says in a superior tone. "The course of history has shown . . . " he pompously continues until another egotist interrupts him.

Confronted with an amazing supernatural situation M. Ionesco's people cannot cope. Their minds are too static. They have no principles. Their imaginations are sluggish. They can only repeat the clichés from the normal periods of their lives. And it should be remarked that the only human being who refuses to become a rhinoceros is the one with the most commonplace mind and the least personality. "I'm the last man left and I'm staying that way until the end," he exclaims.

M. Ionesco is a Roumanian who has become a French citizen. After undergoing the idiotic experience of Europeans in the last half century he is totally disillusioned. Since there is no place to which an iconoclast can go, M. Ionesco has deposited his whole bundle of nonsense in the theatre before people who cannot be shocked and who have a sense of humor. One of the most fatuous people in his play says to another who is equally tedious: "You've no sense of humor, that's your trouble, none at all. You must learn to be more detached, and try to see the funny side of things."

Humor is better than insanity.

o o o o o o o o o o o o o o o o o o o o o o o o o o o o o o o o o o o o o o o o o o

Robert Bolt

A MAN FOR ALL SEASONS

o o o o o o o o o o o o o o o o o o o o o o o o o o o o o o o o o o o o o o o o o

The fate of Sir Thomas More in England in 1535 had a strange relevance to America in the middle 1950's. More was charged with silence about his beliefs and beheaded for unspoken thoughts that the jury suspected were treasonable. During the era of McCarthyism in America four centuries later citizens were not beheaded for thoughts suspected of being disloyal. But many were harassed and others were punished by imprisonment or the loss of jobs. In the twentieth century thought control still seems reasonable to many officers of the Government and to private citizens.

Robert Bolt's somber play about More, *A Man for All Seasons*, was first produced in his native England; it opened at the ANTA Theatre in New York on November 22, 1961. Although it drew no parallels between More's day and ours, everyone knew what the play meant. In one of the last scenes More makes this crucial statement to the king's jury: "What you have hunted me for is not my actions, but the thoughts of my heart. It is a long road you have opened. For first men will disclaim their hearts and presently they will have no hearts. God help the people whose Statesmen walk your road."

Mr. Bolt's play is a beautiful piece of work. It tells the story of More at the time when Henry VIII is proclaiming himself head of the Church of England and arranging a divorce from Catherine of Aragon so that he can marry Anne Boleyn. More is a profoundly religious man—also charming. He submerges his piety in wit, generosity and good will. As the King's chancellor, he is completely loyal and looks after the King's business with scrupulous devotion. He resigns the chancellorship when the King officially declares himself the religious leader of England. More remains silent, however, about his belief that the king cannot supersede the Pope in his control of the spiritual life of England. Since More is famous for his integrity this silence becomes conspicuous. That is how it comes about that he is convicted of, and executed for, treasonable thoughts.

The play has considerable stature beyond the nobility of More's character. It is written with remarkable virtuosity. The literary style is formal; the characters address one another in plain sentences that express social stratifications rather than individual personalities. The form of the play is like a succession of improvisations. The stage setting is architectural, and the succession of scenes is indicated by blackouts and changes in style of lighting and costumes. It is pure theatre without artifice. And the moral of the play is indicated by a comic character called the Common Man. He comes in and out of the play in many guises as servant, boatman, publican, foreman of the jury, prison guard, and, finally, executioner. In his description of the part Mr. Bolt says that the Common Man's face is crafty, loosely benevolent, its best expression being that of base humor. The Common Man keeps the play in perspective by illustrating the greed, guile, rancor, self-interest and distrust of the man in the street.

Although thought control and government authoritarianism remain present dangers after all these years, Sir Thomas More was in some respects the imperfect hero according to our standards. A medieval man, he was a bigot. He regarded Protestantism as heresy. He acquiesced in the execution of non-Catholic communicants. His habits of thought were authoritarian. In *Utopia,* which is his vision of the perfect state, he is, by our standards, fascist. Our civilization is more merciful than his.

In Samuel Johnson's opinion in the eighteenth century, More "was the person of the greatest virtue these islands ever produced."

Paul Scofield in A MAN FOR ALL SEASONS

His allegiance to principle and his grace under pressure make him a man for all seasons, in the twentieth century as well as the sixteenth. His humor is modern and disarming. Mr. Bolt does not include his grisly final jest as he climbed the scaffold: "I pray you, Master Lieutenant, see me safe up, and for my coming down let me shift for myself." The charity and scruple of Mr. Bolt's thinking, the spontaneity of his craftsmanship, and the simplicity of his literary style give his play an undertone of exaltation.

The original performance was modest in style, but full of pride and conviction. Some of the acting was particularly illuminating—Paul Scofield as Sir Thomas More, George Rose as the Common Man, Keith Baxter as Henry VIII, Albert Dekker as the Duke of Norfolk, William Redfield as a shifty courtier. They caught the conscience of everyone who was in the theatre.

o o o o o o o o o o o o o o o o o o o o o o o o o o o o o o o o o o o o o o

Edward Albee

WHO'S AFRAID OF VIRGINIA WOOLF?

o o o o o o o o o o o o o o o o o o o o o o o o o o o o o o o o o o o o o o

Many theatregoers were horrified by Edward Albee's *Who's Afraid of Virginia Woolf?* which opened at the Billy Rose Theatre on October 13, 1962. They were repelled by the depth of the hatred a married couple can have for each other and the cruelties they devise for torturing each other. But the hatred and the cruelty are not gratuitous; they are not stage properties for a melodrama with a routine happy ending. They convey the author's conviction that life is malevolent and they differ from O'Neill's tragic view chiefly by the virulence of the author's feeling.

The opening lines indicate the tension between Martha, the wife, and George, the husband, and the grossness of their speech:

MARTHA: *Jesus...*
GEORGE: Shhhhhh.
MARTHA: H. Christ!
GEORGE: Martha, For God's sake, it's two o'clock in the ...
MARTHA: Oh, George!
GEORGE: Well, I'm *sorry*, but ...
MARTHA: What a cluck! What a cluck you are!

That is the beginning, and an indication of the brutality of the dialogue. But the mood of mutual hatred and the sadistic ingenuity on both sides grow in violence until the last act of a long three-act play. If the play were remarkable for nothing else, it would still be distinguished for sustained ferocity. The maliciousness never weakens. Every performance drained so much energy out of the actors that they could not act the play twice in one day. The management had to provide a second company for matinee performances.

Martha is the daughter of the dictatorial president of a small New England college. George, her husband, is a teacher in the History Department. She had married him in the hope that he would succeed her father, but apparently that will never happen. She despises his mediocrity. After attending a party given by her father they have invited home a young professor and his wife who have just joined the faculty. All four of them have had a lot to drink and they continue drinking until early morning.

After greetings at the door the two couples settle back into a long night of hostilities. George and Martha start destroying one another in a virtuoso dialogue of disgust and malevolence. At first their guests are bewildered. But before the party breaks up they, too, become savage and vindictive. The dialogue is witty as well as infamous. Mr. Albee destroys the civilized world with uncanny grabs at the jugular and an instinct for the weak places in human defenses. All his characters—that is, all four—emerge from this vicious wrangle without pride, without honor, without dignity, without mercy. He dehumanizes everyone in the play.

Why? If the play tells the truth it needs no defense. But since the motivations of the characters are not explained, and only touched on in passing during the fury of the debate, some theatregoers have tried to psychoanalyze it. Some have elevated their own vanity by dismissing the play as some sort of homosexual metaphor. Some see great psychotic significance in George and Martha's fantasy about a son who has never existed. Some believe that the title *Who's Afraid of Virginia Woolf?* (a paraphrase of "Who's Afraid of the Big Bad Wolf?") indicates fear of intellectual women.

The play invites analysis because of the intensity of its animosi-

Arthur Hill and Uta Hagen
in WHO'S AFRAID OF VIRGINIA WOOLF?

ties. The pace is so fast, the situations are so tense, the material is so startling that the author has no time for explanations. The meaning whirls off the top of the dialogue. But explanations need not be esoteric or profound. It is enough to agree that most people have flattering images of themselves and that many of them try to protect their egoes by attacking the vulnerable points in other people. This is a play about viciousness by a man who is repelled by the world. It ends with the exhaustion of all the characters and by the surrender of Martha to one of her husband's cruelest caprices. The more ferocious character yields to the less.

GEORGE: Are you all right?

MARTHA: Yes, No.

GEORGE: (*puts his hand gently on her shoulder; she puts her hand back and he sings to her, very softly*) Who's afraid of Virginia Wolf
Virginia Woolf
Virginia Woolf?

MARTHA. I ... am ... George.

So George wins. But what has he won and does his winning compensate for his loss? That is the enigma of *Who's Afraid of Virginia Woolf?*

Among those exhausted by the play was the author. Mr. Albee has never written another overpowering play.

o o o o o o o o o o o o o o o o o o o o o o o o o o o o o o o o o o o o o o o o o

Bertolt Brecht

MOTHER COURAGE

o o o o o o o o o o o o o o o o o o o o o o o o o o o o o o o o o o o o o o o o o

In 1939, when Germany was beginning World War II, Bertolt Brecht, a German dramatist, wrote a cynical and contemptuous play about war. *Mother Courage* was acted, in Eric Bentley's adaptation, at the Martin Beck Theatre on March 29, 1963. The performance was excellent with Anne Bancroft in the leading part and Barbara Harris as the daughter. But it failed. Broadway audiences were not interested. Perhaps the Vietnam War seemed too remote at that time.

But *Mother Courage* will be a pertinent play as long as wars are fought like holy crusades. Brecht knew that this is a fraud. The play is a series of episodes; the story lacks tension. But the excitement of a brilliant mind holds it together. Brecht's intellectual energy and corrosive humor keep it startling and stinging, and his insights into human cupidity are cold and pitiless.

By setting *Mother Courage* in the Thirty Years' War of the seventeenth century, Brecht avoids the political issues of 1939 and acquires perspective on a philosophical theme. He also avoids official cant by confining his play to the field soldiers and petty officers. They are concerned not with moral fervor but with staying alive. Mother Courage is a traveling saleswoman out to make a buck. She rolls through the battlefields in a gypsy wagon stuffed with food, liquor and clothing for soldiers who have money. The wagon is drawn by her two bastard sons and one bastard daughter.

None of them is concerned with right or wrong. Their only mission is to make money. War is a normal activity for everyone in the play. Everyone feels comfortable in war.

In the first scene the recruiting officer remarks to his sergeant: "They're so friendly around here that I'm scared to sleep nights." And the sergeant replies: "What they need around here is a good war. What else can you expect with peace running wild all over the place? You know what the trouble with peace is? No organization. And when do you get organization? In a war. Peace is one big waste of equipment. Anything goes; no one gives a damn."

Mother Courage is a realist. She has no illusions. When an officer tells her that what the army needs most is "discipline" she retorts: "I was going to say sausages." She dismisses a sergeant derisively: "You're just a corpse on furlough." When the chaplain says: "We're in God's hands," she replies: "Oh, I hope we are not as desperate as that." When some one makes a pessimistic remark she replies: "Who's defeated? There've been cases where a defeat is a victory for the little fellows. It's only their honor that's lost, nothing serious."

Although Mother Courage has no moral principles, there is something heroic about her. She has the stubborn, animalistic soul of a peasant. Although it is against her instinct to be merciful she gives a coat to the chaplain when he is cold. She is devoted to her children; she tries to protect them. In the last resort she believes in human beings: "They're not wolves," she says, "they're human and after money. God is merciful and men are bribable—that's how His will is done on earth." During the war Mother Courage loses all her children; and in the last scene she harnesses herself to the wagon without their assistance. "I hope I can pull the wagon by myself," she remarks. "Yes, I'll manage. There's not much in it now." She is the mother not only of courage but of the human race.

There are two residual ironies about *Mother Courage*. One: In 1939, when Brecht was writing the play, the Germans regarded themselves as invincible. By setting the play in the Thirty Years' War Brecht anticipated the conclusion of World War II. Germany was defeated in both wars—the population decimated, the fields ravaged and the commerce ruined. Two: The Thirty Years' War was fought between Catholics and Protestants. Catholics and Protestants are fighting the same kind of egocentric, ignorant and futile war in Northern Ireland today.

Mother Courage will always be relevant.

o o o o o o o o o o o o o o o o o o o o o o o o o o o o o o o o o o o o o o o o o

Harold Pinter

THE HOMECOMING

o o o o o o o o o o o o o o o o o o o o o o o o o o o o o o o o o o o o o o o o o

Since Harold Pinter refuses to explain the meaning of *The Homecoming* expect nothing but surmises here. The play, which opened at the Music Box on January 5, 1967, is unintelligible in terms of the familiar stage narratives. It could be ignored as a pose or as a failure except for one thing: It seems to be saying something meaningful. It is ruthless and penetrating. It conveys a hateful point of view ably. Nothing that it says is notable, but the composite portrait it presents of evil,

Paul Rogers, Vivien Merchant and Ian Holm
in THE HOMECOMING

egoism, degeneracy, greed and ferocity is overwhelming, There is no violence in *The Homecoming*, but by the time it has sauntered on to its final scene it has destroyed any illusions one might have about the character of the human race. Although the characters are not vicious they are depraved.

Is Mr. Pinter dramatizing the subconscious of his people? They never say exactly what they mean. Their impulses remain below the level of civilized behavior. Leading lives of complete equivocation they puzzle not only the playgoer but themselves. Nothing clear emerges from the deep, dark caverns of their existence.

The Homecoming is set in an old house in North London inhabited by Max, the father, who is a widower, an insipid brother, and two sons—Sam, who is a pimp, and Joey, who hopes to be a prizefighter. Early one morning before they are awake, a third brother, Teddy, and his wife, Ruth, pop in without warning. For six years Teddy has been teaching philosophy in an American university. They left their children at home and have been visiting Italy. All the characters are impassive. And the renewal of a family relationship after six years is perfunctory. "What's for breakfast?" is the most Teddy can say to his father. For nobody in this play has any real interest in anybody except himself.

Although the tone of *The Homecoming* is indolent, the events it chronicles are astonishing. When Teddy's wife, Ruth, enters the house everyone assumes that she is a whore; and, in the words of Teddy's father, "he brings a filthy scrubber off the street and shacks up in my house." No one is outraged by this outburst, nor is Ruth upset. She is artfully taciturn. But she is also complaisant. After a visit with her upstairs, Joey tells the rest of the family: "She's wide open. She's a tart." As the play comes to a close, the father and his two London sons decide to set her up in a flat as a prostitute and make collective use of her at home.

Her husband takes no exception to any of this. It seems to him normal and reasonable. When the time comes for him to return to America he tells her she can stay if she wants to, and she does. All she has to say is: "Don't become a stranger." Like everyone else in the play she is emotionally dead.

In a previous play, *The Caretaker*, Mr. Pinter demonstrated his method of describing character by indirection. The surface may be civil, but the inner drive is self-serving and malevolent. In *The Homecoming* the accumulation of malevolence is so excessive that it has comic overtones. There by the grace of Satan goes Mr. Pinter's image of the human race.

Since the situations and relationships in *The Homecoming* are scandalous the play was more successful in New York than any of Mr. Pinter's other plays have been. But that observation does him less than justice. He has mastered an original style of playwriting that gives *The Homecoming* a terrible plausibility. The English cast, under Peter Hall's direction, was brilliant. The performance was full of subtle intonations and meaningful pauses, all of them in a doleful mood. It confirmed what Mr. Pinter had maintained—that under the conscious movements of society the subconscious is corrupt and ruthless.

Teddy says that the other members of the family lack intellectual equilibrium, but he excludes himself: "You're just objects," he says. "You just move about. I can observe it. I can see what you do. It's the same as I do. But you're lost in it. . . . You won't catch me being. . . . I won't be lost in it."

But who is Teddy to make judgments about other people?

o o o o o o o o o o o o o o o o o o o o o o o o o o o o o o o o o o o o o

Charles Gordone

NO PLACE TO BE SOMEBODY

o o o o o o o o o o o o o o o o o o o o o o o o o o o o o o o o o o o o o

When Charles Gordone's *No Place to Be Somebody* opened on May 2, 1969, it was performed in the Public Theatre's room that seats only 109 people. The room soon turned out to be too small. For *No Place to Be Somebody* was quickly recognized as not only an exciting play but also a creative one.

Since it is set in a Greenwich Village bar owned by Johnny, a black man, and since the characters are white as well as black and since they are continuously in conflict and keep on shouting at each other, Mr. Gordone's play seems on the surface to be a protest play in a familiar vein. It *is* a protest play. But the protest is not confined to discrimination against the blacks. It is against the common injustices of life, and the protest is ably made by a dramatist who can write with lyricism as well as fury.

The lyricism applies to the form of the play. Each act begins with a long, meditative poem spoken by Gabe, an actor and writer who is almost white. Gabe lives in a half world, shunned by the whites because he is black, discredited by the blacks because he looks white. Gabe is a constant failure because he does not seem to have a social base out of which he can operate normally.

Discrimination against the blacks is very much on Mr. Gordone's mind. When white gangsters are moving into Johnny's bar and threatening him, Gabe says: "You know they're gonna git you." Johnny replies: "Gabe, we was got the day we was born! Where you been? Jus' bein' black ain't never been no reason for livin'."

But the white people who hang around the bar are no better off. Those that try to live in the black world have disastrous experiences. The pairing of a white woman and a black man is invariably either unhappy or catastrophic. And Shanty, the white barkeep in a black saloon, is cruelly frustrated. He imagines that he used to be a brilliant drum player. Everyone believes him when he says that if he could only get enough money to buy a set of drums he would astonish the world. A simpleminded black girl believes him and moves in with him and finally makes enough money whoring to buy him the drums. But when he drags them into the bar and starts playing, everyone realizes that he is a mediocre performer. He cannot play as well as many black players can.

Since they can no longer believe in him they turn away from him in disgust. He angrily denounces and discards the girl who has bought the drums for him. He breaks with the black bar owner who has been protecting him: "You put me down for the last time 'cause my skin is white. Yeah, baby, I'm white. An' I'm proud of it. Pretty an' white. . . . If you're an example of what the white race is ag'inst, then baby, I'm gettin' with 'em. They gonna need a cat like me. Somebody that really knows where you black sons-a-bitches are at."

No Place to Be Sombody is ages away from the white liberal's protest of *In Abraham's Bosom* of 1926 and the romantic fable of *Porgy* of 1927. It is a play about the frustration of life. Mr. Gordone's bitter experience screams out of it, but his point of view is not parochial. His play contains the hatreds, the violence, the double-crossing

Nathan George in NO PLACE TO BE SOME[

the depravity and the viciousness of life in a seedy barroom. The dialogue is swift, fiery and obscene. The pitch of the play is melodramatic. But Mr. Gordone writes at such a reckless pace directly out of his own experience and observation that *No Place to Be Somebody* cannot be catalogued conveniently. It is an explosion. All the characters all of the time are on the verge of blowing up because the life that surrounds them is hostile and evil and relentless. At the Public Theatre, and later at the ANTA Theatre and at the Promenade Theatre, the play was acted passionately by a dynamic cast.

No Place to Be Somebody won the Pulitzer Prize in 1970—the first Off-Broadway play to win that honor.

o o o o o o o o o o o o o o o o o o o o o o o o o o o o o o o o o o o o o o o o o o

Galt MacDermot, James Rado and Gerome Ragni

HAIR

o o o o o o o o o o o o o o o o o o o o o o o o o o o o o o o o o o o o o o o o o o

Somewhere in the middle of *Hair* a character describes himself in words that apply to the whole drama: "I'm turney on-ey. I'm flipey outey, stoney switchey on-ey, I'm freakey outey, hungey-upey, I'm hung." Then he blandly supervises an act of sexual intercourse between two of the other characters. A note in the stage directions explains: "Berger has fucked Sheila in public. Or rather raped her in public. Berger has had his orgasm. She was fighting him off and reacts to his attack." This statement is not only frank but confusing because the act of sexual intercourse (simulated) has just been performed by Sheila and Woof. Don't expect either logic or reason amid the musical bedlam of *Hair*.

It was originally produced by Joseph Papp in the Public Theatre on October 7, 1969—book and lyrics by Gerome Ragni and James Rado, music by Galt MacDermot. It was amusingly muddleheaded and at times touching. In the emotional context of 1967 the spectacle of a hippie resisting the draft to the war in Vietnam had the sympathy of a great many people. After the original production completed its scheduled eight weeks the authors revised the text, and Tom O'Horgan, king of razzle-dazzle, restaged it and reopened it at the Biltmore Theatre on April 29, 1968. It had 1750 performances.

In part the long run was the result of a scandalous episode in the performance. Some male and female nudes faced the audience and obligingly lingered on stage. Although the lighting was so dim that the audience could not distinguish the males from the females, nudity broadened the community of theatre lovers remarkably. Thousands of them had never seen anything so exhilarating in their lives.

But there was another reason for the success of *Hair*. It perfectly expressed the hippie rebellion against organized society and it had enormous youthful vitality. The rock music was so deafening that eventually it impaired the hearing of some of the performers exposed to it eight times a week. The music also made the lyrics unintelligible. Nothing could be heard except a loud blare. Since the lyrics were on the level of grammar-school poetry, nothing was lost by demolishing them with sound. But they were legitimate. Elementary and obscene, they were part of a rebellion against polite society that consisted of snappy rejoinders to serious statements. They were part of the general hubbub of a mindless revolution.

In the context of the play there was a sound reason for withdrawal from society. Claude has been drafted. "Uncle Sambo wants you," one of his friends declares sardonically. But Claude does not believe in the draft for the Vietnam War. As one of his pals declares: "The draft is white people sending black people to make war on yellow people to defend the land they stole from red people." In one of the few rational statements made in the play Claude says: "I'm a patriot,

HAIR

but I'm a patriot for the whole world." His opposition to the draft gets lost in the orgy of a freewheeling play. But in the last act Claude obeys the draft summons, has his hippie's hair cut and meekly goes to war. Despite all the uproar his rebellion has not been serious.

Nor is the rebellion of *Hair*. In the original production the characters were disarming. There was an innocence about them that aroused the respect of the audience. Uptown the characters were less likable. During the long run they settled down into a kind of arrogant squalor. One of the characters remarks to another: "Let's go over to the park, man, and scare some of the tourists." They are putting on a show.

But the renunciation of the cant and the brutality of the American involvement in Vietnam constituted a legitimate point of view and it was expressed with youthful abandon and energy. *Hair* seemed to have less pertinence as the war dragged on to a negotiated end. But while the war was going on two lines in *Hair* were completely valid:

> *It's what's happening, Baby.*
> *It's where it's at, Daddy.*

o o o o o o o o o o o o o o o o o o o o o o o o o o o o o o o o o o o o o o o o o o

Heinar Kipphardt

IN THE MATTER OF J. ROBERT OPPENHEIMER

o o o o o o o o o o o o o o o o o o o o o o o o o o o o o o o o o o o o o o o o o o

In the Matter of J. Robert Oppenheimer, which opened at the Vivian Beaumont Theatre on March 6, 1969, presents a moral idea in terms of a documentary. The material consists of the transcript of the 1954 loyalty investigation of Dr. Oppenheimer by the Personnel Security Board. Although the author, Heinar Kipphardt, had to simplify the time sequence and reduce the length of the trial record, he tried not to take sides. The English text, translated by Ruth Speirs, is objective.

But nobody is objective in the theatre. Every play—like every piece of literature—is a species of autobiography; and the impressions theatregoers receive are also highly personal. Although *In the Matter of J. Robert Oppenheimer* is a factual documentary, Dr. Oppenheimer inevitably becomes the hero. Although the play is detached, it becomes a melodrama in the theatre; and theatergoers instinctively believe that Dr. Oppenheimer is an inspired free man and that the investigators are the totalitarian enemy. There are no rhetorical flourishes. In fact, the dialogue is dull. But the spectacle of one idealist surrounded by judges and prosecutors becomes a passionate confrontation between good and evil. The theatre is a liberal institution, although many theatre workers and many theatregoers are conservative people.

In the Matter of J. Robert Oppenheimer is set in a hearing room with props, but with very little scenery. When the play opens the record shows that Senator Joseph McCarthy, the Wisconsin hoodlum, has just said on television the night before that America may perish because the Atomic Weapons Laboratory at Los Alamos has let Russia produce the first hydrogen bomb. Suspicion points to Dr. Oppenheimer. The prosecution tries to prove that he has been a Communist sympathizer and perhaps a Communist agent for years—to quote the play, he is "a new type of traitor—the traitor for ideological, ethical and I don't know what other motives. . . . He has never abandoned the utopian ideal of an international, classless society. . . . It is ideological treason which has its origins in the deepest strata of the personality and renders a man's actions dishonest against his own will." That kindergarten sophistry is the best the prosecution can do.

Everything Dr. Oppenheimer says, however, expresses the ethical convictions of a humanist. He says he had terrible scruples

Joseph Wiseman in
IN THE MATTER OF J. ROBERT OPPENHEIMER

against dropping the atomic bomb on Hiroshima, but agreed because he had been told that it would bring the war to a close quickly—which it did. He had hoped that the hydrogen bomb would never be built because "there are no limits to its destruction." He thinks it may destroy the world we are trying to save.

He is a man not only of principle but of sensibility. When the first experimental atomic bomb was exploded on the desert he said he recalled some lines from the Bhagavad-Gita:

> *The radiance of a thousand suns*
> *which suddenly illuminate the heavens*
> *all in one moment—thus*
> *the splendor of the Lord*

and then two other lines:

> *And I am Death who taketh all*
> *who shatters worlds.*

He concludes his testimony by declaring that whatever decision the Personnel Security Board may come to respecting his loyalty, he will no longer serve because he now realizes that the scientists have no control over the finest and most brilliant of their discoveries: "I ask myself whether we, the physicists, have not sometimes given too great, too indiscriminate loyalty to our governments against our better judgment.... We have spent years of our lives in developing sweeter means of destruction; we have been doing the work of the military, and I feel it in my very bones that this was wrong." Although the play concludes before the Security Board has arrived at its decision the theatregoers have already given their loyalty to a man of principle in a tradition that began with Socrates' trial for corrupting the young and Jesus' trial for claiming to be the son of God.

The most untheatrical play thus becomes exalting because it is illumined by the character of a good man. In the Vivian Beaumont Theatre production, Dr. Oppenheimer was played by the most untheatrical of actors—Joseph Wiseman, who was mild and soft-spoken. Without raising his voice he was eloquent because the character he played stood for love and principle.

o o o o o o o o o o o o o o o o o o o o o o o o o o o o o o o o o o o o o o

Arthur Kopit

INDIANS

o o o o o o o o o o o o o o o o o o o o o o o o o o o o o o o o o o o o o o

Amid the whirl and glitter of his stage fantasy Arthur Kopit makes some painful statements about the experience of American Indians in this turbulent play, called *Indians,* put on at the Brooks Atkinson Theatre on October 13, 1969. The play dramatizes the hopelessness of reconciliation between the white man and the Indian; the gulf between them is wide, deep and unbridgeable. Sitting Bull tells three United States Senators that he is the legitimate leader of the nation: "If the Great Spirits have chosen anyone to be leader of their country, know that it is not the Great Father [the President]. It is myself." His view is totally irreconcilable with the Senators' sense of reality.

Sitting Bull has tried to live at peace with the white man. He has even performed in Buffalo Bill's popular Wild West show. But in the end he has resumed his responsibilities as leader of the Sioux Indians, and his death precipitates the ghastly massacre at Wounded Knee. Historically that was on December 29, 1890. In the hearts of the Indians it is today.

The play is not a statement of facts but a theatrical incantation —a grievous carousal. There is no curtain. The stage is lighted when the audience comes in. The audience is surrounded with strange and varied music that comes from a mysterious source. There are twenty-six major characters in addition to many walk-ons. The actors appear not only on the stage floor but also on platforms constructed on poles. The performance includes Indian dancing. The scenes change impulsively and the time sequences are capricious. Nothing Mr. Kopit has written on paper takes precedence over his stage fantastications of a harrowing incident in the American heritage.

Buffalo Bill is the catalyst. Braggart, swagger, opportunistic, a folk hero because of his romantic Wild West show, Buffalo Bill regards himself as the friend of the Indians. Since he is admired by the white men of the East he tries to intercede on the Indians' behalf.

Stacy Keach and Ed Rombola in INDIANS

He takes his show to the White House and appeals to the President for justice for the Indians. But Buffalo Bill is no demigod. He is a showoff before Nat Buntline, who is writing a flamboyant book about him, and he performs pretentiously before the Grand Duke of Russia, who is a celebrity. He callously slaughters one hundred buffaloes to demonstrate the brilliance of his marksmanship. Although Buffalo Bill is goodhearted he represents the bluster and bombast of the insensitive American promoter.

The Indians are refugees in their own country. Nothing they say or do can convince the three visiting Senators or any other white men that they are anything except children and beasts. Excited and challenged by Buffalo Bill's extravaganzas about his own exploits in the West, the Grand Duke shoots and kills an Indian and becomes delirious with joy over the accuracy of his marksmanship. He equates the Indians with wild game.

In the course of the play everyone becomes insulted. The Senators feel insulted when the Indians complain that none of the Government's remedies are suitable for Indians and that the Government continually breaks its word. Finally, Chief Joseph accepts defeat in mournful phrases: "Hear me, my chiefs, I'm tired. My heart is sick and sad. From where the sun now stands, I will fight no more, forever." But Buffalo Bill reverts to the delusions of grandeur of the conventional white man: "I am sick and tired of these sentimental humanitarians who take no account of the difficulties under which this Government has labored in its efforts to deal fairly with the Indian, nor the countless lives we have lost and atrocities endured at their savage hands," he says.

Indians is not a thesis play. It is a bitter phantasmagoria. It sketches a dark corner in the American dream and demonstrates the impossibility of expunging it. In 1973 the Indians and the white men again confronted each other at Wounded Knee, as in the last part of *Indians*. The 1973 circumstances were less tragic and brutal than the massacre at Wounded Knee in 1890. But the points of view of Mr. Kopit's strange drama were still valid. *Indian* celebrates a painful dilemma.

o o o o o o o o o o o o o o o o o o o o o o o o o o o o o o o o o o o o o o o

David Rabe

STICKS AND BONES

o o o o o o o o o o o o o o o o o o o o o o o o o o o o o o o o o o o o o o o

While the Vietnam War was still killing soldiers and civilians a long way from America, David Rabe wrote a merciless play, *Sticks and Bones*, put on at the Public Theatre on November 7, 1971. It simmers with hatred—not only of the war but of the inhuman Army system and the complacence of the people at home. There are no soft points in it. In *What Price Glory?* which debunked war six years after World War I was over, there was a certain romantic exuberance that dismissed the audience in a happy frame of mind. Sergeant Quirt succumbed to the tradition of loyalty to the Army in the last scene. But *Sticks and Bones* makes no excuses. It totally rejects the America of the Vietnam War.

Most of the scenes are written realistically. But the whole play emerges as a kind of evil hallucination in which the characters can never escape the privacy of their own experience. They are all trapped in the miseries of the times. In the first scene, David, who has been blinded in the war, is delivered back home by a petulant sergeant major who is in a hurry to get rid of a piece of damaged goods. He is pressed for time because he has many other grisly deliveries to make.

David's mother, father and brother—especially his mother—ex-

Drew Snyder and Tom Aldredge in STICKS AND BONES

press the regulation joy over the return of their older son. But they are repelled by his condition—his bitterness as well as his blindness. The father and the brother revert to trivial pleasures to escape responsibility for David. He is surplus property to them; he is junk.

"I'm lonely here," David exclaims as soon as he gets home. "The air is wrong, the smells and the sounds, the winds are wrong. . . . I want to leave, I want to leave. I want to leave." His mother tries to relax him by preparing the kinds of food he used to like. Although she is bewildered, she is sympathetic. But too many memories of pain and horror separate him from his family. The war has made them total strangers.

What he saw overseas is part of the barrier that separates them. While the rest of the family is looking at a home movie he is tortured by one particularly macabre memory—a peasant woman dying after an attack on a defenseless village, her baby shot, her husband with the back of his head shot off. The old people are buried, but the baby is burned—"There's an oven. It is no ceremony. It is the disposal of garbage." A ghoulish memory.

David's family—particularly the mother—are even more revolted by hearing about David's liaison with a native girl. His mother and father try to dismiss it as the usual whoring of soldiers away from home. But David still longs for the girl. He feels guilty; he thinks he has been unfair to her. She is the one thing in which he believes. But David's father and mother are mortified by the thought that David might have given them half-caste grandchildren. The idea of miscegenation makes them strangers to David.

There is no common ground where the family can meet. The mother sends for their priest to counsel David. Father Donald greets David with the condescension of a spiritual leader and offers a number of pious sophistries. David is infuriated. He drives Father Donald away with his cane.

As the home situation becomes more tense, David's father tries to escape into fantasies about his standing as a leading citizen and the brother escapes into debauchery, while both the father and mother try to escape into the consolations of religion by praying.

Mr. Rabe is adamant. He makes no concessions to the characters or to the audience. *Sticks and Bones* is a play of furies. Since Mr. Rabe's craftsmanship equals his convictions he has written a headlong play that gives the theatre distinction as a public forum. It was acted with passion and skill that overwhelmed the audiences in Lafayette Street. It was too merciless for Broadway audiences after it moved uptown.

Although the Government was involved in a war that no one believed in, the Government did not interfere with the play that made the most devastating case against national policy. Freedom of speech still prevailed at home while death prevailed abroad.

o o o o o o o o o o o o o o o o o o o o o o o o o o o o o o o o o o o o o o o o o o o o

Neil Simon

THE PRISONER OF SECOND AVENUE

o o o o o o o o o o o o o o o o o o o o o o o o o o o o o o o o o o o o o o o o o o o

Audiences started laughing at Neil Simon's *The Prisoner of Second Avenue* as soon as the curtain rose at the Eugene O'Neill Theatre on November 11, 1971. They may have started laughing before the curtain went up. For people brighten at the prospect of seeing a Neil Simon comedy and feel cheerful the moment they walk into the theatre. Audiences were still laughing at *The Prisoner of Second Avenue* a year and a half later, for it was still on the same stage through the spring of 1973. At that time there were two Neil Simon plays on Broadway, *The Sunshine Boys* being the other. In 1966–67 there were four on the stage simultaneously. Without being in the least aggressive Mr. Simon appears to have taken over Broadway.

In *The Prisoner of Second Avenue* the comedy consists of the ironic edgings in the dialogue and the ludicrously oversize proportions. Mel Edison and his wife, Edna live on the fourteenth floor of an "overpriced" apartment house at the corner of 82nd Street and Second Avenue. Everything about this luxurious house is intolerable according to Mel. He itemizes the flaws: a faulty air-conditioner, thin walls and noisy neighbors, a toilet that will not shut off automatically, the stink of garbage, barking dogs, the clatter of city traffic all night, not to mention the heat and humidity of New York in the summer. The humorously distorted statement of these familiar annoyances delights audiences, who have had identical experiences. Mr. Simon has not lost the common touch.

But Mel's troubles are more fundamental than that. At the age of forty-seven, after holding one job for twenty-two years, he is unemployed and has no prospects of a job anywhere. Suddenly in the middle of life he is one of the city's dispossessed. In a poignant cry of despair to his wife he says: "I'm losing control. I can't handle things any more. The telephone rings on my desk seven or eight times before I answer it. I forgot how the water cooler works this morning. . . . I don't know where to go, Edna. I'm slipping, I'm scared." As the weeks go by he becomes paranoid. He imagines that he is the victim of a plot: "It is the human race. It is the sudden, irrevocable deterioration of the spirit of man. It is man undermining himself—self-imposed, self-evident, self-destruction."

What is funny about this? The question is valid. For *The Prisoner of Second Avenue* consists of disasters. The radio news programs are full of disasters, including a long hospital strike that deprives the patients of care. To compensate for Mel's joblessness and loss of income, Edna gets a secretarial job, but her employers go bankrupt. Like her husband, she has a bill of particulars: "What kind of life is this? You live like some kind of caged animal in a Second Avenue zoo that's too hot in one room, too cold in another, overcharged for a growth on the side of the building they call a terrace that can't support a cactus plant, let alone human beings. Is that what you call a worthwhile life? Banging on walls and jiggling toilets?"

Mr. Simon writes out of experience in New York City. In his own words he is "that person sitting in the corner who's observing it all," and what he reports rings true to the people in the audience. But *The Prisoner of Second Avenue* raises a problem. Is this funny? Is Mel's feeling of hopelessness funny? Is Edna's despair funny? Are their outbursts of temperament funny—the abusive retorts, the cutting insults between man and wife, the malicious quarreling between brother and sisters? At the end of Acts One and Two the impatient tenant upstairs pours buckets of water on Mel when he is standing on the terrace shouting. This is part of the comic horseplay of the old burlesque theatre. But is it funny in the circumstances of Mel's agonizing situation in the heartless hierarchy of a callous city?

Lee Grant and Peter Falk in THE PRISONER OF SECOND AVENUE

Audiences think so. A half century before Neil Simon, audiences thought the rancorous yelling of Montague Glass's *Potash and Perlmutter* was funny. On the affluent Upper East Side only the style of living has changed.

o o o o u o o u o o o o o o o o o o o o o o o o o o o o o o o o o o o o o o o o o o o o

Jason Miller

THAT CHAMPIONSHIP SEASON

o o o o o o o o o o o u o o u o o o o o o o o o o o o o o o o o o o o o o o o o o o

When Jason Miller's *That Championship Season* opened at the Public Theatre in May of 1972 the long cycle of plays about people had come full circle. It was back where it began. The style was not expressionistic or in any way improvised or inventive. It was realistic, like the plays of Eugene Walter or Edward Sheldon. The setting was solidly realistic; it included the standard staircase—almost stage center with doors and windows leading to realistic places. Also, the play was in three acts instead of two, which had become the custom, or instead of the occasional play with no intermission.

Theatregoers—if any—from the days before World War I would have felt at home except for one fact: the curtain was up when the audience came in. It was the lighting instead of the rising of the curtain that announced the opening scene. That much was conceded to the sophisticated assumption that a play is not actual life but a representatiton of actual life. The fact of no curtain destroyed the traditional barrier between the audience and the play.

The author's point of view, however, is thoroughly contemporary.

That Championship Season is a savagely iconoclastic portrait of the corruption and greediness and petty treachery of life in a small town somewhere in Pennsylvania. Four men in their late thirties are holding their annual celebration of a famous basketball team that won the state championship when they were in high school. The silver trophy stands on a table to stage right. The old basketball coach is still full of sleazy slogans and moral bromides. But the four former players are now stodgy men. One is the mayor of the town, getting ready to run for re-election. Another is a bitter schoolteacher; another is his brother, now a dipsomaniac. The fourth is a prosperous businessman who contributes heavily to political campaigns and is a strong influence in town affairs. They pound each other on the back and slap each other fraternally and do ten push-ups to demonstrate their physical prowess. But by now they are a long way from being athletes. They are men who have contentedly succumbed to the timeless degeneracies of small communities.

After the exuberant opening scene on the bright surface of modern life, the provincial ignobility wells up from the interior of their lives. The businessman, a notorious chippy-chaser, has been sleeping with the wife of his comrade, the mayor. The schoolteacher is a malicious tale-bearer and schemer; his brother is a drunken bum. The mayor is a petty crook. The coach retains the swagger, manners and sanctimonious beliefs of a sports leader, but the slogans he adheres to now sound vicious—hatred of your competitor, do anything to win, hatred of Jews, hatred of Communists.

Although the form of *That Championship Season* is old-fashioned, the author is a man of his times. Born in 1939, he has never known the legendary America of peace and good will to men. He is the totally disillusioned citizen of a demoralized nation that has been eroded by a futile war, economic disaster, political corruption, drugs, hatred and other evils. A stream of humorous comments—put-downs with blistering punch lines—gives the play considerable vivacity. Most of them are spoken by the drunken brother who is tolerated by the other characters as a sort of club jester. The humor is idiomatically obscene and it sardonically accepts whoring, intrigue, backbiting

Michael McGuire, Paul Sorvino, Charles Durning,
Richard A. Dysart and Walter McGinn in THAT CHAMPIONSHIP SEASON

and double-crossing as normal. And audiences accept *That Champion-ship Season* as a hilarious comedy, not only because the lines are witty but also because they describe a debased world with which everyone is familiar and in which most participate.

In the Twenties dramatists thought that the malaise of America could be cured. O'Neill was the great exception; he believed that life is tragic and cannot be changed. But Elmer Rice, Robert Sherwood, Sidney Howard, S. N. Behrman, Clifford Odets, John Howard Lawson, Thornton Wilder were unintentional reformers. They were concerned citizens who believed that life could be improved. There is no indication of outrage in *That Championship Season,* or hope of a better life. The play assumes that the American civilization will be an extension of the present, that it will be bitter, slimy and unscrupulous, and that winning is worth anything it costs and that the champions are the charlatans who are the smartest and stand closest together. It is—unwittingly—a prologue to Watergate.

Like the dramatists of a half century ago, Mr. Miller writes out of personal experience: he represents the mood of his time. In the fifty-three years covered by this book everything has changed on a descending scale in life as well as in the theatre. *That Championship Season* is a realistic play that illustrates the fallen spirit of the nation. It won the Critics' Circle award as the best play of the 1971-72 season; its only competitor was *Sticks and Bones,* which takes an equally harsh view of the Vietnam War. In 1973 *That Championship Season* won the Pulitzer Prize and a Tony award as the best play of the year.

To look back over the chronicle of this book, it is obvious that a quality of hatred has crept into the plays about contemporary America. They despise contemporary America and they do not expect to change it. The characters lack size, sensitivity and warmth. Although they are victims of the environment in which they live, they accept it as normal. They do not light up the dark landscape with the glowing personalities of Anna Christie or Blanche Dubois or "Captain" Jack Boyle (the Paycock) or Willy Loman or Mother Courage—victims who nevertheless have such independent personalities that they keep on living in the memories of theatregoers who have made their acquaintance. Contemporary plays also lack gusto and humor. They do not include characters as amusing and outrageous as the managing editor of *The Front Page* or the old crones of *The Madwoman of Chaillot.*

The contemporary theatre is an abstract of the life of the times. Indeed, it is part of the same thing. What is wrong with America is wrong with the American theatre. For serious drama cannot have an independent life.

INDEX